NEW TESTAMENT COMMENTARY

NEW TESTAMENT COMMENTARY

WILLIAM HENDRIKSEN

Exposition

of

Paul's Epistle

to the Romans

VOLUME II

Chapters 9—16

BAKER BOOK HOUSE

GRAND RAPIDS, MICHIGAN

Library of Congress Catalog Number: 54-924

ISBN: 0-8010-4255-0

Printed in the United States of America

TABLE OF CONTENTS

EXPOSITION (continued)

PRACTICAL APPLICATION

LIST OF ABBREVIATIONS

A. *Book Abbreviations*

A.R.V.	American Standard Revised Version
A.V.	Authorized Version (King James)
Gram. N.T.	A. T. Robertson, *Grammar of the Greek New Testament in the Light of Historical Research*
Gram. N.T. (Bl.-Debr.)	F. Blass and A. DeBrunner, *A Greek Grammar of the New Testament and Other Early Christian Literature*
Grk. N.T. (A-B-M-W)	*The Greek New Testament,* edited by Kurt Aland, Matthew Black, Bruce M. Metzger, and Allen Wikgren
I.S.B.E.	*International Standard Bible Encyclopedia*
L.N.T. (Th.)	Thayer's *Greek-English Lexicon of the New Testament*
L.N.T. (A. and G.)	W. F. Arndt and F. W. Gingrich, *A Greek-English Lexicon of the New Testament and Other Early Christian Literature*
M.M.	*The Vocabulary of the Greek New Testament Illustrated from the Papyri and Other Non-Literary sources,* by James Hope Moulton and George Milligan
N.A.S. (N.T.)	New American Standard Bible (New Testament)
N.E.B.	New English Bible
N.I.V.	New International Version
N.T.C.	W. Hendriksen, *New Testament Commentary*
R.S.V.	Revised Standard Version
S.BK.	Strack and Billerbeck, *Kommentar zum Neuen Testament aus Talmud und Midrasch*
S.H.E.R.K.	*The New Schaff-Herzog Encyclopedia of Religious Knowledge*
Th.D.N.T.	*Theological Dictionary of the New Testament,* edited by G. Kittel and G. Friedrich, and translated from the German by G. W. Bromiley

LIST OF ABBREVIATIONS

B. *Periodical Abbreviations*

EQ	*Evangelical Quarterly*
ET	*Expository Times*
GTT	*Gereformeerd theologisch tijdschrift*
JBL	*Journal of Biblical Literature*
ThG	*Theologie und Glaube*
ThZ	*Theologische Zeitschrift*

Please Note

In order to differentiate between the second person plural (see Rom. 1:11: "I am yearning to see y o u") and the second person singular (see Rom. 2:1: "Therefore you have no excuse"), the letters in "y o u pl." are spaced, those in "you sing." are not.

Summary of Chapters 1—8 and Preview of Chapters 9—11

After a prologue (1:1-15) Paul has shown that *Justification by Faith is* both *Real*, having been provided not by man but by God (1:16, 17), *and Necessary*; and this both for Gentile (1:18-32) and Jew (2:1—3:8); in fact for everybody (3:9-20), without any distinction between Jew and Gentile (3:21, 22). "All have sinned and fall short of the glory of God, being justified freely by his grace through the redemption (accomplished) in Christ Jesus; whom God designed to be, by the shedding of his blood, a wrath-removing sacrifice (effective) *through faith* . . ." (3:23-25a). As a result, there is no room whatever for boasting (3:27). Does this mean, then, that we invalidate the law through our insistence on faith? "On the contrary," says Paul, "we uphold the law" (verse 31).

In chapter 4 the apostle has shown that this way to be saved, the one and only way, is also definitely *Scriptural* (examples: Abraham and David). And it is *Effective*. Among many other blessings which flow forth from God-given faith, according to the divine *system* or *philosophy* of redemption, the following are probably the most pronounced. Note the first four consonants of the word

```
p h i l o s o p h y.
e o   i   u
a l   b   p
c i   e   e
e n   r   r
  e   t   i
  s   y   n
  s       v
          i
          n
          c
          i
          b
          i
          l
          i
          t
          y
```

These fruits are described, respectively, in chapters 5, 6, 7, and 8.

In chapters 9—11 Paul will show that this divinely provided method of obtaining salvation is also *Historical. In the course of history God's most precious promises were intended not for the unbelieving nation but for the believing remnants. Thus, it was, is now, and will always be,* until Christ returns. *The nation* was rejected because of its unbelief (9:27, 31,32; 10:21). Cf. Matt. 8:11, 12; 21:41;

22:8, 9; Luke 20:16; I Thess. 2:14b-16. *All Israel* will be saved. See Rom. 9:6; 11:1-6, 26.

The Gentiles too are saved in no other way than by faith. *This rule holds for everyone, without ethnic distinctions*. (Rom. 9:24-26; 10:4-13; 11:20, 23, 25).

Paul shows how the disobedience of the Jews opens the door of salvation to the Gentiles, and how, in turn, the latter's salvation causes the Jews—in both cases the elect remnant, of course—to become filled with a jealousy that leads to salvation (11:11, 30, 31). This constantly recurring turn of events results in the rapturous doxology of 11:33-36. But, as has been shown, for both Jew and Gentile the way of salvation is ever the same, namely, that of justification by faith, the product not of human works or merit but of divine sovereign grace.

We notice, therefore, that when Paul reaches chapter 9 he has by no means forgotten his main theme.

It is true, nevertheless, that, as in the first eight chapters, so also here, in chapters 9-11, the apostle touches on a variety of subjects, some of them closely related to the main theme, others not so closely. Thus "the special advantages enjoyed by the Jews," in 9:3-5 enumerated in somewhat expanded form, reflect 2:17, 18; 3:1, 2; and "what it means to be a true Israelite" (9:6) echoes 2:28, 29. Compare also the following:

9:5—1:25	9:26—8:14	11:15—5:11
9:19—3:7	9:33—5:5	11:28—5:10
9:23—8:30	10:9—4:24	11:32—3:9; 5:19
9:24—3:29	10:12—3:22, 29, 30	

Even the doctrine of divine predestination, for which one generally turns immediately to Rom. 9:10-24; 11:5-8, 29, is foreshadowed in 8:29, 30.

The question may be asked, "Why was it necessary for Paul to place such emphasis on *Justification by faith, apart from the works of the law?* In light of what the writer himself states in 9:6 f., the answer must be, "Because the Jews, by and large, misconstrued God's most precious promise, believing that it was intended for Abraham's natural posterity, and that its fulfillment was conditioned, at least to some extent, on human merit." Besides, is it not true that the human heart, whether that of a Jew or of a Gentile, is ever proud and by nature unwilling to be "saved by grace"? Finally, not only was it necessary for the Roman church itself to be pure in doctrine but its membership must also be able to defend its convictions when these are attacked by outsiders; that is, by unbelieving Jews and/or Gentiles.

One additional factor, a very important one, must not be left unmentioned in any introduction to chapters 9—11: The apostle was not only a man with a keen intellect and iron will, but, as has been pointed out previously (see p. 13), also with a loving heart. Is it surprising, then, that, as he reflects on the treasures of salvation, about which he writes so touchingly in chapter 8 and also earlier, he, as it were, heaves a sigh of deep sympathy and poignant grief when he considers the fact that many of his own countrymen failed to share in these glorious blessings?

All these factors must be taken into consideration. They shed necessary light on the meaning and purpose of chapters 9—11. Paul is going to show that God's well-meant invitation is still being extended to the Jews. The Lord is by no means "through with the Jews." Until the day of Christ's return, that is, throughout the present era or dispensation of grace, their rejection is *never complete* (chapter 9; see especially verses 6 and 27), *never arbitrary* (chapter 10; see verse 21); and *never absolute and unqualified* (chapter 11; see verses 14 and 26). In his anger God does not withhold compassion. Neither does Paul.

The writer of this commentary is well aware of the fact that in the opinion of many able scholars, both past and present, one of the purposes of chapters 9-11 is to show that when the finishing line of human history is reached, or is about to be reached, the Jews then living on earth will be saved. As they see it, this will happen to (a) the nation Israel as a whole, (b) the mass [of the Jews], (c) the whole nation. It will be (d) a comprehensive eschatological recovering of the unbelieving Jews.[260] Whether this is actually what Paul has in mind will be among the subjects to be discussed in the following pages.

---

260. a. S. Greijdanus, *Kommentaar op het Nieuwe Testament, Romeinen*, Vol. II, pp. 515, 516; C.E.B. Cranfield, *op. cit.*, Vol. II, pp. 576, 577.
b. J. Murray, *op. cit.*, Vol. II, p. 98; cf. p. xiv.
c. C. Hodge, *op. cit.*, p. 589.
d. G. Vos, *The Pauline Eschatology*, Princeton, 1930, p. 89.

Outline (continued)

Justification by Faith

D. *Historical*

1. *Paul's Sorrow*

"I have great sorrow and unceasing anguish in my heart . . . for the sake of my brothers, my fellow-countrymen"

9:1-5

2. *Divine Election and Rejection*

"Not all who are of Israel are Israel . . . Jacob I loved, but Esau I hated"

9:6-18

3. *God's Wrath and Mercy*

"Does not the potter have the right to make, out of the same lump of clay one vessel for honor and another for dishonor?"

9:19-29

4. *Conclusion*

"He who puts his faith in him will not be put to shame"

9:30-33

CHAPTER 9

9 1 I am speaking the truth in Christ—I am not lying; my conscience bears witness
along with me in the Holy Spirit—(when I declare) 2 that I have great sorrow and
unceasing anguish in my heart. 3 For I could wish that I myself would be accursed
(and cut off) from Christ for the sake of my brothers, my fellow-countrymen according to the flesh, 4 since they are Israelites, and theirs is the adoption and the glory and
the covenants and the legislation and the worship and the promises; 5 and theirs are the
fathers, and from them, as far as his human nature is concerned,[261] is Christ, who is over all
God blest forever. Amen.

D. *Historical*

1. *Paul's Sorrow*

"I have great sorrow and unceasing anguish in my heart . . . for the sake of my brothers, my fellow-countrymen"
9:1-5

1, 2. I am speaking the truth in Christ—I am not lying; my conscience bears witness along with me in the Holy Spirit—(when I declare) that I have great sorrow and unceasing anguish in my heart.

With the words, "I am speaking the truth . . . I am not lying" compare II Cor. 11:31; 12:6; Gal. 1:20; I Tim. 2:7.

It is clear that Paul is deeply moved when he dictates these words. The sorrow of his heart is *great* in its intensity, *deep* in its nature, amounting to nothing less than anguish, and *unceasing* in its duration.

Why does Paul say that he is indeed speaking the truth when he thus describes the inner state of his mind and heart?

To discover the answer we should bear in mind that he has already expressed his opinion about the Jews in language that was anything but complimentary (See 2:5, 17-24; also I Thess. 2:14b-16), and he is going to do so again (Rom. 9:31, 32; 10:2, 3, 16, 21; 11:7-10). His kinsmen might easily draw the conclusion, "Paul hates us." Cf. Acts 21:28 f.; 24:5 f. But nothing could be farther from the truth. This explains why Paul considered it necessary to declare that Israel's unbelief and consequent rejection was for him indeed a heavy burden. Truly and deeply Paul loves his kinsmen. But he loves Christ even more. He is speaking the truth "in Christ." To an extent,

---

261. Literally, as concerning the flesh.

at least, his sadness results from love for him whom the Jews have repudiated. His conscience confirms what he is saying; and, as the expression "in the Holy Spirit" shows, that *conscience* belongs to a man who is constantly being indwelt and led (see 8:9, 14, 16) by the Holy Spirit. Contrast 2:15 which refers to the conscience of those who are still living in darkness.

3. For I could wish that I myself would be accursed (and cut off) from Christ for the sake of my brothers, my fellow-countrymen according to the flesh . . .[262]

As the word "For" indicates, Paul is here beginning to give the reason for the strong statement found in verses 1, 2. So deep is his grief resulting from the unbelief of the Jews and from the divine displeasure with them, that he states, "I could wish myself to be accursed (and cut off) from Christ for the sake of my brothers, my fellow-countrymen according to the flesh." He means every word of it. This expression "I could wish . . . to be cut off from Christ" is all the more striking because it issued from the heart and lips of the very man for whom the impossibility of being separated from Christ meant so much, as 8:38, 39 has shown! He is, as it were, saying, "I could wish to be separated from Christ for the sake of others *if this were possible*, but I realize that this is impossible, which in a sense adds to my woe!"

This is clearly the language of *a Christian*. The person who is unconcerned about those who are perishing may well wonder whether he is a Christian.

Paul's sentiment reminds us of Judah, who, as Surety for his brother Benjamin, said, "Please permit your servant to remain here as my lord's slave in the place of the lad" (Gen. 44:33). It recalls to us the thrilling words of Moses, as he interceded for his people, "Yet now, if thou wilt forgive their sin—; but if not, blot me, I pray thee, out of the book which thou hast written" (Exod. 32:32). It brings back to our memory David's agonizing cry, "O my son Absalom! My son, my son Absalom! If only I had died instead of you; O Absalom, my son, my son!" (II Sam 18:33). But most of all, it fixes our attention on *him who really became* his people's Substitute (cf. Rom. 3:24, 25; 8:32; II Cor. 5:21; Gal. 3:13; I Tim. 2:6; and see also Isa. 53:5, 6, 8; Matt. 20:28; Mark 10:45).

---

262. The verb ηὐχόμην, first per. s. imperf. of εὔχομαι, here probably in the sense *to wish* (other meaning: *to pray*). The Attic form would have been ἐβουλόμην ἄν, I could wish. See H. Greeven, Th.D.N.T., Vol. II, p. 778; Ridderbos, *op. cit.*, p. 206. ἀνάθεμα εἶναι . . . ἀπὸ τοῦ Χριστοῦ, an abbreviated expression (see N.T.C. on John, Vol. i, p. 206) meaning "to be accursed (of God) and separated (or banished) from Christ."

According to S.BK., Vol. III, p. 260, in the terminology of the Septuagint the word ἀνάθεμα indicates anything which by God or in God's name has been devoted to destruction and ruin. The rabbinical "*ḥerem*" is a broader concept, inasmuch as it comprises *whatever* is devoted to God, not only that which is devoted to him for destruction. The same distinction is carried over into the New Testament, where the noun ἀνάθημα (in Luke 21:5, according to the best reading) means "that which has been devoted to God as a votive offering," naturally with no curse implications; while ἀνάθεμα (here in Rom. 9:3 and also in Acts 23:14; I Cor. 12:3; 16:22; Gal. 1:8, 9) refers to that which is devoted to God without hope of being redeemed; hence, that which, or he who, is doomed to destruction, accursed.

In this passage Paul certainly proves what a wonderful missionary he is, how passionately he yearns to save the lost. Cf. Rom. 11:14; I Cor. 9:22.

The dismal character of Israel's tragedy and therefore also the heart-rending nature of Paul's anguish become clear when the advantages which caused this nation to stand out above all others (Ps. 147:19, 20) are listed in greater detail than had been done previously (Rom. 2:17, 18; 3:1, 2):

4, 5. since they[263] are Israelites, and theirs is the adoption and the glory and the covenants and the legislation and the worship and the promises; and theirs are the fathers, and from them, as far as his human nature is concerned, is Christ, who is over all God blest forever. Amen.

The list of advantages contains nine items; as follows:

a. *They are Israelites*

Meaning: they are descendants of Jacob, who, until God blessed him, would not let him go, and whose name was changed to Israel ("he struggles with God"). See Gen. 32:22-28. Accordingly, when used in its most favorable sense, the appellatives *Israel, Israelites* were titles of honor, as is clear from such passages as John 1:31, 47, 49; 3:10; 12:13. The honor attaching to the name *Israel* is also reflected in speeches by Peter and Paul recorded in the book of Acts (2:22; 3:12; 13:16). *Historically* was not Israel a nation which by God had been separated from the nations of the world? See Num. 23:9.

However, it should be constantly borne in mind that an advantage is not necessarily a virtue, and a privilege is not a merit. In fact, when, in spite of the many unique advantages conferred upon Israel, that nation turns its back upon the Lord, these very advantages result in increasing Israel's punishment. See 9:30-32; and also what has been said in connection with 3:3, 4 (pp. 110, 111).

b. *and theirs is the adoption*

They had been accorded the high privilege of having been adopted as *God's firstborn* (Exod. 4:22), his *own possession* (Exod. 19:5), his *son* (Hos. 11:1), his *people*, his *chosen* (Isa. 43:20).

The calling and adoption of Israel, its separation from all the nations of the world to be God's very own, was certainly a high honor. When Paul dictated these words, was he not really saying, "Consider the Rock from which y o u were hewn"? See Isa. 51:1.

c. *and the glory*

Another blessing that could not be omitted from the list![264] A detailed study of this concept is indeed very instructive. As the word is here used it indicates *the divine radiance*, generally described as a body of light or fire, often pictured as being surrounded by a cloud. Sometimes the emphasis is

---

263. In addition to the sense *who, whoever*, the relative pronoun ὅστις (here nom. pl. masc. οἵτινες) at times has a causal meaning. So probably also here; and cf. 1:25.

264. For the various uses of the word δόξα in Scripture see on Rom. 1:23, footnote 38, p. 74. See also G. Kittel, Th. D.N.T., Vol. II, p. 237; and G. von Rad, same volume, pp. 238-242.

on the fire, sometimes on the cloud. It has been called "the visible manifestation of the invisible God."

When the building of the tabernacle had been completed, this "glory of the Lord" came and filled it (Exod. 40:34). It took its stand above the mercy-seat in the holy of holies (Lev. 16:2). During the wilderness journeys when it rested, the Israelites did not travel. When it was taken up, they marched (Exod. 40:36, 37). It was a cloud by day and a pillar of light by night (Exod. 14:20). It is pictured as a devouring fire on top of the mount where Moses spoke with God face to face (Exod. 24:17). When Solomon finished his very impressive prayer at the dedication of the temple, this glory filled the temple (II Chron. 7:1, 2). It indicated the presence of the Lord with his people. However, at times it is associated with the presence of God for the purpose of rendering judgment and inflicting punishment (Num. 14:10; 16:19, 42; 20:6; cf. vss. 12, 13).

By means of this "glory," too, the people of Israel had been separated from all other nations.

d. *and the covenants*

There is a degree of doubt whether one should read the plural "covenants," or—with an important papyrus, with Vaticanus, and with several other witnesses—the singular "covenant." At any rate the word seems to point to the various affirmations and re-affirmations of God's covenant with his people and/or with their leaders. Even though there is only one covenant of grace, in essence identical in both dispensations, it was revealed more and more fully in course of time. See, for example, Gen. 15:1 f.; 17:7; 22:15 f.; 26:1 f.; 28:10 f.; Exod. 2:24; 6:4, 5; Deut. 5:1 f.; 8:18; Josh. 24:1 f.; Luke 1:72, 73; Acts 2:38, 39; 3:25; Gal. 3:9, 28, 29.[265]

Godfearing people in Israel rejoiced in this covenant: David did (II Sam. 23:5); so did Mary, the mother of Jesus (Luke 1:54, 55); and so did Zechariah, the father of John the Baptist (Luke 1:72, 73).

e. *and the legislation*

It was indeed an inestimable privilege that at Sinai Israel had received the law, as it were, out of the very hands of God. Even though by the law no one is justified in God's sight, nevertheless the law is good and serves useful purposes. See on 5:20, p. 184.

f. *and the worship*

Opportunity for worship, first in connection with the tabernacle (cf. Heb. 9:6), later in connection with the temple (Luke 18:9-14), was another high privilege. Nevertheless, the word used in the original is broad enough also to include worship in the synagogue. In fact, does not the occurrence of the same word for "worship" or "service" in John 16:2—"The hour is coming when whoever kills y o u will think that he is offering *service* to God"—point

---

265. See my book, *The Covenant of Grace*, Grand Rapids, revised edition 1978, pp. 21-25.

in the direction of a broader connotation than *cultic* service?[266] Moreover, even family worship was, to a certain extent, regulated by law (Exod. 13:14-16). It would appear, therefore, that Paul here in Rom. 9:4 is referring to far more than temple worship or even public worship in general. He was probably thinking of the *true* worship or service of the one and only God wherever and in whatever manner such homage is rendered. Though things were changing, for a long time both the object and the character of properly tendering religious devotion had been revealed only to the Jews (John 4:21-23). What an inestimable privilege!

g. *and the promises*

The reference is to those made to Abraham, Isaac, Jacob, and to the Jewish people as a whole. To Abraham God had promised, "I will be your God and the God of your seed after you" (Gen. 17:7). In various forms essentially that same promise had been repeated to Isaac, Jacob, and Israel as a nation. In view of its comprehensive character it included many other promises, certainly also the one mentioned in Gen. 18:10, 14 and Rom. 9:9.

It is understandable that the fulfilment of that one basic promise (Gen. 17:7) and therefore also of all subsidiary promises was dependent on the certainty of the coming and mediatorial work of the Redeemer. It is through Christ that all the promises are capable of being realized (II Cor. 1:20; Gal. 3:16). And what an abundance of promises is revealed to us in the pages of Holy Writ, all of them centering in Christ!

In the following list each Old Testament reference in the left column is paralleled by *one* new Testament reference, indicating the fulfilment of the indicated promise. With a little effort it will be easy for the reader to add other references to both lists. By no means all of the Old Testament passages here indicated are in the *form* of promises, but every one at least *implies* a promise.

Old Testament Predictions and Promises	*Fulfilment as recorded in the New Testament*
Gen. 3:15	Rom. 16:20
Gen. 12:3	Gal. 3:8, 9
Gen. 17:7	Acts 2:38, 39
Gen. 18:10, 14	Rom. 9:9
Gen. 22:15-18	Heb. 6:13, 14
Gen. 29:35	Rom. 2:28, 29
Exod. 12:13; Lev. 17:11	Heb. 9:22
Num. 21:8	John 3:14, 15
Num. 24:17a	Rev. 22:16

266. Both Jesus (in John 16:2) and Paul (here in Rom. 9:4) use the term λατρεία. See also the apocryphal writing Ecclesiasticus 4:14: λατρεύοντες αὐτῇ λειτουργήσουσιν ῾Αγίῳ: "Those who *serve* her [Wisdom] *will minister* to the Holy one." This too proves that λατρεία and its cognate verb λατρεύω have a wider meaning than λειτουργία and λειτουργέω.

Deut. 18:15, 18	Acts 3:22
II Sam. 7:12, 13	Luke 1:31-33
Ps. 2:7, 8	Eph. 1:22
Ps. 8:4 f.	Heb. 2:6-8
Ps. 16:10	Acts 13:35
Ps. 22:1	Matt. 27:46
Ps. 68:18	Eph. 4:8
Ps. 69:20, 21	Matt. 27:34
Ps. 110:1	Matt. 22:44
Ps. 118:22, 23	Acts 4:11; Matt. 21:42 and see N.T.C. on Luke, p. 876
Isa. 7:14	Matt. 1:23 and see N.T.C. on Matthew, pp. 133-144
Isa. 9:1, 2	Matt. 4:12-16
Isa. 9:6	Luke 2:11
Isa. 10:22	Rom. 9:27
Isa. 28:16	Rom. 9:33; 10:11; I Peter 2:6, 8
Isa. 53	Matt. 8:17 and see N.T.C. on Luke, p. 977, and on Philippians, pp. 82, 83
Isa. 59:20, 21	Rom. 11:26, 27
Isa. 61:1 f.	Luke 4:18, 19
Jer. 23:5	Luke 1:32, 33
Jer. 31:31-34	Heb. 8:8-12
Dan. 2:34, 35, 44	Matt. 28:18
Dan. 7:13, 14	Matt. 26:64
Dan. 9:24-27	Rom. 3:21, 22
Joel 2:28, 29	Acts 2:17 f.
Amos 9:11-15	Acts 15:16-18
Mic. 5:2	Matt. 2:6
Hag. 2:6-9	Heb. 12:26
Zech. 3:8, 9	Heb. 10:12-14
Zech. 6:12, 13	Heb. 6:20-7:3
Zech. 9:9	John 12:15
Zech. 11:12	Matt. 26:15
Zech. 12:10	John 19:37
Mal. 3:1 f.	Matt. 11:10

What a blessing, all these promises, withheld from others but given to Israel.

h. *and theirs are the fathers*

It has been said, "If one wishes to be successful, he should choose his ancestors!" Paul may have been thinking especially of Abraham (4:1-3, 16-23; 9:7; 11:1); Isaac (9:7, 9, 10); and Jacob (9:13; 11:26). In many respects parents, in training their children, were able to point with pride to these three patriarchs. See also Rom. 11:28 and 15:8. Besides, we should never lose sight of the fact that these three ancestors were living on earth before the proclamation of God's holy law from Sinai. For a considerable period of time, therefore, they were *the bearers of tradition, the transmitters of the divine predictions and promises.*

But Paul also makes mention of David (1:3; 4:6-8; 11:9, 10; and see also 3:4). In fact, when the apostle refers to "the fathers," he was probably thinking of all the devout ancestors who played an important role in the history of redemption. Although it is true that none of these forefathers had been perfect in their earthly life and conduct, by and large they could be exhibited as examples to follow. All in all how supremely privileged were the people who were able to claim such ancestors!

i. *and from them, as far as his human nature is concerned, is Christ, who is over all God blest forever. Amen.*

This item serves as a fitting climax. From *them*, that is, from *the Israelites* (see verse 4) Christ derived his human nature. He was and is a Jew. What a source of intense satisfaction and rejoicing this *should be* for Jews!

The apostle hastens to add that although Jesus is indeed a Jew, he is also much more than a Jew. Though he has a human nature, he also has a divine nature. He is God!

It should be clear that when Paul says, "Christ, who is over all God blest forever," he confesses Christ's deity. He does, unless one is willing to adopt the kind of rendering favored by some, namely, "May God, supreme above all, be blessed forever!" (N.E.B.) or "God who is over all be blessed forever" (R.S.V.).

The reasons for rejecting these and similar translations, and adopting one that ascribes deity to Christ are as follows:

(1) The fact that in the preceding clause Paul has commented on Christ's *human* nature makes it reasonable to believe that he would now say something about his *divine* nature.

(2) A word-for-word translation of the original would be: ". . . and from [or *of*] whom (is) Christ according to (the) flesh, the one being above all God blessed forever . . ." It is clear that the words "the one being" or "who is" refer to Christ. They cannot refer to anyone else.

(3) The rendering, "Let God be blessed forever" would be a doxology in honor of *God*. It is Paul's custom, in such doxologies, to include in a preceding line or clause a reference to God; for example,

". . . since they had indeed exchanged God, (who is) the truth, for a lie, and worshiped and served the creature rather than the Creator, who is blessed forever. Amen" (Rom. 1:25).

". . . according to the will of our God and Father, to whom be the glory forever and ever. Amen." (Gal. 1:4, 5. See also II Cor. 11:31; II Tim. 4:18. The present passage, interpreted as a doxology, would therefore clash with Paul's style.

(4) Those who, in line with N.E.B. and R.S.V., translate the Greek words in question as if they were an *independent* doxology should bear in mind that in both Old and New Testament the word *Blessed* in such doxologies is found at the beginning of the sentence; as, for example, "Blessed (be) the Lord, the God of Israel" (Luke 1:68). See also II Cor. 1:3; Eph. 1:3. That is not the case here in Rom. 9:5.

(5) It is not unusual for the writers of New Testament books, including Paul, to ascribe deity, or the qualities pertaining to deity, to Christ. See, for example, Matt. 28:18; Mark 1:1; John 1:1-4; 8:58; 10:30, 33; 20:28; Phil. 2:6; Col. 2:9; Titus 2:13; Heb. 1:8; II Peter 1:1.

(6) A doxology to God would sound very strange in a paragraph in which Paul expresses "great sorrow and unceasing anguish" because of Israel's unbelief! Today it is unlikely that a missionary, reporting back to his board, would say, "Even though the people among whom I carry on my evangelistic activity have been blessed with many advantages—such as prosperity, good health, intelligence, etc.—there have been very few conversions. *Praise the Lord*!"

For the solemn addition "Amen" see on 1:25, p. 77.

What Paul has been saying, then, may be summed up as follows, "It grieves me deeply that in spite of all the remarkable advantages which God has showered on Israel, it has failed to reciprocate."

How can this negative reaction be explained? Also, does this mean that God has *totally* rejected Israel? The answers are given in the verses that follow; in fact, in a sense, in the entire argument beginning at 9:6 and ending at 11:36.

---

6 But it is not as though the word of God had failed. For not all who are of Israel are
Israel; 7 nor, because they are Abraham's seed, are they all (his) children; but
"It is through Isaac that your seed will be reckoned."
8 This means that it is not the natural children who are children of God, but it is the
children of the promise who are reckoned as seed. 9 For the language of promise is this:
"At the appointed time I will return, and Sarah will have a son."
10 But not only this; (there is) also Rebecca, who conceived (her two sons) at one time by
one and the same husband, namely, our father Isaac. 11 For, before the twins were born or
had done anything either good or bad, in order that God's purpose according to election
might stand, 12 (a purpose) based not on (human) works but on him who calls, she was told,
"The elder shall serve the younger";
13 as it is written,
"Jacob I loved, but Esau I hated."
14 What then shall we say? There is no injustice on God's part, is there? Not at all! 15 For
to Moses he says,
"I will have mercy on whom I have mercy; and I will
have compassion on whom I have compassion."
16 So then, it does not depend on (man's) will or exertion but on God's mercy. 17 For the
Scripture says to Pharaoh,
"For this very purpose have I raised you up, that I might display my power in you, and
that my name might be proclaimed in all the earth."
18 So then, on whom he wills he has mercy, and whom he wills he hardens.

---

2. *Divine Election and Rejection*
"Not all who are of Israel are Israel . . . Jacob I loved, but Esau I hated"
9:6-18

6-8 But it is not as though the word of God had failed. For not all who are of Israel are Israel; nor, because they are Abraham's seed, are they all (his) children; but

"It is through Isaac that your seed will be reckoned." This means that it is not the natural children who are children of God, but it is the children of the promise who are reckoned as seed.

Paul was apparently afraid that the statement with respect to his great sorrow and unceasing anguish might be interpreted as if he meant that God's *word*—his promise regarding Israel—had failed, his purpose frustrated.[267] So the apostle explains that although a marvelous promise had indeed been made to Israel (as has been indicated; see p. 313), that promise was never meant to be realized in the entire nation but only in the true Israel.

The thought expressed here is essentially the same as that found in Rom. 2:28, 29. Not in all the descendants of Abraham or of Israel was the covenant promise destined to be fulfilled but only in the hearts and lives of those who by God's grace would repose their trust in him and strive to obey his will out of gratitude. See Gen. 15:6; 17:1, 2, 9; Deut. 30:2, 3, 9, 10; I Kings 8:47-50; Jer. 18:5-10.

Moreover, in harmony with all this, the line of the covenant would run through Isaac. It was he who would be counted as Abraham's *seed*, in whom the covenant promise would be fulfilled. The true seed was *Isaac*, not Ishmael. Similarly, it was *Jacob*, not Esau (9:13). Cf. Gal. 3:9, 29.[268]

---

267. Note at beginning of verse 6: οὐχ οἷον . . . ὅτι, a combination of οὐχ οἷον and οὐχ ὅτι. The meaning is: it is not as though; it is not so that. Cf. Gram.N.T. (Bl. Debr.), par. 480. κληθήσεται (lit. "will be named or called") is a Hebraism. To be named after someone means to be counted as his offspring. Cf. Gen. 48:6.

268. In connection with verse 8 the question arises, "When Paul says, 'This means that it is not the children *of the flesh* (thus literally) who are the children of God, but it is the children of the promise who are reckoned as seed,' what does this expression 'children of the flesh' mean?" On this point commentators are divided. Some, appealing to the contrast pictured in Gal. 4:23, 29 between flesh-born Israel and Spirit-born Isaac, are of the opinion that the term "children of the flesh" as used here in Rom. 9:8 refers to the Jews who rejected Christ, while the term "children of the promise" points to those people who were reposing their trust in him. We have no quarrel with the latter part of this equation. But as to the former, which would pour the full meaning of Gal. 4:21-31 into Rom. 9:8, with this it is hard to agree.

The expression "children of the flesh" as used here in Rom. 9:8, should be explained in light of its own context. It then becomes clear that the terms "all who are of Israel" (verse 6), "Abraham's seed," here meaning *descendants* (verse 7), and "children of the flesh" (verse 8) are parallel, in the sense that all indicate *natural* or *physical* offspring. Correct are, therefore, those translations and interpretations which, for verse 8a, have adopted the rendering, "It is not the natural [or physical] children who are children of God," etc.

Thus N.I.V., Phillips, N.E.B., Williams, and Berkely must all be considered correct. Of course, those who retain the more literal rendering—"It is not the children of the flesh"—are also correct. That one of these "children of the flesh," who was not a child of promise, was indeed Ishmael, is, of course, admitted.

It is important to point out that although the statement "For not all who are of Israel are Israel" is cast in a negative mold, the positive implication is, *"There is, indeed, a true Israel. God's rejection of Israel is not total or complete."* His word has not failed and never will fail. The remnant will be saved (verse 27). He who puts his faith in Christ will not be put to shame (verse 33).

God's people are here called "the children of the promise," a strikingly beautiful designation! Their spiritual birth was due not to anything residing in them but entirely to God's covenant promise. It was the promise that gave them birth! They "were born not of blood nor of the will of the flesh nor of the will of man, but of God" (John 1:13), a fact exemplified clearly in the story of the birth of Isaac, to which reference is made in verse

9. For the language of promise is this:
"At the appointed time I will return, and Sarah will have a son."

As the conjunction "For" shows, what follows proves that not Abraham's natural children are necessarily God's children, and that only those can claim that distinction who are products of God's promise, his sovereign grace.

Note emphatic position of ". . . the language of promise is this." This is followed by the astounding statement that at the appointed time—that is *next year* (see Gen. 18:10, 14)—Sarah, the very wife, who according to Gen. 11:30 was *barren*, according to Gen. 18:11 was *past the age of childbearing*, and according to Gen. 17:17 was *ninety years old*, would give birth to a child. Not only this, but the child would be *a son*!

That this would happen seemed to be so impossible that when the Lord had told Abraham that he would have a child by Sarah, he had answered, "Will a son be born to a man a hundred years old? And will Sarah, at the age of ninety, bear a child?" (Gen. 17:17). And though Abraham probably quickly conquered his earlier misgiving,[269] even later Sarah had greeted the promise of a child with the laughter of unbelief (Gen. 18:10-12).

Nevertheless, the promise was fulfilled, proving that Isaac was indeed the child of promise, the product solely of divine, sovereign power and grace. God had *returned*; that is, his promise had been fulfilled in every detail.

Paul has made clear, therefore, that the ability to trace one's line of descent to Abraham does not entitle a person to believe that he will inherit that which was promised to Abraham. What matters is whether he belongs to that seed of Abraham which originates in the sovereign grace, will, and disposal of God Almighty.

Not to any extent is it a matter of human merit. The very history of Abraham and Sarah makes this clear. If from what has been said so far about Sarah the conclusion should be drawn that, judged by spiritual standards, she ranked far below Abraham, it should be pointed out that, all in all, Scripture's estimate of her is high. See Isa. 51:2; Heb. 11:11; I Peter 3:6. Abraham certainly must have loved her. Note what efforts he put forth in

---

269. That this patriarch had been briefly afflicted with misgiving is also the opinion of G. Ch. Aalders, *Genesis II (Korte Verklaring)*, p. 66.

order to secure for her an honorable burial (Gen. 23). And observe how Isaac needed to be comforted because of her death (Gen. 24:67).

And, on the other hand, measured by these same standards, Abraham does not fare as well as we had probably expected. In spite of whatever extenuating circumstances may be mentioned in his defense, what he did, as reported in Gen. 12:10 f. and again (!) in Gen. 20:1 f., was shocking.

Isaac too, though certainly a child of God (Gen. 25:21; 26:23-25; 28:1-4) was by no means perfect (Gen. 26:7; 27:1-4).

The only conclusion we can reach is that in the case of Abraham, Sarah, and their son Isaac, salvation, appropriated by faith, was definitely a matter of divine, sovereign grace. Human merit had nothing to do with it. Cf. Gen. 15:6; Rom. 4:3; Gal. 3:6.

Moreover, that salvation and preferential standing in the line of the covenant are indeed matters of grace, gifts proceeding from God's sovereign will and power, is even more strikingly illustrated in the story of Rebecca:

10-13. But not only this; (there is) also Rebecca, who conceived (her two sons) at one time by one and the same husband, namely, our father Isaac. For, before the twins were born or had done anything either good or bad, in order that God's purpose according to election might stand, (a purpose) based not on (human) works but on him who calls, she was told,

"The elder shall serve the younger";

as it is written,

"Jacob I loved, but Esau I hated."[270]

In defense of his reasoning Paul states, "But not only this"; that is, "Consider not only the case of Isaac and Ishmael." In their case one might be tempted to argue that the reason why the line of the covenant ran through Isaac, not through Ishmael, was that Isaac's mother was Sarah, but Ishmael's mother was Sarah's Egyptian slave-handmaid Hagar. Jacob and Esau, however, not only had the same father but also the same mother, and were conceived at the same moment. They were twins, though Esau was born just before Jacob and was, accordingly, "the elder."

Note also the following: in the case of Abraham's children it was possible to point to the contrast in the cause of their birth. Ishmael was, in a sense, the product of his parents' sinful scheming (Gen. 16:14), but Isaac was the realization of God's promise.

Nothing resembling this was true in the case of Jacob and Esau. Both were born in answer to prayer (Gen. 25:21).

---

270. The compressed style of verse 10 leads to certain difficulties in translation. Also, the word κοίτη has more than one meaning, although the various senses in which it is used are closely related. In Luke 11:7 it means *bed*; cf. κεῖμαι, to lie down. In Heb. 13:4 the reference is to the *marriage-bed*; in Lev. 15:24, to *sexual intercourse*; and in Lev. 15:16, to the *emission of semen*. Here, in Rom. 9:10, what Paul probably means is that Rebecca, having one husband, namely, Isaac, conceived (her twins) at one time; that is, from one seminal emission.—In Rom. 13:13 κοίτη = indecency, sexual excess.

Nevertheless, in spite of their remarkable similarities, before these twins were ever born, or had done anything either good or bad, their mother was already told, "The elder shall serve the younger" (quoted from Gen. 25:23). And this is also what actually happened, for not only did Esau forfeit, and Jacob receive, the birthright (Gen. 25:29-34), but the latter also obtained the blessing which father Isaac wrongfully had intended to pronounce upon Esau (Gen. 27:1-29).

The contrast was, however, even sharper, for, quoting from Mal. 1:2, 3, the apostle adds, "as it is written, 'Jacob I loved, but Esau I hated.' " The divine *purpose*, springing from election and executing its design, determines who are saved. Everything depends on God who *calls* (effectively draws) some, not others. Cf. 8:28.

What Paul is saying, then, in verses 6-13, is this: In the final analysis the reason why some people are accepted and others rejected is that God so willed it. The divine, sovereign will is the source of both election and reprobation. Human *responsibility* is not canceled, but there is no such thing as human *merit*. God's eternal purpose is not ultimately based on human works.

Additional Reflections on Election and Reprobation

As is well-known, this passage (Rom. 9:13) is considered a prooftext for the doctrine of predestination: election and reprobation. *Predestination* is God's eternal purpose whereby he has foreordained whatever comes to pass (Eph. 1:11). *Election* may be defined as God's eternal purpose to cause certain specific individuals to be *in Christ* the recipients of special grace, in order that they may live to God's glory and may obtain everlasting salvation (Luke 10:20; Acts 13:48; Rom. 11:5; Eph. 1:4; II Thess. 2:13). *Reprobation* is God's eternal purpose to pass by certain specific individuals in the bestowment of special grace, ordaining them to everlasting punishment for their sins (Rom. 9:13, 17, 18, 21, 22; I Peter 2:8).[271]

Although both of these decrees are equally ultimate, it would be wrong to say that they are co-ordinate in every respect. For example, although sin is indeed the meriting cause of the punishment mentioned in the definition of the decree of reprobation, faith is not the meriting cause of the salvation to which the definition of the decree of election refers. Also—to quote from my published translation of Dr. H. Bavinck's *Doctrine of God*[272]—"In a certain sense, the fall, sin, and eternal punishment are included in God's decree and willed by him. But this is true *in a certain sense* only, and not in the same sense as grace and salvation. These are the objects of his delight, but God does not delight in sin, neither has he pleasure in punishment."

The question is often asked, "How was it possible for a Loving God to ordain certain individuals to everlasting punishment?" A more logical ques-

---

271. Also often mentioned as a prooftext for the doctrine of reprobation is Jude 4, but the translation of this passage is disputed. Also Rom. 11:7 does not prove reprobation. See the context: 11:11f.

272. Grand Rapids, 1979, p. 390.

tion would be, "How was it possible for a God whose righteousness demands that sin be punished, to ordain some individuals to everlasting life and glory?" Surely "the wonder of it all" is the substitutionary death of Christ!

The Westminster Confession of the year 1647 has this to say about Election and Reprobation:

> God from all eternity did, by the most wise and holy counsel of his own will, freely and unchangeably ordain whatsoever comes to pass; yet so as thereby neither is God the author of sin, nor is violence offered to the will of the creatures, nor is the liberty or contingency of second causes taken away, but rather established—Ch. iii, I

> Those of mankind that are predestinated unto life, God, before the foundation of the world was laid, according to his eternal and immutable purpose, and the secret counsel and good pleasure of his will, hath chosen in Christ, unto everlasting glory, out of his mere free grace and love, without any foresight of faith or good works, or perseverance in either of them, or any other thing in the creature, as conditions, or causes moving him thereunto, and all to the praise of his glorious grace.—Ch. iii, V

> The rest of mankind God was pleased, according to the unsearchable counsel of his own will, whereby he extendeth or withholdeth mercy as he pleaseth, for the glory of his sovereign power over his creatures, to pass by, and to ordain them to dishonor and wrath for their sin, to the praise of his glorious justice—Ch. iii, VII

Essentially the same truths are expressed in Canons of Dort, First Head of Doctrine, articles 7 and 15, and in the Belgic Confession, article XVI. The Heidelberg Catechism contains very little on this subject. See Answers 52 and 54.

In addition the Canons (in its Fifth Head of Doctrine, Rejection of Errors, Conclusion) warn against those who teach that the doctrine of the Reformed Churches "makes God the author of sin," and that he

> . . . by a mere arbitrary act of his will, without the least respect or view to any sin, has predestined the greatest part of the world to eternal damnation, and has created them for this very purpose; that in the same manner in which election is the foundation and cause of faith and good works, reprobation is the cause of unbelief and impiety; that many children of the faithful are torn, guiltless, from their mothers' breasts, and tyrannically plunged into hell . . . and many things of the same kind which the Reformed Churches not only do not acknowledge but even detest with their whole soul.

A couple additional matters should not be omitted:

a. "The reprobate receive many blessings, which do not result from the decree of reprobation, but from the goodness and grace of God. They receive many natural gifts: life, health, strength, food, happiness, etc. (Matt. 5:45; Acts 14:17; 17:28; Rom. 1:19; James 1:17, etc.). Also with respect to the reprobate, God does not leave himself without witness. He endures them with much longsuffering (Rom. 9:22). He causes the gospel of his grace to be proclaimed to them, and has no pleasure in their death (Ezek. 18:23;

33:11; Matt. 23:37; Luke 19:41; 24:47; John 3:16; Acts 17:30; Rom. 11:32; I Thess. 5:9; I Tim. 2:4; II Peter 3:9)."[273]

Cain was a reprobate. Of this there can be no doubt (I John 3:12; Jude 11). Yet, how tenderly God addressed him! (Gen. 4:6, 7).

b. There is a problem that must be faced. Our Creeds, as has been shown, proceed from the infralapsarian position, according to which those people who were destined for glory were chosen out of the state of sin and destruction into which they had plunged themselves; and those destined for perdition were, by God's decree, left in that state. The question, however, arises, "Why did God at all allow the fall to take place?"

To that question there is no answer, except it be that of Deut. 29:29, "The secret things belong to the Lord our God, but the things revealed belong to us and to our children forever . . ." And that of Job 11:7, 8,

> Can you by searching fathom God?
> Can you probe the limits of the Almighty?
> They are higher than the heavens—what can you do?
> Deeper than Sheol—what can you know?

Permit me to quote once more from my translation of Bavinck's *Doctrine of God*, this time p. 396:

> Round about us we observe so many facts which seem to be unreasonable, so much undeserved suffering, so many unaccountable calamities, such an uneven and inexplicable distribution of destiny, and such an enormous contrast between the extremes of joy and sorrow, that anyone reflecting on these things, is forced to choose between viewing this universe as if it were governed by the blind will of an unbenign deity as is done by pessimism; or, upon the basis of Scripture and by faith, to rest in the absolute and sovereign, yet—however incomprehensible—wise and holy will of him who will one day cause the full light of heaven to dawn upon these mysteries of life.

Among the many objections that have been raised against the doctrine of election and reprobation, and particularly against the view that Rom. 9:13 supports this doctrine, are the following:

Objection a. Election, yes; reprobation, no! Neither Rom. 9:13 nor any other biblical passage teaches reprobation.

Comment. That Scripture does indeed teach both election and reprobation has been shown. See above, p. 320. Besides, election and reprobation stand and fall together. Those whom the Lord does not elect he rejects. God's counsel is all-comprehensive (Prov. 16:4; Eph. 1:11).

Moreover, when God elects a person, he not merely decides to cause him to enter heaven at last, but guides him all the way from conception to glorification. David proclaims this truth in Ps. 139:16, which, in rhyme, is as follows:

---

273. This quotation is taken from my translation of Bavinck's material on this subject. See *Doctrine of God*, p. 400.

Ere into being I was brought,
Thine eye did see, and in thy thought,
My life in all its perfect plan
Was ordered ere my days began.

Now the believer does not live in a vacuum, and between his life and that of the unbeliever there is no Chinese Wall. The life of the elect and that of the non-elect are so thoroughly intertwined—at play, in school, in the place of business, in factory, in government, etc.—that any divine plan that affects the elect must also affect the non-elect, without canceling human accountability in either case. A half plan is no plan at all. Many a battle has been lost because this or that small (?) item had been excluded.

For the want of a nail the shoe was lost,
For the want of a shoe the horse was lost,
For the want of a horse the rider was lost,
For the want of a rider the battle was lost,
For the want of a battle the kingdom was lost
And all for the want of a horseshoe nail.

—Franklin, Poor Richard Almanac

Objection b. The divine oracle (Mal. 1:2, 3), quoted by Paul in Rom. 9:13, really means, "Jacob have I loved intensely, but Esau have I loved less."

Comment. The verb used in the original for *to hate* can indeed have the meaning *to love less.* See N.T.C. on Luke, pp. 734, 735. The question is, "Does it have that meaning *here* (Rom. 9:13)?" Clearly, it does not! The context of Mal. 1:2, 3 is one of judgment, punishment, indignation: ". . . Esau have I hated, and made his mountains a desolation . . . They will build, but I will throw down." Also, when Esau receives his father's "blessing," that blessing amounts to what might almost be called a curse. Correctly translated, it begins as follows,

"Away from the fatness of the earth will be your dwelling, and away from the dew of heaven from above" (Gen. 27:39). In fact, the "blessing" was of such a negative nature, and the deception by Jacob so painful, that Esau hated Jacob because of what had happened, and threatened to kill him. Conclusion: "loved less" will not do for Mal. 1:3 or for Rom. 9:13. These passages refer to reprobation, nothing less.

Objection c. Gen. 25:22, 23 and Mal. 1:2, 3 do not refer to individuals, Jacob and Esau, but to nations, Israel and Edom.

Comment. Though it is true that in Gen. 25:22, 23 the text turns quickly from babes to nations, nevertheless the starting-point has to do with persons, not nations. The words, "Two nations are in your womb" can, of course, not be taken literally. The meaning is, "The two babes within your womb will become rival nations."

The Malachi context is similar. Here too the starting-point is certainly personal: "Was not Esau Jacob's brother . . . yet I loved Jacob but Esau I hated." Paul had every right, therefore, to apply these passages to persons, as he did.

Objection d. The doctrine of a twofold predestination—election and reprobation—is wrong because Jacob is always Esau also, and Esau is also Jacob; or, again, in each of us there is a Jacob and an Esau, etc.

Comment. Can anyone really believe that this is actually what Scripture is saying in these passages?

Having examined the objections, the result is that the doctrine of divine election and reprobation, based, among other passages, on Rom. 9:13, stands. The arguments against it are shallow and fallacious. See also the excellent "Paper" by F. H. Klooster, "Predestination: A Calvinistic Note," in *Perspectives on Evangelical Theology*, Grand Rapids, 1979, pp. 81-94.

14, 15. What then shall we say? There is no injustice on God's part, is there? Not at all. For to Moses he says,

"I will have mercy on whom I have mercy; and I will have compassion on whom I have compassion."

For "What [or What then] shall we say?" see also 3:5; 4:1; 6:1; 7:7; 8:31; 9:14, 30. The apostle anticipates an objection, whether from the side of an opponent or from that of those addressed; in fact, perhaps even a possible objection that might arise in *anybody's* mind. For the rest, two interpretations have been advanced.

According to the first, the meaning of verses 14, 15 is as follows: The question arises, "When God chose Isaac instead of Ishmael, and when he elected Jacob instead of Esau, making known his decision to their mother before the twins had even been born and had done either good or bad, that was not possibly unjust, was it?" According to this interpretation Paul answers, in substance, "Not at all, for that is God's way of acting, as is clear from what he said to Moses (verse 15) and to Pharaoh" (verse 17).

So interpreted, however, the answer would make little sense. It would amount to saying, "God is not unjust, for that is the way he is used to doing things!"

According to the second, the meaning is this: "Paul, by reasoning as you did [in Rom. 9:6-13] about God's sovereignty, you are not, perhaps, doing injustice to God, drawing inferences from the passages (about Abraham's seed and Rebecca's twins) that you have no right to draw?" The answer then is, "*Not at all* (see on 3:4), for, in speaking to Moses, God has definitely declared that he has the right to show his mercy and compassion to whomsoever he wishes." Cf. Matt. 20:15. What the apostle declares, therefore, is that when he underscores the doctrine of God's sovereignty he is simply saying what God himself also said.[274] I accept this explanation.

Continued: **16. So then, it does not depend on (man's) will or exertion but on God's mercy.**

Literally what Paul says is, "So then (it is) not of a person's willing nor of a person's running, but of God's showing mercy."

---

274. For this interpretation see S. Greijdanus, *Kommentaar Romeinen* II, pp. 422, 423; and Ridderbos, *op. cit.*, pp. 14, 15.

To the question, "What is the subject of the sentence?"—for in the original there is no subject—the answers differ. Some say it is "Mercy." They point to the immediate context (verse 15). Others go back a little farther, to verses 6-15, and answer, "It is being a child of God" (see 9:8), or "salvation," "life everlasting." But do not all these answers basically agree?

Hymn writers have caught the idea; see on 1:17, pp. 60, 61, and on 3:24, 25, p. 133. Neither man's volition nor his exertion brings about salvation. *God* does. Election, and therefore also salvation, is a matter of God's sovereign will. Equally ultimate is reprobation.

Therefore, parallel with verse 15 is verse **17. For the Scripture says to Pharaoh, "For this very purpose have I raised you up, that I might display my power in you, and that my name might be proclaimed in all the earth."**

Since this passage is presented as being a direct quotation, the Lord's own message to Pharaoh, a message conveyed to that king by Moses, and recorded in Scripture—note "the Scripture says"—it is advisable to study the text (Exod. 9:16) in which it is first recorded.

Its context shows us that there had been six plagues on Egypt: water turned into blood, frogs, lice, flies, murrain of cattle, boils on man and beast. There were going to be four more: hail, locusts, three days of intense darkness, all the firstborn of Egypt slain. Between the sixth and the seventh plague God ordered Moses to say to Pharaoh, "By now I could have stretched out my hand and struck you and your people with a plague that would have wiped you off the earth. But for this reason did I cause you to stand [or survive], to show you my power, and that my name might be proclaimed in all the earth" (Exod. 9:15, 16).

It is clear, therefore, that in Exod. 9:16 the expression "made you to stand" or "survive" means "spared you." There is accordingly no reason to interpret Rom. 9:17 differently. To be sure, the Greek verb has other meanings also, but these meanings do not fit the Exodus account.[275]

I agree, therefore, with the interpretation of Rom. 9:17 found also in the following commentaries: E. F. Harrison, *op. cit.*, p. 106; Ridderbos, *op. cit.*, pp. 216, 217. God spared Pharaoh so that he might display his power in him, by punishing him and his people. Cf. Rom. 9:22.[276]

That God did indeed fulfil his purpose of displaying his power in Pharaoh, so that his (God's) name might be proclaimed in all the earth, is clear from Deut. 6:22; 7:18, 19; 11:3; 34:11; I Sam. 4:8; Ps. 135:9; Acts 7:36. These passages prove that what God did in Egypt with Pharaoh and his people

---

275. The Hebrew verb used in Exod. 9:16 is the Hiph. pret. first per. s., with sec. per. s. suffix, of the verb עָמַד, to stand. This verb at times has the meaning: to spare, keep alive. See W. H. Gispen, *Exodus (Korte Verklaring)*, Kampen, 1932, p. 102. Also in harmony with this interpretation is the LXX rendering διετηρήθης, you have been spared.

276. For a different interpretation of the verb ἐξεγείρω, used in Rom. 9:17, see L.N.T. (A. and G.), p. 273, and several commentaries, including Cranfield, Greijdanus, Murray. Popular is the interpretation: to cause to be born, to cause to appear on the stage of history.

made a very deep impression on the minds and hearts of later generations. Even today when, in the home, in Sunday School, Christian School, or church, the story of the ten plagues is told, or when that story is read, is not God's name and greatness being proclaimed?

It is clear that when God hardens the heart of a person who has hardened himself against his Maker, God cannot be accused of being unjust. Whether God will actually do this, or whether, instead, he will show mercy, is not for that person or for us to decide. It is a matter pertaining to God's own will, power, and eternal decree. It is exactly as stated in verse

18. So then, on whom he wills he has mercy, and whom he wills he hardens. Cf. verse 15. A striking expression of *God's sovereignty*!

There is no reason to doubt that the hardening of which Pharaoh was the object was final. It was a link in the chain: reprobation—wicked life—hardening—everlasting punishment. This does not mean, however, that divine hardening is always final. See on 11:7b, 11.

---

19 You will say to me then, "Why does he still find fault, for who is resisting his will?" 20 But who are you, O man, to talk back to God? Will what is molded say to its molder, "Why did you make me thus?" 21 Does not the potter have the right to make, out of the same lump of clay, one vessel for honor and another for dishonor?[277] 22 And what if God, choosing to show his wrath and to make known his power, bore with great patience vessels of wrath, prepared for destruction, 23 (doing this) in order to make known the riches of his glory (lavished) upon vessels of mercy, which he prepared beforehand for glory, 24 even us, whom he also called, not only from the Jews but also from the Gentiles? 25 Just as he says in Hosea:

" 'Not my people' I will call 'My people,'
and
'Not my loved one' (I will call) 'My loved one.' "

26 And it will happen that in the very place where it was said to them, "You are not my people," they will be called "sons of the living God."

27 But Isaiah cries out concerning Israel:

"Though the number of the children of Israel be as the sand of the sea, (only) the remnant will be saved. 28 For the Lord will carry out his sentence on earth completely and quickly."

29 And as Isaiah predicted:

"If the Lord of hosts had not left us a seed, we would have fared like Sodom, and have been made like Gomorrah."

---

3. *God's Wrath and Mercy*

"Does not the potter have the right to make, out of the same lump of clay, one vessel for honor and another for dishonor?"

9:19-29

A plausible objection is now presented: **19. You will say to me then, "Why does he still find fault, for who is resisting his will?"**

The objection arises from failure to distinguish between God's secret (decretive) and his revealed (preceptive) will. Man can, of course, do nothing

---

277. Or: one for ornamental . . . one for everyday use.

about the former. But he certainly and rightly is held responsible for what he does about the latter. This two-fold fact is clearly set forth in two easy-to-remember passages: Deut. 29:29 and Luke 22:22.

It is, therefore, not surprising that the apostle continues as follows:

20, 21. But who are you, O man, to talk back to God? Will what is molded say to its molder, "Why did you make me thus?" Does not the potter have the right to make, out of the same lump of clay, one vessel for honor and another for dishonor?

The answer rebukes the questioner for his impudence and for his imbecility; for his shamelessness and for his senselessness. The objector calls in question God's justice, and is therefore impudent, arrogant. He forgets that if that which is molded has no right to say to its molder, "Why did you make me thus?," then *all the more*, human beings have no right thus to address their Sovereign Maker. The objector is stupid.

This passage about the potter and his lump of clay brings back to the memory several biblical passages; such as Job 10:9; Isa. 64:8; II Tim. 2:20; and especially Isa. 29:16; 45:9. See also the apocryphal book Wisdom of Solomon 15:7-17.

Note: "out of the same lump of clay, one vessel for honor and another for dishonor?" Several translators and commentators agree with this or a very similar rendering.[278] Others prefer "ornamental . . . everyday; or noble . . . common." The difference is minor. In favor of the first alternative is the fact that the context, here in Rom. 9:20, 21 (see 9:13 f.) is replete with sharp contrasts; such as, love, hatred, Moses, Pharaoh; mercy, hardening; vessels of wrath, vessels of mercy.[279]

The main idea Paul is putting across is this: If even a potter has the right out of the same lump or mass of clay to make one vessel for honor, and another for dishonor, then certainly God, our Maker, has the right, out of the same mass of human beings who by their own guilt have plunged themselves into the pit of misery, to elect some to everlasting life, and to allow others to remain in the abyss of wretchedness.

22-24. And what if God, choosing to show his wrath and to make known his power, bore with great patience vessels of wrath, prepared for destruction, (doing this) in order to make known the riches of his glory (lavished) upon vessels of mercy, which he prepared beforehand for glory, even us, whom he also called, not only from the Jews but also from the Gentiles?[280]

---

278. For example, A.V., A.R.V., Berkeley, Williams, Phillips, Greijdanus, Lekkerkerker.

279. See also the meaning of the word ἀτιμία in Rom. 1:26; I Cor. 11:14; 15:43; II Cor. 6:8; 11:21; namely, shame, disgrace, dishonor. And study N.T.C. on II Tim. 2:20, p. 270.

280. In the original this sentence, beginning with verse 22, and extending at least through verse 24, has no subject. Its anacoluthic character reminds us of 5:12 f. Nevertheless, the unexpressed but assumed subject can be conjectured on the basis of the context. See especially verses 19, 20, which indicate the unreasonableness of questioning God's justice or fairness. The subject—or subject clause—is therefore probably, "*Who* would dare to find fault with

Note the following:

a. *God . . . bore with great patience*

The patience of God, his reluctance to punish sinners, is stressed in several passages; among them being Rom. 2:4—see p. 90; Gen. 6:3b; 18:26-32; Exod. 34:6; I Kings 21:29; Neh. 9:17b; Ps. 86:15; 10:8-14; 145:8, 9; Isa. 5:1-4; Ezek. 18:23, 32; 33:11; Luke 13:6-9; Rev. 2:21.

b. *vessels of wrath*

Who are these vessels of wrath? Some identify them with the prospective believers of Eph. 2:3. But is it not more natural, in the present context, to think of men like Pharaoh, the impenitent; in other words, of reprobates? It is comforting to know that, as remarked previously—see p.321—God shows patience even with those who are ultimately lost! This explanation also harmonizes with the next point:

c. *prepared*[281] *for destruction*

Paul does not state who it was that prepared these people or made them ripe for destruction. From 9:18 some have drawn the conclusion that it was God. But here in verse 22 we are not told that it was God. And even if it was God, then must we not assume that his action of hardening their hearts, and thus preparing them for destruction, followed, and was a punishment for their own action of hardening themselves? But it is not at all impossible that the apostle wishes to present a contrast between the present passage and verse 23, where the active agent is mentioned, in order to show that here, in verse 22, *the people themselves*—in co-operation with Satan!—were the active agents; as, for example, also in I Thess. 2:14b, 15, 16; whereas in Rom. 9:23 *God* is said to be the One who prepares, and there in a favorable sense; see below.

d. *choosing to show his wrath and to make known his power*

It is exactly to hardened sinners, men like Esau (9:13), Pharaoh (9:17, 18), and Judas the traitor (Luke 22:22; John 13:18; 17:12; Acts 1:15-20, 25), impenitents all; that is, to those people who to the very end refuse to respond favorably to God's patient appeals, that God shows his wrath and makes known his power.

e. *(doing this)*, that is, bearing with great patience vessels of wrath, *to make known the riches of his glory (lavished) upon vessels of mercy.*

God" (continued: "if he, etc."). In English such a sentence would generally begin with "What if," etc.

After the introductory words the main clause is "[he] bore with great patience vessels of wrath, prepared for destruction." This is modified as follows:

a. choosing—that is, because he chose; cf. verse 17—to show his wrath.

and

b. . . . . to make known his power

c. in order to make known the riches of his glory (lavished) upon vessels of mercy, which he prepared beforehand for glory, even us, whom he also called, not only from the Jews but also from the Gentiles.

281. κατηρτισμένα, having been prepared; hence ripe, acc. pl. neut. perf. pass. participle of καταρτίζω, here: to prepare.

This reason is co-ordinate with that mentioned above under d. Both modify the main clause (a. God bore with great patience).

It was exactly God's *great patience* with Pharaoh and his people, his delay in pouring out upon them the full measure of the punishment they had deserved, that provided the opportunity to make known the riches of God's glory lavished on the Israel of that early day. If Pharaoh had been immediately destroyed, who would have become aware of God's *mercy* toward Israel? But as the ten plagues followed each other, one by one, that *mercy* became increasingly evident. Note the following:

In connection with the

fifth plague: "But the Lord will make a distinction between the livestock of Israel and the livestock of Egypt, so that no animal belonging to the Israelites will die . . . All the livestock of the Egyptians died, but of the animals belonging to the Israelites died not one" (Exod. 9:4, 6).

seventh plague: "Only in the land of Goshen, where the children of Israel lived, was there no hail" (Exod. 9:26).

ninth plague: "No one could see anyone else or leave his place for three days; but all the children of Israel had light in their dwellings" (Exod. 10:23).

tenth plague: "There will be loud wailing throughout all the land of Egypt . . . but among the Israelites not a dog will bark at any man or animal, that y o u may know that the Lord makes a distinction between the Egyptians and Israel . . . The blood will be a sign for y o u on the houses where y o u are; and when I see the blood, I will pass over y o u" (Exod. 11:6, 7; 12:13).

The same principle is always operating. God is ever bearing with great patience vessels of wrath, to make known the riches of his glory lavished on vessels of mercy.

f. *the riches of his glory*

This phrase refers to the glorious sum-total of all God's attributes. See their meaningful enumeration in such passages as Ps. 85:10; 145:8, 9; Rom. 11:33; Eph. 1:6-8; 2:4, 5, 7; 3:8.

g. (vessels—or objects—of mercy) *which he prepared beforehand*[282] *for glory*

For contrast see above, under c. The expression "which he prepared beforehand for glory" reminds us of Eph. 2:10, "For his handiwork are we, created in Christ Jesus for good works, which God prepared beforehand, that we should walk in them." The thought of Rom. 8:28-30 returns here.

h. *even us, whom he also called*

The calling to which this passage refers is that operation of the Holy Spirit whereby he so applies the gospel to the minds and hearts of sinners that they become aware of their guilt, begin to understand their need of Christ, and embrace him as their Lord and Savior. It is the *effective* call, the invitation savingly applied to heart and life. See on 1:7 and 8:28.

---

282. προητοίμασεν, third per. s. aor. indicat. of προετοιμάζω, to prepare in advance or beforehand.

i. *not only from the Jews but also from the Gentiles*

As far as the Jews are concerned, *historically* only the true Israel is effectively called and saved; as, in many different ways, the apostle impresses upon us again and again (Rom. 2:28, 29; 9:6, 27, 28; 11:5, 7, 26). There is indeed such a remnant. *Israel's rejection is never total or complete.*

But not only Jews, also Gentiles are saved. In fact, Paul, throughout this epistle, and also elsewhere, emphasizes the thought that there is no distinction between Jews and Gentiles. All God's children constitute *one* people, the church universal: Rom. 1:5, 13-16; 2:10, 11; 3:22-24, 30; 4:11, 12; 8:32 ("us all"); 10:4, 9 (cf. John 3:16); 10:12; 11:32; 16:26. Cf. Gal. 3:9, 29; Eph. 2:14-18.

25, 26. Just as he says in Hosea:

"*Not my people*" I will call "*My people,*"
and
"*Not my loved one*" (I will call) "*My loved one.*"

And it will happen that in the very place where it was said to them, Y o u are not my people, they will be called sons of the living God.

Hosea was a prophet to Israel, the kingdom of the ten tribes. See Hos. 7:1. He prophesied during the eighth century before Christ; that is, during what may be called the Glamor Age and the Growth of Assyria Period. Great victories were being won by Israel—hastening Israel's doom! The nation resembled a polished piece of furniture, inside of which the termites were at work. On the inside Israel was being devoured by moral and spiritual decay. From the outside Assyria, capturing nation upon nation, was approaching and threatening Israel's very existence. The *prosperity*, of which the Israelites boasted, was, accordingly, illusive.[283]

At God's command Hosea married a woman named Gomer. She was not true to her husband. She became a woman of whoredom and conceived children of whoredom (Hos. 2:4): Jezreel, Lo-ruḥamah, and Lo-ammi (son, daughter, son). We are concerned here only with the last two. Their names are symbolical of Israel's condition as seen by the Lord. Lo-ruḥamah means "Not my loved one"; and Lo-ammi, "Not my people."

Hosea, instead of rejecting his wife, slips away to the haunt of shame, buys her back, and mercifully restores her to her former position of honor, so that "Not my loved one" becomes "My loved one," and "Not my people" becomes "My people."

In Rom. 9:25 Paul quotes this passage from Hos. 2:23, reversing the lines, so that what Hosea had said about "Not my loved one" becomes Paul's second line, and what the Old Testament prophet predicted with reference to "Not my people" is placed first by the apostle. The sense is, however, unchanged.

---

283. For more on the Israel of that day and on Hosea see Leon J. Wood, *The Prophets of Israel*, Grand Rapids, 1979, pp. 275-283; and W. Hendriksen, *Survey of the Bible*, pp. 235-238.

Paul's next line ("And it will happen that in the very place where it was said to them, 'Y o u are not my people,' they will be called 'sons of the living God' ") is quoted from what in our Bibles is Hos. 1:10b.[284]

It is clear, therefore, that what Hosea describes is Gomer's sin, punishment, and restoration: a symbol of Israel's sin, punishment, and restoration to divine favor.

Hosea clearly was speaking of *restoration* (to God's favor) *of Israelites*. However, when Paul makes use of this passage, he makes no such limitation. He speaks about "us, whom he also called not only from the Jews but also from the Gentiles." And Peter (I Peter 2:10), addressing congregations of predominantly Gentile origin (see I Peter 1:14, 18; 2:9, 10; 4:6), applies the Hosean passage directly to converts from the Gentile world. The question may be asked, therefore, How is it possible for Paul and Peter to take a passage which predicts restoration for *Israelites* and apply it to audiences in which *Gentiles* predominated?

The answer is simple: the same principle operates throughout. Whether it be restoration to divine favor of Israelites, or conversion of Gentiles, or even both, the cause or source of restoration and salvation in each case is the same. That which brings about the restoration or conversion is ever the active, powerful, and sovereign grace of God Almighty! The rule is always, " 'Not my people' *I* will call 'My people,' and 'Not my loved one' (*I* will call) 'My loved one.' " When that principle goes into operation, then in the very place—that is, in *every* place—where it was said to sinners, "Y o u are not my people," they will be called—and will actually be—sons of the living God. What is stressed in these quotations is the sovereign and pitying grace of God shown to those who—whether Jews or Gentiles—lack the right to consider themselves God's people.[285]

The next quotation has reference especially to Israel. After reading or hearing Rom. 9:25, 26, the question might very well occur, "Does Paul have in mind a *total* restoration of Israel?" The answer is clear:

27, 28. But Isaiah cries concerning Israel:

"Though the number of the children of Israel be as the sand of the sea, (only) the remnant will be saved. For the Lord will carry out his sentence on earth completely and quickly."

The quotation is from Isa. 10:22, 23. The prophet predicts that, due to the Assyrian invasion, Israel will be greatly reduced in number. The nation which at one time was as numerous as the sand by the sea (cf. Gen. 22:17) would be reduced to a remnant. Yes, only a remnant would return.

---

284. Our Rom. 9:25 is a "free" quotation of what in the Hebrew Bible and the LXX is found in Hos. 2:25, and in our Bibles in Hos. 2:23. Our Rom. 9:26 is quoted from what in the Hebrew Bible is found in Hos. 2:1b. So also in the LXX, of which Rom. 9:26 is an exact transcription.

285. Thus also Ridderbos, *op. cit.*, p. 223.

At this point we should guard ourselves against committing an error in our interpretation. It is a rather common practice to say that Paul now begins to spiritualize, by stating that only the remnant *will be saved.* However, a close look at Isaiah's own prophecy shows that he by no means restricts his prophecy to a prediction of a physical *return* from captivity, but states that the remnant will return "to the mighty God" (Isa. 10:21). They will *lean on Jehovah*, will rely on the Lord (verse 20). Paul is therefore exactly reproducing Isaiah's thought when he says that of the total number of Israelites only the remnant *will be saved*. The apostle adds that the Lord will carry out his sentence "completely and quickly" or "with vigor and dispatch."[286] In the days of Isaiah's prophecy the rigors of warfare, deportation, living in a strange country under distressing conditions, being cut down by the sword and/or seeing one's friends and relatives being thus cut down, must have been included. When *Paul*, guided by the Holy Spirit, makes use of this language, it is hard to believe that the Fall of Jerusalem in the year A.D. 70 was not at least part of the picture. But see also 9:13b, 18b. 22b.

29. And as Isaiah predicted: "If the Lord of hosts had not left us a seed, we would have fared like Sodom, and have been made like Gomorrah."

The quotation is from Isa. 1:9. The Hebrew original may be rendered as follows:

"Unless the Lord of hosts had left us a remnant ever so small, like Sodom should we have been, to Gomorrah should we have been compared."

The LXX is essentially the same, except that for "remnant ever so small" it uses the word "seed." It is this LXX text which is exactly reproduced by Paul here in Rom. 9:29. Of course, "seed" and "small remnant" are alike in meaning. If there is any difference at all, it might be that "seed" points directly to the Sower, namely, God, and has hopeful implications for the future.

What Isaiah, and after him Paul, are saying, then, is this: It is due exclusively to God's sparing love and providential care that the people—the authors include themselves and those addressed; note "we"—have not become like Sodom and Gomorrah. Stronger rejection of any personal merits or

---

286. This is the R.S.V. rendering. See below in this footnote. Note the word κράζει, third per. s. pres. indicat. of κράζω, to cry. According to Calvin (*Romans*, p. 373) Paul describes Isaiah as *exclaiming*, not speaking, "in order that he might excite more attention." Now although it is certainly true that even today the biblical truth that of Israel *only the remnant* (never the whole nation) is saved, needs to be exclaimed and emphasized, because so many persist in denying it, it is, nevertheless, also a fact that, according to S.BK. Vol. III, p. 275, the verb used in the original was probably no more than a then current indication of prophetic speech.

The expression λόγον συντελεῖν καὶ συντέμνειν is not easy to interpret, and has therefore been explained in various ways. The general idea is clear enough from the context: God will take definite and vigorous action. He will carry out his sentence completely and quickly. Punishment will not be postponed and will be severe. In the present context this also implies that Israel will be "cut down to size." Only a remnant will be saved.

pretensions was certainly impossible, for these cities were considered the very culmination of wickedness. See Gen. 13:13; 18:20, 21, 32 (cf. 19:29); Isa. 3:9; Jer. 23:14; Matt. 10:15; 11:23, 24; II Peter 2:6; Jude 7.

When a person reviews the ground covered in this chapter, he is surprised about the great number of scriptural quotations (verses 7, 9, 11-13, 15, 17, 20, 21, 25-29, and, still coming, 33). It is as if Paul purposely somewhat holds his own judgments in abeyance, so that the readers and listeners may be able to see for themselves what God had been saying in the past. And if even Paul, who, after all, was divinely inspired, made this use of Scripture, should not we today? Is not a sermon all the more powerful and effective if the preacher can prove to his audience, "Thus saith the Lord"?

Also here, as often previously, the lesson is: There is, indeed, a seed, a remnant, by God's sovereign grace. *Israel's rejection is not total.* Election is still having its effect.

---

30 What then shall we say? That Gentiles, who were not pursuing righteousness, have obtained righteousness, but the righteousness that is by faith. 31 Israel, however, though ever in pursuit of (the) law of righteousness, has not attained to (that) law. 32 Why? Because (they pursued it) not by faith but by relying on (their) works. They stumbled over[287] The Stumbling Stone; 33 as it is written:

"Behold, I lay in Zion A Stone of Stumbling
And A Rock of Offense.
But he who puts his trust in him
will not be put to shame."

---

4. *Conclusion*

"He who puts his faith in him will not be put to shame"
9:30-33

30, 31. What then shall we say? That Gentiles, who were not pursuing righteousness, have obtained righteousness, but the righteousness that is by faith. Israel, however, though ever in pursuit of (the) law of righteousness, has not attained to (that) law.

Though the words "What then shall we say?" are the same as those in verse 14, their import is not the same. In verse 14 Paul was anticipating an objection, which he then obliterates. Here, in 9:30, 31, he states the conclusion to which he has arrived on the basis of his previous reasoning.

That conclusion amounts to this: Gentiles—that is, those Gentiles who have embraced Christ—have obtained righteous standing before God. Yet, beforetime they had not been seeking to obtain righteousness where alone it could be found. At that time they had been living in moral and spiritual darkness. See Rom. 1:18-32; and cf. Acts 14:16; 17:30; Eph. 2:1-3. But when they heard the gospel, many of those Gentiles had, by God's grace, accepted it, and had thus obtained righteousness. Cf. Rom. 9:25, 26. However, it was

---

287. Or *against.*

not a righteousness based on their own goodness in the sight of God. It was *God's* righteousness, appropriated by God-given faith. It was a righteousness purchased by Christ's redeeming blood.

On the contrary, Israel, though ever in pursuit of the law of righteousness, zealously seeking to overtake it—so far, so good!—had failed to attain to it, to reach it. It ever eluded Israel. The reason is stated in verse

32a. Why? Because (they pursued it) not by faith but by relying on (their) works.

There was, of course, nothing wrong with seeking to attain to a state of righteousness in God's sight. The trouble with Israel was that these people proceeded from the false presupposition that by trying very, very hard they would be able, some day, to observe God's entire law, so that they would be able to shout, "Success! We made it!" Paul preaches an entirely different gospel. See Rom. 3:27, 28; Gal. 1:8, 9; 3:10; 5:6. The law, with its uncompromising demand of perfect love and obedience, should have driven each Israelite to God with the fervent prayer, "Oh, God, be thou merciful to me, the sinner." Instead, Israel took for granted that men would be able, by their own power, and on the basis of their own resources, to fulfil the law's demands.

Result: though ever pursuing, Israel never achieved. The law ever remained miles ahead of Israel. It could not be reached.[288]

32b, 33. They stumbled over The Stumbling Stone; as it is written:
"Behold, I lay in Zion A Stone of Stumbling
and A Rock of Offense.
But he who puts his trust in him
will not be put to shame."

Paul now goes to the very root of Israel's failure to attain to righteousness. They stumbled over—or against—the Stumblingblock. They failed to recognize Christ as their Savior. Of course, as long as Israel relied on works it could not embrace Christ. It was either the one or the other. It could not be both.

For Jews Christ was a stumblingblock (I Cor. 1:23). To be sure, for many a Gentile too he was foolishness. But on the whole Jews were far more adament in their belief that they had found the solution of the problem of achieving the status of righteousness in God's sight. And their failure humbly to flee to Christ and to embrace him by faith proved their undoing, spelled their doom.

The words quoted by Paul here in verse 33 are a combination of two biblical passages: Isa. 28:16 and 8:14:

"Behold, I lay in Zion a tested stone, a precious cornerstone for a solid foundation. The one who trusts will never be dismayed" (Isa. 28:16).

"For both houses of Israel he will be a stone that causes people to stumble, and a rock that makes them fall" (Isa. 8:14).

---

288. Note οὐκ ἔφθασεν, third per. s. aor. act. indicat. of φθάνω, here probably in the sense of *to attain to, reach, come up to, overtake.* Also see N.T.C. on Luke, p. 634.

Skillfully Paul combines the essence of both in his quotation. Even though in Isa. 8:14 it is the Lord of hosts who is described as being a stone of stumbling, the apostle does not hesitate to apply this passage to Jesus. Cf. Matt. 21:42; Mark 12:10; Luke 20:17; Acts 4:11; I Peter 2:6-8. Solution: Christ is God!

Israel's pursuit of the law, as if a person could be saved by keeping the law, amounted to unwillingness to accept the righteousness offered by God on the basis of the redemptive work of Christ. Gentiles, on the other hand, in great numbers, had accepted Christ by faith. As noted earlier, the church in Rome too consisted for the most part of converts from the Gentile world. Paul asserts that by putting their trust in Christ *they will not be dismayed or put to shame.* This reading of the passage (Isa. 28:16), seems to have been the basis of the LXX translation and also of Paul's quotation here in Rom. 9:33.[289]

By far the main point to be emphasized is this, that the truth here expressed holds for Jew and Gentile alike. Is it not a statement in prophetic, and now also in Pauline, language, of the precious truth embodied in John 3:16?

Practical Lessons Derived from Romans 9

Verse 1

"I am speaking the truth in Christ—I am not lying; my conscience bears witness along with me in the Holy Spirit. . . ." The apostle knew that his statements were going to be challenged, and, what is more important, shows that he is deeply conscious of writing in the very presence of God and under the constant direction of the Holy Spirit. See also 1:25; 6:17; 7:25; 8:35-39; 11:33-36; 15:13, 32; 16:25-27; Gal. 1:20; Eph. 1:3 ff.; 1:15 ff.; 3:14-21; I Tim. 2:7. Does not this fact make Paul's epistles even more precious to us?

Verses 1 and 3

"I am speaking the truth in Christ . . . I could wish that I myself would be accursed . . . for the sake of my brothers, my fellow-countrymen . . ." Here is *a great theologian* . . . who is at the same time *a very warm-hearted lover of souls*! To be sure, books are very important. Every minister should have access to a fine theological library. But what is even more important: he should love people, and be deeply concerned about their everlasting welfare. The same spirit should mark *every* believer!

---

289. It is, therefore probably incorrect to say that Paul's wording "varies from the Hebrew." (Murray, *op. cit.*, p. 45). The real question is, "Was the LXX rendering of Isa. 28:16 based on the masoretic text, and was that the text Paul, too, had in mind?" If not, then the difficulty disappears entirely, and one no longer has to say, "The Hebrew really means 'will not make haste,' but the apostle is following the LXX text."

Verse 5

"Christ, who is over all God blest forever. Amen." This reminds us of "But we see Jesus . . . crowned with glory and honor" (Heb. 2:9). It is the consciousness, in all circumstances of life, of the reality and closeness of the ever-living and ever-active Christ that imparts courage to stand firm, knowing that *he* is in complete control!

Verse 6 and Verse 27

"Not all who are of Israel are Israel." "Though the number of the children of Israel be as the sand of the sea, (only) the remnant will be saved."

Is it not high time that, in the preaching of the Word, the doctrine of *the remnant* be revived? See such passages as the following: I Kings 19:18; Isa. 1:9; 10:20-22; 11:11; 46:3; Jer. 23:3-6; Ezek. 6:8-10; Joel 2:32; Amos 5:15; Micah 2:12; 4:5-7; 7:18; Zeph. 3:12, 13; Matt. 7:14; 9:37; 22:14; Luke 12:32; 13:23, 24; Rom. 9:27-29; 11:4, 5; Rev. 12:17.

Verse 16

"So then, it does not depend on (man's) will or exertion but on God's mercy."

This passage shows how deeply conscious was Paul of the need of God, every step of the way. What do we find today, often even in church-going families? The children are brought up in schools were evolution is taught, and where creation, if it is ever mentioned, is frowned upon. The speaker who has been invited to address the graduates tells them "Y o u will undoubtedly be very successful if only y o u do y o u r darndest" (an example taken from life). What can be done to correct this evil?

When the youth looks for a wife or husband, he (she) demands that his (her) marriage partner possesses all kinds of qualities . . . without ever asking the most important question of all, "Is he (she) a Christian?" And so life continues. Religion—if present at all—is a side issue. To be sure, by no means all young people are like that. Many show in their lives that they love the Lord and figure with him and his will as revealed in his Word! But is it not true that many too are in the opposite camp? As verse 16 shows, Paul was ever fully conscious of the fact that his welfare for time and eternity was subject to God's good pleasure!

Verse 22

"And what if God . . . bore with great patience vessels of wrath, prepared for destruction?"

If God bore with *great* patience those whom he knew would never be saved, should not we have at least *a little* patience with people who, though now unconverted, may still, by God's grace, experience a fundamental change, a genuine conversion?

Summary of Chapter 9

Paul opens this chapter by solemnly declaring that Israel's unbelief and consequent rejection is for him a heavy burden. So genuine, profound, and heart-rending is his anguish that he states, "I could wish myself to be accursed (and cut off) from Christ for the sake of my brothers, my natural kinsmen." In saying this he reminds us of Judah (the son of Jacob and brother of Joseph), of Moses, of David, and, in fact, of Jesus Christ. See Gen. 44:33; Exod. 32:32; II Sam. 18:33; Isa. 53:5-8, 12b.

The depth of Israel's tragedy and of Paul's grief becomes especially clear when the advantages that enabled this nation to place all others in its shade are listed. Greatest of them all is surely this: ". . . from them, as far as his human nature is concerned, is Christ, who is over all God blest forever. Amen." (verses 1-5).

No one should imagine, however, that Israel's rejection meant that God's Word—his promise to Israel—had failed. Fact is that this promise was never meant to be realized in the nation as a whole. It was meant for the true Israel, the body of God's elect from Israel: "Not all who are of Israel are Israel" (verse 6). This true Israel includes Jacob but not Esau. It includes all those, and only those, who are born of the Spirit. In the final analysis who these true Israelites are is determined by God's eternal decree. "Jacob I loved, but Esau I hated" (verses 6-13).

"So then," says Paul, "it [probably our *salvation*] does not depend on man's will or exertion but on God's mercy." After the first six plagues God had spared wicked Pharaoh's life in order, by means of the remaining plagues, now more than ever to display his power in connection with the outpouring of his wrath on Egypt's king and people, so that God's name might be proclaimed in all the earth. It is clear that God should not be accused of being unjust when he hardens the heart of a person who has hardened himself against his Maker. Whether God will show mercy to such a person or will harden him is up to God (verses 14-18).

Paul continues, "You will say to me, then, 'Why does he [God] still find fault, for who is resisting his will?' " The objector forgets that God certainly has a right to find fault with the man who disobeys God's revealed will (Deut. 29:29; Luke 22:22). Besides, "Who are you, O man, to talk back to God? Will what is molded say to its molder, 'Why did you make me thus?' "

Two facts stand out in God's dealings with people:

a. He bears with great patience the objects of his wrath.

b. While doing this, he is not forgetting his elect, the objects of his mercy. In fact, "God . . . bore with great patience objects ["vessels"] of wrath . . . in order to make known the riches of his glory (lavished) upon objects ["vessels"] of mercy, which he prepared beforehand for glory, even us, whom he also called [effectively drew to himself], not only from the Jews but also from the Gentiles" (verses 19-24).

With quotations from the prophecies of Hosea (first from 2:23 and then from 1:10b) the apostle now shows that just as for the Israelites of the old dispensation there was a promise of restoration, so also now that promise of restoration to divine favor still holds. However, with a quotation from Isa. 10:22, 23 Paul emphasizes (cf. Rom. 9:6) that he is not speaking about a *national* but about a *remnant* restoration. He states, "Though the number of the children of Israel be as the sand of the sea, (only) *the remnant* will be saved." Also, quoting Isa. 1:9, the apostle adds, "If the Lord of hosts had not left us *a seed*, we would have fared like Sodom, and have been made like Gomorrah" (verses 25-29).

Paul's conclusion is that, although Gentiles had formerly not been seeking to become righteous in the eyes of God, they had, nevertheless, obtained righteousness; that is, they had by faith accepted the Christ of the gospel.

On the contrary, Israel, though ever pursuing (seeking to fulfil) the law of righteousness, had failed to reach the status of righteousness in the eyes of God. Why? Because they relied on their own vaunted works and imagined merits, instead of placing their trust in Christ. He, *The Precious Cornerstone*, had become for them *A Stone of Stumbling and Rock of Offense*.

Paul closes this chapter with a quotation from Isa. 28:16, "But he who puts his trust in him will not be put to shame." The apostle, as is clear, has not forgotten his theme. Cf. Rom. 1:16, 17; 3:21-24, 28-30; 4:3-8, 22-24; 5:1, 2, 9, 18, 19; 8:1 (verses 30-33).

Outline (continued)

Justification by Faith

5. *Self-righteousness versus the Righteousness that Comes from God and Is Appropriated by Faith*
"For it is with the heart that a person exercises faith leading to righteousness, and with the lips that he makes confession issuing in salvation."
10:1-13

6. *Israel Is Responsible for Its Own Rejection. That Rejection Is Not Arbitrary.*
"All day long I have stretched out my hands to a disobedient and defiant people"
10:14-21

CHAPTER 10

ROMANS 10:1-13

10 1 Brothers, my heart's desire and prayer to God for them is that they may be
saved. 2 For I can testify about them that they have a zeal for God, but it is not
based on knowledge. 3 For, failing to acknowledge the righteousness that comes
from God, and seeking to establish their own, they did not submit to God's righteousness. 4 For Christ is the goal[290] of the law, so that there is righteousness for everyone
who puts his trust (in him). 5 For Moses describes in this way the righteousness that is by
the law: "The one who does these things shall live by them." 6 But the righteousness that
is by faith says, "Do not say in your heart, 'Who will ascend into heaven?' " that is, to bring
Christ down; 7 "or, 'Who will descend into the abyss?' " that is, to bring Christ up from the
dead. 8 But what does it say? "The word is close to you; (it is) on your lips[291] and in your
heart;" that is, the word of faith we are proclaiming. 9 Because, if on your lips is the confession, "Jesus is Lord," and in your heart the faith that God raised him from the dead, you will
be saved. 10 For it is with the heart that a person exercises faith leading to righteousness,
and with the lips[292] that he makes confession issuing in salvation. 11 For the Scripture says,
"No one who puts his trust in him will ever be put to shame." 12 For there is no distinction
between Jew and Greek. For the same Lord (is Lord) of all and richly blesses all who call on
him. 13 For everyone who calls on the name of the Lord will be saved.

---

5. *Self-righteousness versus the Righteousness that Comes from God and Is Appropriated by Faith*

"For it is with the heart that a person exercises faith leading to righteousness, and with the lips that he makes confession issuing in salvation."

10:1-13

1. Brothers, my heart's desire and prayer to God for them is that they may be saved.

For the use of the emotion-filled word of affection "brothers" see on 1:13 and 7:1. Especially now that Paul is about to enlarge on the subject of Israel's guilt, showing that *their rejection was not arbitrary but deserved*, he wisely first of all reaffirms (cf. 9:1 f.) his deep attachment to, and affection for, his kinsmen. By stating that his heart's desire and prayer to God is that they may be saved, is he not implying that he loves them intensely? The apostle knew that in Israel there was always a remnant that would be saved (9:23, 27). But even aside from this, is it not the believer's duty and joy to love *everyone*? See Matt. 5:43-48. Then certainly also one's kith and kin! Very properly the

---

290. Or: meaning and substance.

291. Literally: *in your mouth*, both here and in verse 9.

292. Literally: with the mouth.

apostle desires and earnestly prays for their salvation. He enlarges on this theme by adding:

2. For I can testify about them that they have a zeal for God, but it is not based on knowledge.

Zeal or enthusiasm can be a very good thing. See Ps. 69:9; John 2:17. The apostle admits that his fellow-countrymen wear themselves out to assure themselves of God's favor. Was not this already implied in 9:31? Is it not definitely confirmed by such passages as Acts 21:20; 22:3; Gal. 1:14?

So far, so good! The fly in the ointment, however, was this: this zeal for God, this enthusiasm about him, this strong and deep-seated urge to live in accordance with God's will, was not based on proper understanding! It was not in harmony with God's revelation concerning the way of salvation. Paul explains this in verse

3. For, failing to acknowledge the righteousness that comes from God, and seeking to establish their own, they did not submit to God's righteousness.

In words so clear that explanation is hardly necessary, Paul points out that Israel's basic fault consisted in this:

a. It failed *to acknowledge*, that is, to accept and welcome, the righteousness that has God as its Author (3:21-24; 8:1; 9:30), is based on Christ's substitutionary atonement (3:24; 5:8, 17, 18; 8:3, 4, 32; cf. Isa. 53:4-8; Matt. 20:28; Mark 10:45; II Cor. 5:21; Gal. 3:13; I Tim. 2:5, 6), and is appropriated by faith (some of these same passages and also Rom. 1:17; 4:3-5, 16, 23-25; 5:1; cf. Hab. 2:4; Gal. 3:11).

b. It substituted its own work-righteousness for God's grace-righteousness. For the sad results, as pointed out by Paul, see Rom. 2:17 f.; 3:20; 9:31, 32.

That God did indeed provide righteousness is clear from that which, by an easy transition, follows in verse

4. For Christ is the goal of the law, so that there is righteousness for everyone who puts his trust (in him).

Does one wish to understand the goal, the meaning and substance, of the Old Testament law? Then study Christ. Is not the very purpose of the law the establishment of *love*? See Deut. 6:5; Lev. 19:18 (in *that* order); cf. Matt. 22:37-39. Is not Christ the very embodiment of that love, both in his life and in his death? And is it not true that because of this love which caused him to suffer and die in his people's stead, there now is right standing with God for everyone who reposes his trust in the Savior? Is not this the very theme of Romans?[293]

---

293. Instead of "For Christ is the *goal* of the law," many prefer, "For Christ is the *end* of the law." As a *translation* this can stand. The further question is, "What is meant by the Greek word τέλος and the English word *end*? In addition to other meanings, both of these words can mean: (a) termination, finish; or (b) goal, intention, purpose, meaning and substance. However, meaning (a) does not apply in the present case, for the notion that because of the work of Christ the Old Testament law has in every respect lost its usefulness, and is therefore "finished," is contrary to Paul's teaching, as is clear from Rom. 3:31; 7:7. See especially on 5:20, Vol. I, p. 184. Accordingly, to avoid ambiguity and misunderstanding, it is probably better, even in the translation, to substitute the term *goal* for *end*.

Since verse 4 refers to Christ, as the law's goal, in the sense explained, it would seem to be logical, in the present case, to refer to Christ also in the next verse.

5. For Moses describes in this way the righteousness that is by the law: "The one who does these things shall live by them."

The reference is to Lev. 18:5 (quoted also in Gal. 3:12; cf. Luke 10:28). It was Christ, *he alone*, who by his life and death completely fulfilled the demands of the law, and thereby secured *for himself* the Father's approval and the place at the latter's right hand (Heb. 12:2); and *for his followers* everlasting life (Heb. 5:8, 9). Accordingly, for all those who place their trust in Christ the path that leads to salvation has, in a sense, become incredibly easy. That which was infinitely difficult, hard, and painful, in fact for sinners *impossible*, has been accomplished by Christ. No mere sinner should now try to do what for him is both impossible and unnecessary.

Now listen to what "the righteousness that is *by faith*" says:

6, 7. But the righteousness that is by faith says, "Do not say in your heart, 'Who will ascend into heaven?' " that is, to bring Christ down; "or, 'Who will descend into the abyss?' " that is, to bring Christ up from the dead.

Note the word "But." It marks a sharp contrast between (a) the state of righteousness *earned* by Christ (verses 4, 5), and (b) that same state which, on the basis of Christ's righteousness, is *freely obtained* by all those who believe in him.

This latter "righteousness," the one that is "by faith," is here personified and presented as speaking. It delivers a New Testament message in Old Testament terms. It is able to do this because in both testaments the way of salvation is the same, as Paul has already established (1:17; 3:21, 22; 4:1f.).

The words that are quoted carry us back to the time when Moses was giving instructions to the people of Israel with respect to their entrance into the land of Canaan. He sets forth the curses that would be poured out upon the disobedient (Deut. 27:9-26), as well as the blessings that would be bestowed upon the obedient (Deut. 28:8-14). He then addresses each Israelite as follows:

"Now what I am commanding you today is not too difficult for you, nor is it beyond your reach. It is not up in heaven, so that you have to ask, 'Who will ascend to heaven for us and bring it down to make us obey it?' Nor is it beyond the sea, so that you have to ask, 'Who will cross the sea for us and bring it to us to make us obey it?' " (Deut. 30:11-*13*).

The point Moses emphasizes is that the law has been given to Israel in the context of grace, and that Canaan, which the people are about to enter, is *God's gift* to them. It is in no sense whatever the product of their own righteousness or strenuous effort. See also Deut. 8:17, 18; 9:4-6.

That there is a striking analogy between entrance into earthly Canaan and obtaining salvation was clear not only to the writer of the epistle to the

Hebrews (see Heb. 4:6-10) but also to Paul; or, in the present context, to "the righteousness that is by faith."

Here too the truth to be emphasized is that *the really difficult task is not for us to undertake. It has been accomplished for us by Christ.* It is he who came down from heaven, dwelt among us as in a tent (John 1:14), suffered the agonies of hell for us, died, was buried, rose again, ascended to heaven. *The hard work was accomplished by him*! Therefore, any attempt on *our* part to ascend to heaven to bring Christ down would amount to a most ungracious denial of the reality and value of Christ's incarnation. Similarly, any attempt to descend into the realm of the dead in order to bring Christ up from the dead would be a disavowal of the genuine character and meaning of Christ's glorious resurrection from the dead and triumph over the grave. (See Ps. 16:10; Acts 2:27; Rom. 4:25; I Cor. 15:20, 55-57; Rev. 1:17, 18).[294]

When we study this reassuring teaching of the apostle Paul, it reminds us of Christ's own unforgettable words:

"Come to me all who are weary and burdened, and I will give y o u rest. Take my yoke upon y o u, and learn from me, for I am meek and lowly in heart, and y o u shall find rest for y o u r souls. *For my yoke is kindly, and my burden is light*" (Matt. 11:28-30).

8. But what does it say? "The word is close to you; (it is) on your lips and in your heart;" that is, the word of faith we are proclaiming.

The apostle continues to "quote" *the righteousness that is by faith*. The quotation found in Rom. 10:6, 7 ended with words from Deut. 30:*13*. So here in Rom. 10:8 the words of Deut. 30:*14* are quoted: "The word is close to you; it is on your lips and in your heart." By means of his very gracious assurances, promises, and admonitions—present in abundance in Deuteronomy; study, for example, such precious gems as Deut. 5:6; 6:4-9; 7:7-9; 10:12, 13; 11:13-15, 22-25; 18:15-18; 26:16-19; 28:1-14—the Lord had, as it were, drawn his people very close to his heart. Let them now answer with the response of love.

The more one takes time to study Deuteronomy, the more also he will agree with Paul's statement that this is indeed "the word of faith we are proclaiming." It *must* be, for the heart and center of this book and of the entire Old Testament, is Christ, exactly as the apostle has affirmed (see Rom. 10:4).

There is only one way, however, in which this can be appreciated. That is the way of faith; for God's word, as revealed both in the Old Testament and in the New, is "*the word of faith*"; that is, it is the word which, in order to exert its saving effect, must elicit the response of faith!

Paul now shows that the statement, "The word is close to you; (it is) on your lips and in your heart" is true:

---

294. Although "the abyss" can indicate the depth of the sea (cf. Ps. 107:26=LXX 106:26), in the present passage death and the grave are indicated. See Acts 2:27.

9, 10. Because, if on your lips is the confession, "Jesus is Lord," and in your heart the faith that God raised him from the dead, you will be saved. For it is with the heart that a person exercises faith leading to righteousness, and with the lips that he makes confession issuing in salvation.

Note the following:

a. "Because" (rather than "That") is natural here, the sense being that the statement that the word is close to you (verse 8) is true is shown by the fact that, instead of requiring superhuman exertion, salvation is obtained simply by confessing with the lips and having faith in the heart.

b. In verse 9 the confession on the lips precedes the faith in the heart; in verse 10 the opposite sequence prevails. Probable reason: first Paul is thinking of Deut. 30:14 where "on your lips" precedes "in your heart." Next, he follows the natural order, according to which a person confesses with his lips that which is already present in the heart.

c. Not the Roman emperor but Jesus was to receive all honor and glory. Moreover, it is clear from I Cor. 16:22 (māránā thā, "Our Lord, come!") that the exaltation of Jesus as Lord was customary even in the early, Aramaic-speaking, church. That the title *Lord* is here (in Rom. 10:9) used in the most exalted sense, indicating Jesus' equality with God, is clear not only from the fact that the apostle frequently, without any hesitancy, ascribes to Jesus qualities which in the Old Testament are predicated of God, but also from the circumstance that already in 9:5 he has called Jesus "over all God blest forever."

d. Note "heart" and "lips" (literally "mouth"). The *heart* is not merely the seat of affection or emotion. According to biblical usage, it is the hub of the wheel of human existence and life (intellectual, emotional, and volitional). See Prov. 4:23.

First of all there must be faith in the heart. Without such faith a confession with the lips would be mockery (Matt. 7:22, 23). But also, even if there is faith in the heart, confession with the lips is not only required (Ps. 107:2) but altogether natural if the faith is genuine (Acts 4:20). Faith and confession should be combined (Luke 12:8; John 12:42; I Tim. 6:12; I John 4:15).

e. By means of the resurrection from the dead the Lordship of Jesus had been made abundantly clear. See Rom. 6:9; I Cor. 15:20; Eph. 1:20-23; Phil. 2:9-11; Col. 3:1-4; Heb. 2:9; Rev. 1:17, 18.

f. When in verse 10 *faith* is said to issue in *righteousness*, and *confession* in *salvation* (lit . . . is unto righteousness—is unto salvation), the two concepts, righteousness and salvation, are conceived of as synonyms. This is also clear from verse 9, where salvation is described as being the product both of confession and faith.

g. Note "you will be saved" (verse 9), and "issuing in salvation" (verse 10). For the meaning of *salvation* and *to save* in Paul's epistles see p. 60 on 1:16.

The fact that faith does indeed lead to justification, hence to salvation is confirmed by verse

11. For the Scripture says, "No one who puts his trust in him will ever be put to shame." Or, if one prefers, **"Everyone who puts his trust in him will never be put to shame."** Again, as in 9:33 Paul quotes Isa. 28:16; this time, however, in somewhat strengthened form, "he who . . . will never" being changed to "No one . . . will ever" (or to "Everyone . . . will never"). But is not Paul's version here in Rom. 10:11 already implied in Isa. 28:16? For the meaning see, accordingly, on Rom. 9:33.

That the truth which the apostle has just now reaffirmed cannot be successfully denied is demonstrated in the three sentences which follow in verses 12, 13. Each of the three supports the one that precedes it:

12, 13. For there is no distinction between Jew and Greek. For the same Lord (is Lord) of all and richly blesses all who call on him. For everyone who calls on the name of the Lord will be saved.

Note the following:

a. "For there is no distinction between Jew and Greek."

The word "for" shows that what immediately follows proves the preceding line which states that *no one* who puts his trust in him will ever be put to shame.

Though the fact that, as concerns the way of salvation, *there is no distinction between Jew and Greek*, is emphasized by Paul again and again, it must have been very difficult for Jews to believe this. What? Did Paul really mean to say that *they*, the highly privileged descendants of Abraham, were in God's eyes not any better than Greeks or Gentiles?

Even today are there not many church members who endorse the theory that the Jews, as a people, are still the objects of God's *special* delight and that a glorious future is in store for them? Note how, in many books written by authors who cling to this opinion, the truth expressed here in 10:12 is touched on very lightly, is passed over very quickly. Nevertheless, so thoroughly convinced was Paul of its importance that he dwelt on it, at least mentioned it, again and again. Let the reader see this for himself by carefully examining the following passages: Rom. 1:16; 2:11; 3:10-18, 22-24; 3:29, 30; 4:9-12; 5:18, 19; 9:24; 10:12; 11:32; and elsewhere in Paul's epistles: I Cor. 7:19; Gal. 3:9, 29; 5:6; 6:15; Eph. 2:14-18; Col. 3:11.

That there is indeed no distinction between Jew and Greek is clear from the fact which the apostle states in the following words:

b. "For the same Lord (is Lord) of all and richly blesses all who call on him." Not only is it true that one and the same *God* is God of the Gentiles as well as of the Jews (cf. Rom. 3:29), but also, as the apostle states here in 10:12, that the same *Lord* (=Jesus) is Lord of all.

God is rich! In fact, his wealth is incalculable. If there is anything at all which, for the moment, he does not possess, all he has to do is assert his sovereign will, and there it is! See Gen. 1:3, 6, 9, 11, 14, 20, 24, 26. All the gold and silver belongs to God (Hag. 2:8). Every beast of the forest is his, and so are the cattle on a thousand hills (Ps. 50:10-12).

And if *God* is rich, then so is *Christ*, for Christ is God. Eph. 3:8 mentions *the unsearchable riches of Christ*. Rev. 5:12 shows that the Savior is indeed *worthy to receive* all this wealth.

But not only is God infinitely rich, he is also intensely desirous to bestow his riches on his creatures. He is rich in revealing to them his kindness, patience, glory, and mercy (Rom. 2:4; 9:23; Eph. 2:7). He is, in fact, generous beyond the capacity of human words to express. See such a precious passage as John 1:16, according to which one manifestation of divine grace or favor is hardly gone when another one arrives, like the waves of the ocean which follow one another in close succession as they dash against the shore. Truly "He giveth and giveth and giveth again."

Especially when one lives in a state that borders on the ocean (or makes a visit to such a state)—for example, Florida—it is rewarding, when watching the constantly approaching billows, to reflect on John 1:16. See N.T.C. on John, Vol. I, pp. 88, 89. It hardly needs to be added that here too what is said with reference to God applies also to Christ, who, "though he was rich, yet for our sake became poor, that we through his poverty might become rich" (cf. II Cor. 8:9).

Note also that, according to Paul's inspired teaching, not only a few people, or a certain group of people, whether Jews or Gentiles, are the beneficiaries of this enormous wealth, but that, on the contrary *all* who call on God in Christ receive a rich blessing. The Lord richly blesses—literally, is rich toward—them all.

Of course, this calling on God—or specifically on Jesus—must be done in the spirit of the centurion (Matt. 8:8) and of the publican (Luke 18:13).

Proof of this universality (in a sense) of divine generosity is offered by Paul in his third sentence:

c. "For everyone who calls on the name of the Lord will be saved."

See Acts 7:59; I Cor. 1:2. That which here in Rom. 10:13 follows the word "For" is an exact reproduction of what in our Bibles is found in Joel 2:32 but in the Hebrew Bible and the LXX in Joel 3:5. In fact, in the present case even the word *everyone* was already in the original of the Old Testament passage. Contrast this with Rom. 10:11 where, in quoting Isa. 28:16, Paul himself inserted this word.

For "will be saved" see the explanation of 10:9.

---

14 How, then, can they call on one in whom they have no faith? And how can they have faith in one whom they have not heard? And how can they hear without a preacher? 15 And how can people preach unless they have been commissioned? As it is written, "How beautiful are the feet of those who bring good news!"

16 But not all accepted the good news. For Isaiah says, "Lord, who has believed our message?" 17 Consequently, faith (comes) from hearing the message, and the message is heard through the word of Christ.

18 But I ask, "Can it be that they never heard (it)?" Of course they did:

"Into all the earth there went out their sound,
And to the ends of the inhabited world their words."

19 But I ask, "Can it be that Israel did not understand?" First, Moses says,

"I will make y o u envious of a non-nation,
And with a nation (that is) senseless will I make y o u angry."
20 And Isaiah is so bold as to say,
"I was found by those who did not seek me;
I revealed myself to those who did not ask for me."
21 But concerning Israel he says,
"All day long I have stretched out my hands to a disobedient and obstinate people."

---

6. *Israel Is Responsible for Its Own Rejection. That Rejection Is Not Arbitrary.* "All day long I have stretched out my hands to a disobedient and defiant people" 10:14-21

Rom. 10:13 stated, "For everyone who calls on the name of the Lord will be saved." The connection between the line and the beginning of the subsection, verses 14-21, is clear, for in 10:14 the subject of *calling on the Lord* is continued by means of the question, "How, then, can they call on one in whom they have no faith?" The spirit of this question, especially in light of what follows in verses 16 and 21, indicates that the apostle is leveling a charge against Israel. He is saying that because of Israel's lack of faith it is fully responsible for its rejection by God. In other words, that rejection, to the extent in which it was real, was not arbitrary but deserved.

14, 15a. How, then, can they call on one in whom they have no faith? And how can they have faith in one whom they have not heard? And how can they hear without a preacher? And how can people preach unless they have been commissioned?[295]

A few points should be noted:

---

295. ἐπικαλέσωνται verse 14), third per. pl. aor. middle subjunct. (deliberat.) of ἐπικαλέω, here in the sense of: to call on God in prayer. Cf. II Tim. 2:22. For calling on "the name" of the Lord see the preceding verse (10:13), in which the third per. s. aor. subjunct. middle of the same verb occurs.

ἐπίστευσαν (verse 14), third per. pl. aor. indicat. of πιστεύω. For the εἰς ὅν . . . ἐπίστευσαν construction see also Gal. 2:16 and Phil. 1:29. In both cases the faith to which reference is made is *in Christ.* In the Gospel and First Epistle of John this construction ("in him" or "in his name"), with reference to faith in Christ, occurs frequently. See John 3:16.

In verse 14 note πιστεύσωσιν and ἀκούσωσιν; and in verse 15 κηρύξωσιν. All are third per. pl. aor. act. subjunctives (deliberative). The meaning (after πῶς in each case, and add Πῶς . . . ἐπικαλέσωνται at the beginning of verse 14, already discussed), is "How can they . . . ?" In other words, "They cannot . . ." οὗ οὐκ ἤκουσαν (verse 14) = whom they have not heard; not "of whom they have not heard." In that case would not περὶ οὗ have been more natural? See Gram.N.T., p. 506. Compare Luke 9:35 "Hear him," not "Hear of or about him." Note also the difference in the construction and meaning of (a) οὗ οὐκ ἤκουσαν, where, after the gen., this verb means *to hear*; and (b) οὐκ ἤκουσαν (verse 18), where, without the gen., the same verb indicates *to understand*.

κηρύσσοντος (verse 14), gen. s. masc. pres. act. participle of κηρύσσω, to announce, make public proclamation, preach. Cf. κῆρυξ, herald; also κηρύξωσιν ("How can they preach?") in verse 15.

ἀποσταλῶσιν (verse 15), third per. pl. aor. pass. subjunct. of ἀποστέλλω, to send out, especially on a divine mission, to commission.

a. In this series of questions what is the subject? To whom is Paul referring? The apostle writes: they . . . they . . . they . . . they . . . they . . . they . . . they; though, for the sake of variation and clarity, one of these they's can be changed to *the people* (or something similar).

To whom, then, is Paul referring? The usual answer is: to Israel. Some translations even insert the word "Israel" in places where the original does not have it. Now it must be admitted that to a considerable extent this answer is correct. See, first of all, what has been said in the introduction to this section (p. 348). Examine also the following passages: 9:3-5, 27, 31-33; 10:1-3, 19, 21; 11:1 f. On the basis of all this the conclusion "the reference is to Israel" cannot be escaped.

But is this a *complete* answer? Not every commentator is of that opinion.[296] And rightly so. Does not the fact that in this section (10:14-21) Paul does not even mention Israel until he reaches the very close (verses 19-21) prove that he wants *every hearer or reader* to wrestle with these questions in his own heart and conscience?

b. We have here a series of questions. The Old Testament also contains groups of questions (Job 38:2-39:27; 41:1-7; Isa. 40:12-14, 21). However, the present series is different. It is a kind of chain in which each link bears a close relationship to its immediate neighbor(s).

Is this chain similar, then, to the one found in Rom. 5:3b-5, and to the one described in 8:29, 30? No, the difference is that in the latter two instances the chain is *progressive*: its links follow one another in historical, cause and effect, manner. The sequence may be compared to the series 1, 2, 3, etc. Here, in Rom. 10:14, 15a, and also in 10:17, the chain is *regressive*. It proceeds from effect to cause, and is comparable to the series 5, 4, 3, 2, 1. Calling upon Christ in prayer is mentioned first though in reality, of course, it follows having faith in him, which, however, is the second link in this chain. Having faith in Christ results from hearing him, the third link as here arranged. This hearing implies that there must have been a preacher, the fourth link, who addressed the people. He did this because even earlier someone, the fifth link, had authorized him to bring the message.

c. What may have been the reason for Paul's decision to arrange these links in this regressive order?

To answer this question we should bear in mind that the apostle was not only a fully inspired, very learned, deep-thinking theologian; he was also a very practical, warm-hearted Christian friend. As such he may well have had a twofold purpose in mind for writing as he did.

First of all, he is thinking of the audience, the one in Rome, to be sure, but, along the line of the centuries to follow, any audience, including also today's. For the audience, then, and for every person in that audience, the apostle has so arranged the series that the reference to God—or, if one

296. See, for example, Ridderbos, *op. cit.*, p. 240.

prefers, to Jesus Christ—who commissioned the preacher, would be mentioned last of all, in order that all the emphasis might fall upon him! Every person in the audience must be made aware of the fact that when he rejects the preacher who, as a faithful minister of the word, with insight and enthusiasm presents the glad and glorious tidings of salvation in Christ, *then he is rejecting Jesus Christ himself*! In addressing the seventy (or seventy-two) missionaries Jesus said, "He who listens to y o u listens to me, but he who rejects y o u rejects me; and he who rejects me rejects him who sent me" (Luke 10:16).

Secondly, Paul is thinking of the preacher. The climactic reference to the duly commissioned preacher contains a lesson for him also. Any preacher better be sure that he has actually been called of God to do this kind of work. To arrive at a true answer to this question he should turn to Jer. 23:21, 22. If this preacher is earnestly and prayerfully trying to do that which is mentioned in the twenty-second verse, he will find it much easier to arrive at a positive and encouraging answer to the question with reference to the genuine character of his ordination.

For the preacher Rom. 10:14, 15a contains still another lesson. Just what is meant by *preaching*? As the footnote (p. 348) shows, preaching is actually *heralding, proclaiming*. Genuine preaching, therefore, means that the sermon is lively, not dry; timely, not stale. It is the earnest proclamation of the great news initiated by God. It must never be allowed to deteriorate into an abstract speculation on views merely excogitated by man!

That there could be no doubt about the fact that the people—here especially Israel, as has been shown—have actually heard the gospel, and that it has been proclaimed to them by divinely authorized ambassadors, is indicated in verse

15b. As it is written, "How beautiful are the feet of those who bring good news!"

This passage is quoted from Isa. 52:7[297] where the prophet describes the exuberance with which the exiles welcome the news of their imminent release from captivity. This news was regarded by them as being very wonderful not just because they could now return to their homeland but also, and probably especially, because for them it meant that God's favor was still resting on them, and that not this or that earthly power but God—their own God—was still reigning. See the Isaiah context, and add Ps. 93:1; Rev. 19:6. Moreover, can there be anything more spiritually exhilarating and invigorating than the message of God's ambassadors, as reported, for example in II Cor. 5:20, 21?

How beautiful[298] are those feet! As over the mountains those messengers approached with their electrifying news, how dust-covered and dirty these

297. Here, rather than in the LXX, correctly translated from the Hebrew.

298. ὡραῖοι, nom. pl. masc. of ὡραῖος, timely, seasonable, blooming, beautiful; cf. ὥρα, season, time, *hour*.

feet must have been! Yet also, how beautiful . . . for they were the feet of those who brought the long-awaited marvelous news!

16. But not all accepted the good news. For Isaiah says, "Lord, who has believed our message?"

There was nothing wrong with the good news. It should have been accepted with joy and gratitude by all. "But," says Paul, "Not all" accepted the good news, the wonderful gospel. Note "not all." What an understatement! A merciful meiosis indeed; for we already know that by far the most of the Israelites did not accept the gospel. See Rom. 9:27. Cf. Isa. 53:1; Rom. 10:21; I Cor. 10:5.

We learn, therefore, that although items 4 and 5 (of 10:14, 15a) had been fulfilled—there had been preachers, and they had been duly commissioned—yet, as far as most of the people were concerned, items 1 and 2—*calling on Christ* in prayer because of the presence of *faith* in him—had not.

That this was true, indeed, with respect to *most* of the people follows also from the words of Isa. 53:1 quoted by Paul: "Lord, who has believed our message?" This basically means, "Lord, who has believed that which was heard by us?"[299]

17. Consequently, faith (comes) from hearing the message, and the message is heard through the word of Christ.

Of the many interpretations of this passage, some very involved, the best is probably the one which views it as a summarizing conclusion. Does not the opening word "Consequently" point in this direction? What Paul is saying, then, is that faith in Christ presupposes having heard the word that proceeds from and concerns Christ. Here a word, in the original, that has just (verse 16) been used in a passive sense—"that which was heard"—is now also used in the active sense: *hearing* the message.[300]

The great importance Paul attached to *hearing* immediately reminds one of Jesus. In all Christ's teaching, both on earth and from heaven, it would be difficult to discover any exhortation which he repeated more often, in one form or another, than the one about hearing; better still: listening (Matt. 11:15; 13:9, 43; Mark 4:9, 23; Luke 8:8; 14:35; Rev. 2:7, 11, 17, 29; 3:6, 13, 22; 13:9). Add 8:18 in both Mark and Luke.

18. But I ask, "Can it be that they never heard (it)?" Of course they did:

"Into all the earth there went out their sound,

---

299. ἀκοῇ, dat. s. of ἀκοή. As is true with respect to many words, the meaning of this word, in any given case, depends on the context in which it is used, and, at times, as here, from which it is quoted. The Greek noun can mean: faculty of hearing, act of hearing, that which is heard, account, report, message.

In the Hebrew passage (Isa. 53:1) from which Rom. 10:16 is quoted, the noun is שְׁמוּעָה from שָׁמַע, to hear; and the word including suffix is שְׁמוּעָתֵנוּ, our report; literally: *that which was heard* by us, and was revealed to us. It is in that sense that it becomes: our report, message. We convey to others what was previously revealed to us.

300. The reference is to the Greek word ἀκοή; here in the combination ἐξ ἀκοῆς: from hearing.

And to the ends of the inhabited world their words."

This passage found in Ps. 19:4 is here quoted literally according to the LXX text (there Ps. 18:5). We should not misinterpret what Paul is saying. He is not trying to tell us that the Old Testament Psalm was describing the universal spread of the gospel. What he means is that what in Ps. 19 applies to the language of the heavenly bodies is also applicable to the spread of the gospel.

But perhaps the comparison is more than superficial. Should we not rather say that God's revelation in the realm of creation and in that of redemption is such that in both cases it forces itself on our attention?

That in the days of Christ and the apostles the gospel was indeed spreading fast is clear from such passages as Rom. 15:22-24; Phil. 1:12, 13; Col. 1:6; cf. John 12:19; Acts 2:41, 47; 4:4; 17:6.

The rapid progress of the gospel in the early days has ever been the amazement of the historian. Justin Martyr, about the middle of the second century, wrote, "There is no people, Greek or barbarian, or of any other race, by whatever appellation or manners they may be distinguished, however, ignorant of arts or agriculture, whether they dwell in tents or wander about in covered wagons, among whom prayers and thanksgivings are not offered in the name of the crucified Jesus to the Father and Creator of all things." Half a century later Tertullian adds, "We are but of yesterday, and yet we already fill y o u r cities, islands, camps, y o u r palace, senate, and forum. We have left y o u only your temples." R. H. Glover (*The Progress of World-Wide Missions*, New York, 1925, p. 39) states, "On the basis of all the data available it has been estimated that by the close of the Apostolic Period the total number of Christian disciples had reached half a million."

19. But I ask, "Can it be that Israel did not understand?" First, Moses says,

"I will make y o u envious of a non-nation,
And with a nation (that is) senseless will I make y o u angry."

"But I ask" matches the opening of verse 18. The question regarding *hearing* (verse 18) is followed by one regarding *understanding*. Note that now Israel, already implied in the earlier verses, is definitely mentioned.

The purport of the question is whether Israel, even though it has indeed heard the gospel, has nevertheless not been able to understand it sufficiently so that it could be held responsible for its unbelief. What is found in verses 19b-21, though not a direct answer to this question, implies the answer. It shows that not ignorance but unwillingness was the cause of Israel's lack of faith. The quotation is from Deut. 32:21b.

A non-nation is a mere mass of people. It is a vast multitude which had not received the many privileges that had been bestowed on Israel, "the people for God's own possession." That non-nation was going to receive those blessings which earlier had been granted to Israel. It was going to take Israel's place.

This very fact, of course, implies Israel's guilt, since it also implies that Israel had received sufficient understanding of the way of salvation to be held fully accountable for its unbelief.

Does not this passage immediately remind us of Luke 20:15, 16 (cf. Matt. 21:41; Mark 12:9): "What, then, will the owner of the vineyard do to them? He will come and kill those sharecroppers and give the vineyard to others." The privileged position, once granted to Israel, was going to be transferred to those very people who had been despised by Israel. Cf. Acts 13:46.

The envy and anger to which our passage refers is illustrated in Mark 12:12. But envy can also have a positive result. For this see Rom. 11:11.

20. And Isaiah is so bold as to say,
"I was found by those who did not seek me;
I revealed myself to those who did not ask for me."

These lines from Isa. 65:1 (quoted here in reverse order) are even more incisive. If among those who first heard them there were any self-righteous Jews, they must have been shocked by this statement, especially in its present context. It is in the form of a paradox. By reminding the hearers that God was found by those who did not seek him, and was revealed to those who did not ask for him, it emphasizes God's sovereign right to bestow salvation on whomsoever he wills. In no sense is it true that man, by means of any merit he may dare to claim, brings about God's saving attention. The Gentiles, their minds and hearts darkened by sin, and therefore not even asking for God's help, receive it. Israel is passed by because of its obstinacy, as is clear from verse

21. But concerning Israel he says,
"All day long I have stretched out my hands to a disobedient and obstinate people."

Sound exegesis demands that this passage—a quotation from Isa. 65:2—be interpreted in light of the immediate context (see verses 19, 20; and in Isa. 65 see verses 3-7). The passage indicates that Israel was fully responsible for the divine judgment that was pronounced upon it. The fact that the nation day after day, week after week, year upon year, continued *to be disobedient* and *to contradict God, even in spite of God's outstretched hands of patience and invitation*, made matters worse for Israel. The predominant impression Rom. 10:21 leaves upon a person is therefore one of gloom, not one of cheer. It is darkness rather than light upon which the emphasis falls here.[301] When God pronounces a judgment on Israel he is not acting arbitrarily. Israel has earned that judgment. We cannot help thinking of these words of Jesus:

"Jerusalem, Jerusalem, who kills the prophets and stones those that are sent to her! how often would I have gathered your children together as a

---

301. It is for this reason that I do not agree with Cranfield's explanation of this passage, *op. cit.*, Vol. II, pp. 541, 542.

hen gathers her brood under its wings, but y o u would not. Behold, y o u r house is left to y o u a deserted place" (Matt. 23:37, 38).

This does not mean that the light has been completely replaced by darkness, that God's hands have ceased to be outstretched in loving patience and appeal, and that God is, accordingly, "through with the Jews."

We are not forgetting such passages as the following—and more could be added—which show that even now mission work among the Jews is not fruitless: 1:16; 3:3, 30; 4:12; 5:18, 19; 7:4; 9:6, 23, 27, 29; 10:1, 11-13, 16. There is a remnant of Israel that is destined for grace and glory. God has not thrust *his people* away from himself (11:1). There is a sense in which "all Israel" will be saved (11:26).

Besides, once the hardening process has begun in the life of this or that Israelite, no one has a right to say that it will continue until that man dies and perishes everlastingly. God's grace is sufficiently powerful to reach even the temporarily hardened sinner. See further on 11:28-31.

Practical Lessons Derived from Romans 10

Verse 1

"Brothers, my heart's desire and prayer to God for them is that they may be saved." The Jewish opponents were constantly persecuting Paul. Again and again they tried to kill him. Nevertheless, Paul continued to pray that they might be saved. He was putting into practice the rule laid down by Jesus (Luke 6:27-31). A lesson for us all.

Same passage. How was it possible for Paul to pray for the salvation of the Jews when he knew that, to a considerable extent, God had rejected them? See Matt. 8:10-12; Mark 12:9; Luke 20:15, 16; Rom. 9:27; I Thess. 2:14-16.

Answer: The identity of reprobates is known to God alone. Therefore it was right for the apostle to pray for individual Jews and for Jews in general.

Verse 2

"For I can testify about them that they have a zeal for God . . ." Being filled with zeal and being sincere may be excellent, but not if the zeal is without understanding. As to sincerity: it is possible for a person to be sincerely . . . wrong!

Verse 8

"The word is close to you; (it is) on your lips and in your heart . . ." Is it not strange that, by nature, man wants to go to heaven the hard way? Yet, Rom. 10:8-10 is clear as daylight. See also Matt. 11:28-30 and John 3:16.

Verse 9

"Because, if on your lips is the confession, 'Jesus is Lord,' and in your heart the faith that God raised him from the dead, you will be saved." The original says: your . . . your . . . you; not y o u r . . . y o u r . . . y o u. It is fine to recite the

Apostles' Creed in unison during public worship. More than this is necessary, however; namely, the personal, individual profession of heart and lips.

Same passage. This confession, with specific mention of two supernatural facts—Christ's lordship and his bodily resurrection—deals the deathblow to all liberalism, showing that liberalism and Christianity cannot live together harmoniously under the same roof.

Same passage once more. Even though the two truths that are here mentioned may well be regarded as implying all the central doctrines of the Christian religion, does Paul not also imply that believers do not need to think alike on every minor point of theology? Room must be left for differences of opinion. See Luke 9:49, 50.

Verse 12

"For there is no distinction between Jew and Greek." God's love in Christ overarches distinctions with respect to race, nationality, sex, age, social and/or financial standing, degree of accomplishment, etc. With respect to any and all of these matters God is impartial. Rom. 10:12 is very clear on this point. So is John 3:16.

Verse 21

"All day long I have stretched out my hands to a disobedient and defiant people." How marvelous is God's patience. However, this does not mean that it has no limits. See Prov. 29:1; Luke 13:8, 9; 17:26-29. The only "safe" procedure, therefore, is the one described in Ps. 95:7, 8; Heb. 3:7, 8.

Summary of Chapter 10

This chapter consists of two main parts: verses 1-13; verses 14-21.

As at the beginning of chapter 9 so also here Paul reveals his tender affection for his kinsmen. He states that his prayer to God is that they may be saved. He testifies that they have a zeal for God, but deplores the fact that this zeal is not based on proper insight into God's revelation concerning the way of salvation (verses 1, 2).

Israel's tragic error consisted in this, that they sought to establish their own righteousness and refused to accept the righteousness provided by God in Christ. It is Christ, he alone, in whom the law attained its goal, so that, as a result, there now is righteousness for everyone who exercises saving faith (verses 3, 4).

It was Christ who came from heaven and who, in his people's stead, suffered the agonies of hell. The hard work was done by him, and should therefore not be attempted by us. Moses (Deut. 30:11-14) already made clear that Canaan was God's free gift, not the product of human exertion. As it was with Canaan so it is with salvation in general. It is given to those who trust in the Lord Jesus Christ. Therefore, "if on your lips is the confession, 'Jesus is Lord,' and in your heart the faith that God raised him from the dead, you will be saved . . . For the Scripture says, 'No one who puts his trust in him will ever be put to shame' " (verses 5-11).

Ethnic considerations play no part in the bestowment of salvation: "there is no distinction between Jew and Greek. For the same Lord (is Lord) of all and richly blesses all who call on him. For everyone who calls on the name of the Lord will be saved" (verses 12, 13).

In the second part of this chapter Paul, by means of a series of questions, arranged in effect-to-cause order, stresses the supreme importance of taking to heart the message of the duly authorized preacher. He who accepts his message accepts Christ. He who rejects it rejects Christ. It is understood, of course, that this is true only when the preacher truly represents Christ and actually conveys Christ's message.

To those who in the proper frame of mind listen to the gospel, blessings abound. To them the feet of those who bring good news are indeed beautiful (verses 14, 15).

There are many, however, who refuse to accept the gospel, as Isaiah proves by saying, "Lord, who has believed our message?" Everyone should therefore examine himself to see whether he really belongs to the company of those who heed whatever it is that God, through the proclamation of the word, is saying.

Excuses will not avail. The gospel is being circulated far and wide, reminding us of the heavens which all around are declaring God's glory (verses 16-18).

Israel too not only heard God's message, but understood it well enough to be responsible for its lack of faith. Rejection and replacement are God's penalties imposed on the rejecters. Moses declared, "I will make y o u envious of a non-nation. And with a nation (that is) senseless will I make y o u angry" (Deut. 32:21b). And Isaiah was so bold as to say, "I was found by those who did not seek me; I revealed myself to those who did not ask for me" (Isa. 65:1). Concerning Israel he said, (65:2) "All day long I have stretched out my hands to a disobedient and obstinate—literally *contradicting*—people" (verses 19-21).

Outline (continued)

Justification by Faith

The Election of Israel's Minority (or Remnant)
versus
The Hardening of its Majority
"The elect have obtained it. The others were hardened"
11:1-10

Ingrafted Branches
"But they, if they do not persist in their unbelief, will be grafted in, for God has the power to graft them in again"
11:11-24

God's Mercy on "the Fulness of the Gentiles" and on "All Israel"
"For God has locked up all in the prison of disobedience in order that he may have mercy on all"
11:25-32

Doxology
"For from him and through him and to him are all things. To him be the glory forever. Amen."
11:33-36

CHAPTER 11

11 1 I ask then, "Did God reject his people?" Of course not! Why, I myself am an
Israelite, of the seed of Abraham, of the tribe of Benjamin. 2 God did not reject
his people whom he foreknew. Or do y o u not know what the Scripture says in (the section about) Elijah, how he complains to God about Israel,

3 "Lord, thy prophets they have killed,
thine altars they have demolished,
and I am the only one left,
and they are seeking my life"?

4 But what is God's reply to him? "I have left for myself seven thousand men who have not
bowed the knee to Baal." 5 So, too, at the present time a remnant has come into being,
chosen by grace. 6 And if by grace, (then it is) no longer by works; since (if it were) grace
would no longer be grace.

7 What then? What Israel is seeking so earnestly it has not obtained, but the elect have
obtained it. The others were hardened, 8 as it is written:

"God gave them a spirit of stupor,
eyes not to see,
and ears not to hear,
to this very day."

9 And David says,

"Let their table become a snare and a trap,
a stumbling block and a retribution for them.

10 Let their eyes be darkened so as not to see,
and their back do thou bow down forever."

The Election of Israel's Minority (or Remnant)
versus
The Hardening of its Majority
"The elect have obtained it. The others were hardened"
11:1-10

The description (in 10:21) of Israel as "disobedient and obstinate" naturally introduces the question whether God has perhaps rejected his people (11:1).

This theme, divine rejection, is not new. The apostle has already shown that divine rejection, though in a sense real, is *not complete* (chapter 9) and not *arbitrary* (chapter 10). Here in chapter 11 he will point out that it is also *not absolute* or *unqualified*. It is not the whole story. Running side by side with rejection there is also election. Divine saving activity parallels divine hardening. See 11:7, 25, 26. In a sense some of the ideas of chapter 9—see especially verses 6-13; 23-27—recur in chapter 11. But chapter 11 goes farther. It shows that between hardening and saving, between breaking off and grafting in, there is a kind of cause and effect relationship: the disobedience of the Jews brings about the obedience of the Gentiles (verses 11, 12, 15, 30); the mercy shown to the Gentiles is a blessing for the Jews (verse 31b); so that, in the end, not only *the fulness of the Gentiles* but also *the salvation of "all Israel"* is secured.

Of course, this double *interaction* (German *Wechselwirkung*) does not come about automatically. It is God who produces this favorable result: "For God has locked up all in the prison of disobedience in order that he may have mercy on all" (verse 32). It is not surprising therefore that the chapter is climaxed by an enthusiastic doxology (verses 33-36).

1a. I ask then, "Did God reject his people?"

Were not the Jews God's "peculiar treasure," his very own? See Exod. 4:22; 19:6; Deut. 14:2; 26:18; Ps. 135:4; Isa. 43:20; Hos. 11:1. Nevertheless, in complete harmony with previous statements (2:17-25; 9:30-32; 10:3, 16) Paul has just now stated that the Jews are disobedient and obstinate (10:21), a people deserving to be condemned. Does the apostle mean, then, that God has totally rejected, has thrust away from himself, *his people*?

Paul wants the addressees to become concerned about this question. He, accordingly, to arouse their interest, asks *them* to answer it. He says, "I ask then,[302] Did God reject his people?"

Paul now answers his own question:

1b, 2a. Of course not! Why, I myself am an Israelite, of the seed of Abraham, of the tribe of Benjamin. God did not reject his people whom he foreknew.

Note the terse, almost indignant, negative answer, "Of course not!"[303] Or "Perish the thought!" See on 3:4. Does not I Sam. 12:22 state, "For the sake of his great name the Lord will not reject his people," and is not this assurance repeated in Ps. 94:14, which adds, "He will never forsake his inheritance"?

The words, "Why, I myself am an Israelite . . . of the tribe of Benjamin," remind us of a similar statement in Phil. 3:5. See N.T.C. on Philippians, pp. 154-159. Paul was a direct descendant not only of Abraham but of Abraham, Isaac, and Jacob; in fact, of Jacob's son Benjamin! That son was the youngest child of Jacob's most beloved wife, Rachel. Benjamin was the only son of Jacob born in the land of promise.

Being able to claim such ancestry, the apostle was therefore "a Hebrew of Hebrews," a Hebrew if there ever was one, unquestionably *an Israelite*.

302. The verb λέγω does at times have this meaning. See Matt. 18:1; Mark 5:30 f.; and here in Rom. 10:18, 19; 11:11.

303. This negative answer is already implied in the very wording of *the question* as found in the original. Added stress appears in *the answer*. In both cases note μή.

Moreover, even though this was true, Paul had been a fierce persecutor of God's dear children. Nevertheless, the former enemy had become a friend, a true believer and even an enthusiastic apostle and proclaimer of the gospel. All this because divine sovereign love rested upon him, and this not only during his lifetime but from all eternity.

Indeed, God did not reject his people, including Paul, *whom he foreknew*; that is, on whom, from before the foundation of the world, he had set his love. He had made them the object of his special delight, a delight beginning in eternity, continuing in connection with their conception and birth, and never leaving them. For more on divine foreknowledge see on 8:29. Also see John 8:27, 28.

So here in verses 1b, 2a Paul is, as it were, saying, "Does anyone need proof that God fulfils his promise and has not rejected Israel? Well, then look at me. God did not reject me, and I am an Israelite!"

2b-4. Or do y o u not know what the Scripture says in (the section about) Elijah, how he complains to God about Israel,

"Lord, thy prophets they have killed,
thine altars they have demolished,
and I am the only one left,
and they are seeking my life"?

But what is God's reply to him? "I have left for myself seven thousand men who have not bowed the knee to Baal."[304]

Further proof of the fact that God is still concerned about Israel and has not completely rejected it is drawn from the story recorded in I Kings 19:1-18; see especially verses 9, 10, 14, and 18. According to this narrative, when disconsolate Elijah had entered a cave of Mt. Horeb, the Lord came and asked him, "What are you doing here, Elijah?" He replied, "I have been very zealous for Jehovah, the God of hosts; for the children of Israel have forsaken thy covenant, thrown down thine altars, and slain thy prophets with the sword; and I, only I, am left, and they are seeking my life, to take it away." The Lord's answer had included these words, "Yet I reserve for myself seven thousand in Israel—all whose knees have not bowed down to Baal and whose mouths have not kissed him."

The appropriate character of Paul's reference to this Old Testament account is immediately evident. In a sense the times of Elijah had returned.

---

304. ἐν Ἡλίᾳ, in the section about Elijah; cf. Mark 12:26. ἐντυγχάνει τῷ θεῷ κατὰ τοῦ Ἰσραήλ, appeals to God against Israel; i.e., complains to God about Israel.

κατέσκαψαν, third per. pl. aor. act. indicat. of κατασκάπτω, to tear down, demolish. Cf. Acts 15:16.

ζητοῦσιν τὴν ψυχήν μου, they are seeking my life; that is, they are trying to kill me.

χρηματισμός (in the New Testament only here), a divine *statement* or (as here) *reply*; cf. χρησμός, oracle. For the cognate verb see N.T.C. on Luke, pp. 175, 176 (on Luke 2:26).

τῇ Βάαλ. Note the fem. article. Yet the Baals or Baalim were generally regarded as masculine, in distinction from the feminine Ashtaroth and Asherim. Explanation: when Scripture was read aloud, the name of the god was not pronounced. Instead, the reader would say *shame*; Grk. αἰσχύνη; Heb. בֹּשֶׁת, both fem.

Unbelief was again rampant. In Elijah's day Jehovah's prophets had been slain, and recently the Jews had killed (Matt. 27:25; I Thess. 2:14, 15) the greatest Prophet of all (Deut. 18:15, 18; Acts 7:37). Nevertheless, as was true in the days of Elijah so also now, not all was dark: there were true believers.

The words, "Or do y o u not know," (cf. 6:3, 16; 7:1; I Cor. 3:16; 5:6; 6:2, 3, 9, 15, 16), arousing interest and telling the addressed that they *should* have known, remind us of the same and similar words ("Have y o u not read?") spoken by Jesus (Matt. 12:3, 5; 19:4; 21:16, 42; 22:31; John 3:10).

There are those who attach significance to the fact that for the words "altars . . . prophets," in the Old Testament account, Paul substitutes "prophets . . . altars." One explanation is that the apostle wanted to point out that not only had wicked Jezebel seen to it that *the prophets* had been slain, but, in order to make it impossible immediately to substitute new prophets for the old, she had even ordered *the altars*, frequently used by the prophets, and here mentioned last for the sake of emphasis, to be demolished. Other interpreters explain the transposition as evidence of poor memory on Paul's part. Fact is that Paul correctly reproduces the substance of the original; i.e., as much of it as he needs for his purpose. In this particular instance the exact order of these two words was probably of no significance.

"I am the only one left, and they are seeking my life," Elijah had said. The Lord, on the other hand, had assured him that no less than seven thousand faithful men were left. Seven thousand *men*,[305] probably to be understood in the sense "in addition to the women and children," for it would be hard to imagine a situation in which only the men had remained faithful to God. Cf. Mark 6:44 with Matt. 14:21. To be sure, these seven thousand constituted only a remnant of Israel's population, but it was a *significant* remnant. In accordance with the symbolical meaning which Scripture attaches to the number seven and its multiples, we can say that this seven thousand amounted to *the full number* of Elijah's contemporary kinsmen chosen from eternity to inherit life everlasting. There must have been at least seven thousand.

Note especially "*I* have left *for myself*." The fact that seven thousand had remained loyal to God must not be ascribed to Elijah's energetic activity—he evidently did not even know anything about these seven thousand—or to the innate goodness of these faithful people, but to the sovereign will of God, to his delight in preserving for himself a remnant.

5. So, too, at the present time a remnant has come into being, chosen by grace.

As it was *then*, says Paul, so it is *now*. God did not then, does not now, and never will completely reject Israel. He is not "through with the Jews." Was it not he himself who had caused them to be an ore-bearing vein? Was it not he too, who, by means of his sovereign grace, had seen to it that also at the

305. Grk. ἄνδρας.

present time a remnant of Israel had come into being, a remnant "chosen by grace"? Cf. 9:11; 11:28.

The doctrine of *the salvation of the remnant* is taught throughout Scripture:

At the time of *Noah* the many perished, the few were saved (Gen. 6:1-8; Luke 17:26, 27; I Peter 3:20).

The same thing happened in the days of *Lot* (Gen. 19:29; Luke 17:28, 29).

Elijah too, as we have just now been told, was acquainted with the idea of the saved remnant, though he did not realize that it amounted to no less than seven thousand.

Previously (Rom. 9:27; cf. Isa. 10:22 f.) the apostle has reminded us of the remnant in the days of *Isaiah*.

It does not surprise us therefore that also "at the present time," that is, in the apostle's own day, there was a saved remnant, and that *Paul* belonged to it. In Romans the remnant doctrine is either taught or implied also in the following passages: 9:6 f.; 9:18a; 9:27; 10:4, 11, 16; 11:14, 24, 25.

Further substantiation of the doctrine that salvation is for the elect remnant can be found in such Old Testament passages as Isa. 1:9 (=Rom. 9:29); 11:11, 16; 46:3; 53:1; Jer. 23:3; 31:7; Joel 2:32; Amos 5:15; Mic. 2:12; 4:5-7; 7:18; Zeph. 3:13, to mention but a few. Was not a son of Isaiah named Shear Jashub, meaning *A remnant shall return?*

As to the New Testament, it may or may not be significant that in the parable of The Sower (or The Four Kinds of Soil)—see Matt. 13:1-9, 18-23; Mark 4:1-9, 13-20; Luke 8:4-15—it is *only the final kind of soil* that yields a good crop. But even if no conclusion can be drawn from this parable as to the proportion of saved to unsaved among those who hear the gospel, we have the Master's clear statement,

"For many are called, but few chosen" (Matt. 22:14). Cf. Luke 12:32.

The view of some—and among them those whose writings we regard highly—that a day is coming when this rule will no longer apply, in fact that the very principle of the remnant implies that one day the nation of Israel as a whole will be saved, seems rather strange. Are those who favor this opinion guilty of reading the words of Rom. 11:26 ("And so all Israel shall be saved"), *as they interpret it*, into 11:5?

6. And if by grace, (then it is) no longer by works; since (if it were) grace would no longer be grace.

Paul feels the need of adding this, probably because *salvation by works*, and therefore by human merit, was the very cornerstone of the Jewish (rabbinical) religion. Not only did Christians constantly have to defend themselves and their beliefs against this false doctrine, but, as is clear from such passages as Gal. 1:6-9; 3:1-5, they themselves were in danger of slipping back into the heresy which they, upon becoming Christians, were supposed to have left behind.

It is as if Paul were saying, "If salvation is by grace, it is no longer by works or by *merit*. Why not? Because the very essence of grace is *unmerited divine favor*." Cf. 4:4.

7-10. What then? What Israel is seeking so earnestly it has not obtained, but the elect have obtained it. The others were hardened, as it is written:

> **"God gave them a spirit of stupor,**
> **eyes not to see,**
> **and ears not to hear,**
> **to this very day."**

And David says,

> **"Let their table become a snare and a trap,**
> **a stumbling block and a retribution for them.**
> **Let their eyes be darkened so as not to see,**
> **and their back do thou bow down forever."**

"What then?" Paul means, "What follows?" When he continues, "What Israel is seeking so earnestly it has not obtained," he is repeating the thought of 9:30, 31. See especially 9:31: "Israel, however, though ever in pursuit of (the) law of righteousness, has not attained to (that) law." See the explanation of that passage. However, here (in 11:7) the apostle adds, "but the elect have obtained it. The others were hardened." By comparing our present passage with 9:30, 31 it becomes clear that *historically* the thing which Israel as a nation was constantly seeking but was not obtaining was *right standing with God*, righteousness.

One rather important difference between the former passage (9:30, 31) and this one (11:7) is that in the earlier one we were told that the Gentiles had obtained that which Israel as a nation had not obtained; but now, in 11:7, Paul, without in any way denying what he had said previously about the Gentiles, limits himself to Israel. He now states that "the elect"—that is, the elect[306] among the Jews—had obtained it." Cf. 9:6.

After saying, "The others were hardened," Paul immediately describes this hardening as an act of *God*. He quotes two Old Testament passages. In the first Moses is the speaker; in the second David.

The first quotation (verse 8) is from Deut. 29:4, which, as found there, reads as follows, "But to this day the Lord has not given y o u a mind that understands or eyes that see or ears that hear." With this passage may be compared Isa. 6:9. The spirit of stupor, mentioned in Rom. 11:8, is that of mental and moral dulness or apathy. The giving of this spirit describes the divine hardening process. The stupor resembles a deep sleep in which a person is insensitive to the impressions that come to him from the outside; hence, no seeing and hearing. Cf. Isa. 29:10.

Moses tells the Israelites that this condition has prevailed "to this very day." Paul was able to say the same with respect to the "day" when he was writing Romans: the Jews who had rejected Christ and the righteousness of God in

---

306. Literally "the election." This is simply an idiom for "the elect," as "the circumcision" is for "the circumcised." See footnote 119 on 4:9, p. 149.

and through the Savior, were continuing to attempt to establish their own righteousness.

The second passage (verses 9, 10) reflects Ps. 69:22, 23. However, Paul, in quoting these words, is for the most part following the LXX translation (there Ps. 68:23, 24), which is as follows:

English from Greek Translation (LXX)
"Let their table become a snare before them,
a retribution and a stumbling block.
Let their eyes be darkened so as not to see;
and their back do thou bow down forever."

A superficial glance at Ps. 69:22, 23, quoted by Paul here in Rom. 11:9, 10, might lead to the conclusion that its moral tone is not very high. The Psalmist seems to be pronouncing curses upon his enemies because, without good cause, they hate, reproach, and persecute him. However, a closer look at the psalm reveals that the reason—at least part of the reason—why his enemies hate him so implacably is the closeness of the fellowship existing between him and his God (see verses 7, 9). It is therefore not surprising that Ps. 69 is a Messianic Psalm (see especially verses 20, 21). Note also its stirring climax (verses 29-36).

It remains true, nevertheless, that in this psalm the author (David) is flinging an imprecation at his foes. He invokes a curse upon them. The meaning of the four lines (after "And David says") can be reproduced as follows:

Let their wasteful lifestyle prove to be their undoing.
Let it become the disaster they deserve.
Fill them with moral and spiritual blindness
And cause them to be bent down with continuous grief.

The concept to be emphasized in this connection is *retribution*: the disaster they deserve.

Verses 7-10 establish the following facts:

a. The elect have obtained salvation.
b. God hardens those who have hardened themselves.
c. They get what is coming to them.

Even for the hardened ones there is hope; that is, if they repent. It will then become clear that they too belong to the elect. In a marvelous manner (see the interpretation of 11:25, pp. 377, 378) God gathers to himself a remnant even from the hardened majority.

Accordingly, to include Rom. 11:7 (or 11:7-10) in a list of passages proving reprobation is an error. Scripture teaches reprobation as well as election, as has been shown; and see Rom. 9:13, 17, 18, 21, 22; I Peter 2:8, but Rom. 11:7f. does not prove this. It can be included in the list of proof passages only if the context (11:11f.) is ignored. On this point I agree with Ridderbos, *op. cit.*, p. 249 and with Cranfield, *op. cit.*, p. 549.

---

11 I ask then, "Did they stumble so as to fall?" Of course not! Rather, because of their trespass salvation (has come) to the Gentiles to make Israel envious. 12 Now if their trespass

(means) riches for the world, and their defeat (means) riches for the Gentiles, how much more (does) their fulness (mean)? 13 It is to y o u, Gentiles, that I am speaking. Inasmuch as I am an apostle to (the) Gentiles, I take pride in my ministry, 14 in the hope that I may somehow arouse my own people to envy and save some of them. 15 For if their rejection (means the) reconciliation of the world, what (is) their acceptance but life from the dead? 16 And if the cake that is offered as firstfruits (is) holy, so (is) the entire batch; and if the root (is) holy, so (are) the branches.

17 Moreoever, if some of the branches have been lopped off, and you, being a wild olive shoot, have been grafted in among them, and have come to share the nourishing sap[307] from the olive root, 18 do not gloat over this at the expense of those branches. But if you do gloat, (then remember that) it is not you who support the root, but the root that supports you. 19 You will say then, "Branches were lopped off so that *I* might be grafted in." 20 True! But it was for lack of faith that they were lopped off, and it is by faith that you stand. Don't be arrogant but fear! 21 For if God has not spared the natural branches, neither will he spare you.

22 Consider then the kindness and the severity of God: toward those who have fallen there is severity, but toward you God's kindness, if you remain in his kindness. Otherwise you also will be cut off. 23 But they, if they do not persist in their unbelief, will be grafted in, for God has the power to graft them in again. 24 For if you were cut out of an olive tree that was wild by nature, and, contrary to nature, were grafted into a cultivated olive tree, how much more readily will these, the natural olive branches, be grafted (back) into their own olive tree?

Ingrafted Branches

"But they, if they do not persist in their unbelief, will be grafted in, for God has the power to graft them in again"
11:11-24

11, 12. I ask then, "Did they stumble so as to fall?" Of course not! Rather, because of their trespass salvation (has come) to the Gentiles to make Israel envious. Now if their trespass (means) riches for the world, and their defeat (means) riches for the Gentiles, how much more (does) their fulness (mean)?

Paul now informs us about God's purpose in hardening those who had hardened themselves. That purpose is ultimately one of grace, and this for the benefit of both Gentile and Jews.

In quoting from Ps. 69 (LXX Ps. 68) Paul had said, "Let their table become a stumbling block" (see also Rom. 9:33). He now asks, "Did they stumble so as to fall?"[308] In other words, "Was their final and irrevocable doom what God had in mind? With another and very comforting "Of course not!" or "Far from it!" the apostle buries that idea and emphatically proclaims the opposite, namely, that blessings were in store for both Gentile and Jew; all of this because of God's marvelous providential guidance and love, able to cause something good, yes very good, to come forth out of evil.

First of all, then, because of Israel's trespass (see footnote 157 on 5:15)—clearly, their rejection of the gospel—salvation has come to *the Gentiles*. That

---

307. Or fatness.

308. In the original the construction of this part of the sentence is the same as in 11:1, "I ask then, Did God reject his people?" So footnote 302 applies here also.

this was what had actually happened and was occurring right along is clear from such passages as Acts 13:44-48; 18:6; 28:23-28.[309] But indirectly *the Jews* themselves were also being blessed. Paul says, "salvation has come to the Gentiles *to make Israel envious*." In the present context *envy* has a positive effect. Such an effect is, however, not universal, as 10:19 has already shown. To reconcile these two passages (Rom. 10:19 and 11:11b) we must assume that 11:11b has reference to the true Israel (9:6). In his marvelous kindness God causes their envy to be the means of their salvation. These people take note of the peace that passes understanding present in the hearts and lives of the Gentiles who, by God's sovereign grace, have embraced Christ as their Lord and Savior. The elect Jews then become envious, yearning to participate in this peace of God and in all the other blessings God is bestowing on the converted Gentiles. Result: the Holy Spirit uses envy to save these Jews.

The apostle draws this conclusion: If *their trespass*—the sin of the Jews in rejecting the gospel—means riches for the world, and *their defeat* riches for the Gentiles, for by this rejection the door to the evangelization of the Gentiles had been opened, then how much does *their fulness*[310] mean?

In the manner already explained, Israel's *defeat* had brought riches to the Gentiles. Then surely the salvation of the full number of Israelites who had been predestined to be saved (cf. 9:6)—hence, not just the salvation of a remnant at any *one* particular time (see 11:5)—would progressively bring an abundance of blessings to the entire world. Think of such blessings as spiritual unity and fellowship (Eph. 2:14, 18), co-operation in providing aid to the sick and needy, and presenting a strong, united evangelical testimony to the world. Just imagine that on history's final day one could look back on all those blessings!

The interpretation according to which Rom. 11:12 is limited to the conversion and restoration of the people of Israel at *history's close* is vulnerable on two counts:

---

309. In view of the clear language in these passages of the book of Acts, in which Paul is himself the speaker (or, as in one case, one of the speakers, the other being Barnabas), the explanation offered by K. Barth, namely, that the reference would be to the action of the Jews in nailing Jesus to the cross and thereby activating the reconciliation of the world, must be rejected. See K. Barth, *Kirchliche Dogmatik* II, p. 307; *Church Dogmatics* II, p. 279.

310. For the term πλήρωμα (pleroma) see N.T.C. on Colossians, p. 79, footn. 56. It lends itself to a variety of interpretations. By examining (a) the article on this word found in L.N.T. (A. and G.), p. 678, where for the present passage two meanings are discussed; (b) the various commentaries, containing many different opinions; and (c) G. Delling's article on this word in Th.D.N.T., Vol. VI, p. 305, one becomes aware of the existing confusion. As I see it, the best results will probably be obtained if:

a. the same English equivalent is assigned to the word in verse 12 as in verse 25.

b. in the *explanation* of the term, as used here in verse 12, the contrast Paul undoubtedly had in mind, between ἥττημα and πλήρωμα is recognized.

The result is that I have adopted *fulness* as the English equivalent in both instances. In my explanation of the term, as used here in verse 12, I suggest that the contrast is that between *defeat*, on the one hand, and *arrival at full strength* (implying full number), on the other.

a. As 11:5, 14, 30, 31 indicate, Paul is referring to events that include those which are taking place "at the present time," during Paul's current ministry, "now."

b. His words "their fulness" pertain to the salvation not of a physical unit, "the people of Israel"; but of the sum of all Israel's remnants. See 11:1-7, 26.[311]

At this point Paul begins to address specifically the Gentile portion of the Roman church:

13, 14. It is to y o u, Gentiles, that I am speaking. Inasmuch as I am an apostle to (the) Gentiles, I take pride in my ministry, in the hope that I may somehow arouse my own people to envy and save some of them.

Note the following:

a. As some see it, when Paul says, "It is to y o u, Gentiles that I am speaking," he is addressing the congregation as a whole, calling its members *Gentiles* because most of them were Gentile converts. However, this view is hard to accept since in the same verse the word *Gentiles* occurs again ". . . Inasmuch as I am an apostle to (the) Gentiles" in a context where it must mean *Gentiles in distinction from Jews*. Also in verse 17 the designation "a wild olive shoot" is best explained as referring to a Gentile.

It would seem, accordingly, that, beginning at verse 13 and continuing through verse 24, Paul is addressing especially the Gentile portion of the church at Rome. In fact, starting with verse 17, he is speaking to *a*—that is "any"—representative member of that part of the congregation.

b. "Inasmuch as[312] I am an apostle to (the) Gentiles . . ."

Although the sphere of Paul's apostolic labors and authority included Jews as well as Gentiles (Acts 9:15; 26:15-20), in a preeminent sense he had been appointed to be, and actually became, "apostle to the Gentiles" (Acts 18:6; 22:21; Rom. 1:5; 15:15, 16; Gal. 2:2, 8; Eph. 3:1, 8; I Tim. 2:7; II Tim. 4:17).

c. "I take pride in my ministry," etc.

The apostle is enthusiastic about, and adds prestige to, his ministry to the Gentiles, one reason being that he hopes to be a means in God's hand for the realization of God's purpose mentioned in verse 11, namely, to promote salvation for the Gentiles in order thus to make Israel envious with a view to salvation. Note similarity between verses 11b and 13b, 14.

Not as if conversion of Israelites is the one and only goal of Paul's Gentile mission activity. For the apostle missionary endeavor among the Gentiles to the glory of God is also an end in itself. See I Cor. 9:22. However, in the present context Paul indicates that his ministry to the Gentiles is not in conflict with, but in the interest of, the salvation of his kinsmen.

d. ". . . and save some of them."

---

311. For the opposite interpretation see J. Murray, *op. cit.*, Vol. II, p. 79.

312. ἐφ' ὅσον, basic meaning: to the extent that, inasfar as; and so: inasmuch as. See also Matt. 25:40, 45.

Paul's hope that some Jews might be saved through his current ministry, a hope strengthened by his affection for his own people (9:1-5; 10:1), was not without solid foundation. It was based on God's promise concerning the salvation of Israel's *remnant*.

Continuing in the style of verse 12 Paul writes:

15, 16. For if their rejection (means the) reconciliation of the world, what (is) their acceptance but life from the dead? And if the cake that is offered as firstfruits (is) holy, so (is) the entire batch; and if the root (is) holy, so (are) the branches.

It will be recalled that all but a remnant of the Jews had hardened themselves against the gospel (verse 7) and in turn had become hardened. Now God, in his beneficent and overruling providence, brings about a twofold result:

a. The gospel was now being proclaimed to the nations of the world. Those Gentiles who accept it by faith become reconciled to God; that is, the bond of fellowship between God and themselves is restored. Cf. 5:11; II Cor. 5:18-20.

b. Sin-hardened Israelites, taking note of the peace and joy experienced by these Gentiles, become filled with envy, but, in a marvelous manner that envy is by God changed into living faith in the Lord Jesus Christ.

Imagine for a moment the radical change here implied for these Israelites. They now love what they formerly hated. They hate what they formerly loved. Above all, they know that no longer are they God's enemies. They have now been accepted by the very God against whom earlier they had hardened themselves and by whom they had been further hardened. The change was simply astounding, as especially Paul, the former persecutor, knew by his own experience! It was a turnabout to life from the dead, a truly spiritual resurrection. Cf. Luke 15:32; Eph. 2:1-10. It reminds one of the hymn, "Out of My Bondage, Sorrow, and Night" by William T. Sleeper. Think especially of the stanza beginning with the line:

"Out of the fear and dread of the tomb, Jesus I come, Jesus I come."

A Jew who used to hate every Christian experienced a dramatic conversion. Afterward he was heard to say, "The change from darkness to day is great, but the change brought about in me is greater by far."

This change implies the consciousness that one has been *set apart* to devote one's life to God. See I Peter 2:9.

This is in line with the illustration Paul uses: if the cake that is offered as firstfruits is holy, that is, *set apart for sacred use*, then surely the entire batch is holy. If the root is holy, so are the branches that are upheld by that root and receive their nourishment from it.

This illustration owes its origin to the offering to the Lord of a cake prepared from the firstfruits of grain worked into dough (Num. 15:17-21). When the Israelites brought this offering they thereby consecrated to the Lord the entire grain harvest. All of it was now regarded as *set apart* to the

Lord, so that whatever was subsequently used by the people was regarded as a gift out of his hand.

Similarly, if the root of a tree *is consecrated* to the Lord, so are all its branches. The cake and the root probably symbolize Abraham; better still: Abraham, Isaac, and Jacob. See Rom. 11:28. The branches are the descendants of these forefathers. They are the people of Israel, highly privileged (Rom. 9:4 f.). They—cf. "the entire batch"—had been *set apart* by the Lord, to live for him (Exod. 19:5, 6; Deut. 14:2; cf. I Peter 2:9).

When the apostle mentions "their rejection" and "their acceptance" he is not referring to what is going to happen in connection with The Great Consummation. We should not forget the context. The *immediately preceding* context is: "I take pride in my ministry, in the hope that I may somehow arouse my own people to envy and save some of them." The *immediately following* context is: "Moreover, if some of the branches have been lopped off, and you, though being a wild olive shoot, have been grafted in among them and have come to share the nourishing sap from the olive root, do not gloat over this at the expense of those branches." It will not do, therefore, to interpret the intervening reference to "their acceptance . . . life from the dead," as being a reference to what by some is expected to happen at the close of the world's history. Those interpreters who, nevertheless, have adopted that theory will at times inform their readers that the "life from the dead" change means that in the last days the radical turnabout or conversion of the people of Israel will result in unexampled blessings for mankind, worldwide quickening, with Israel advancing from one missionary triumph among the Gentiles to another. Are they forgetting that, according to the interpretation of Rom. 11:25, 26, favored by them and/or by their friends, there will be no more Gentiles left to become candidates for conversion, since, as these exegetes see it, it is only *after* the totality of Gentile believers has been gathered into God's fold that Israel will finally be saved?

17-21. Moreover, if some of the branches have been lopped off, and you, being a wild olive shoot, have been grafted in among them, and have come to share the nourishing sap from the olive root, do not gloat over this at the expense of those branches. But if you do gloat, (then remember that) it is not you who support the root, but the root that supports you. You will say then, "Branches were lopped off so that *I* might be grafted in." True! But it was for lack of faith that they were lopped off, and it is by faith that you stand. Don't be arrogant but fear! For if God has not spared the natural branches, neither will he spare you.[313]

313. ἐξεκλάσθησαν, in verses 17, 19, and 20, third per. pl. aor. pass. indicat. of ἐκκλάω, to break off; and, in connection with a tree, to lop off.

ἀγριέλαιος = ἄγρος, field, plus ἐλαία, here olive shoot; hence, *field* = *wild* olive shoot. In verse 17 ἀγριέλαιος is probably an adjective; in verse 24 a noun. Cf. the English word *oak* which can also be a noun or an adj. (oaken).

συγκοινωνὸς τῆς ῥίζης τῆς πιότητος τῆς ἐλαίας "(having come) to share the root of fatness

Continuing to address the Gentiles (see on verse 13), Paul feels the need of issuing a warning to them with respect to their attitude toward his kinsmen, the Jews. The contents of the present passage (verses 17-21) will be discussed under the following three captions: Why was this warning necessary? In what form is it presented? What is its content? Discussion of the third question will also cover verses 22-24.

Paul Warns the Gentile Members of the Roman Church To Shun Sinful Pride

A. *Why was this warning necessary?*

As has been indicated, p. 25, the spiritual condition of the Roman church was, on the whole, very favorable. This does not mean, however, that perfection had been attained. In connection with the discussion of 8:23-25 it has already been shown that there seems to have been some people in this church who were lacking in the basic Christian virtue of humility. Similarly, from the present passage it appears that there were Gentile Christians who, filled with sinful pride, were tempted to look down with a degree of contempt on their Jewish fellow-members. At first the real clash may well have been between these Gentiles and the unbelieving Jews, those outside the church. It would seem, however, that little by little the Gentile church members caused their feeling of superiority to be manifested also within the church. See verses 17, 18. It is not ruled out, of course, that not only Gentiles but even Jews may have become infected with this evil. Paul does not always differentiate between the two, but most of all it was a Gentile blemish. For evidences of the presence of a boastful frame of mind among those addressed see the following passages: 12:3; 14:1, 3, 4, 10, 13; 15:1, 2, 5, 7, 15, 16, in addition to the present passage (11:17-21; in a sense 11:17-24).[314]

For the present, then, we are dealing with the spirit of arrogance as it manifested itself in a typical *Gentile* member of the Roman church, as is clear from the fact that the apostle describes this representative member as "a *wild* olive shoot." Contrast verse 17b where the root of a *cultivated* olive tree is presupposed; and see also verse 24.

B. *In what form is it presented?*

The answer is: in the form of a metaphor, an implied comparison, in the present case *reminding one* of the practice of arboreal grafting, in which, for

---

(= the fat root) of the olive"; or else: "(having come) to share the root of the olive, that is, its fatness." For "fatness" one can substitute "nourishing sap."

ἐνεκεντρίσθης, sec. per. s. aor. pass. indicat. of ἐγκεντρίζω, to ingraft. In verse 19 the first per. s. aor. pass. subjunct. (ἐγκεντρισθῶ) of the same verb occurs.

ἐν αὐτοῖς, among them.

κατακαυχῶ, sec. per. s. pres. imperat., and κατακαυχᾶσαι, sec. per. s. pres. indicat. of κατακαυχάομαι, to glory over, gloat over.

ἐφείσατο, third per. s. aor. act. indicat., and φείσεται, third per. s. fut. indicat. of φείδομαι, to spare.

314. See S. K. Williams, "The 'Righteousness of God' in Romans," *JBL*, No. 99 (June 1980), pp. 241-290. Note especially pp. 245-255.

any one of several reasons, a shoot ("scion") of one tree is inserted into the stem ("stock") of another.

The transition between verses 16 and 17 is, however, not abrupt. The apostle has just now been speaking about "branches," meaning people, and here in verse 17 he continues to do so. In verse 16 he described these branches as being *holy*, in the sense of "set apart for sacred use or duty." This cannot mean, however, that all the people so described were also marked by inner holiness, sanctity of heart, life and conduct. The apostle makes clear that some of "the branches" revealed the opposite character, and had to be lopped off. Clearly such branches symbolize unfaithful covenant members. They were descendants of the patriarchs but had abandoned the faith of the fathers.

Note that the *y o u* of verses 2 and 13 changes into the *you* of verses 17-24, the reference now being to a—that is, *any*—Gentile member of the Roman church. Let each take the lesson to heart! Paul says that this typical member, "being a wild olive shoot" *was grafted in among* the branches of the cultivated olive tree.

For this "application of the practice of grafting" Paul has been severely criticized. It has been remarked that it is customary to graft a slip of a cultivated olive tree into a wild olive tree, but not the reverse. To reestablish Paul's reputation some have answered that it is exactly in Palestine that a wild olive shoot is at times grafted into an old cultivated olive tree in order to reinvigorate it.[315] Others, however, in their effort to rescue the apostle, employ the very opposite method of reasoning. They argue as follows: Granted that Paul refers to a kind of grafting that is contrary to customary practice, he admits it, does he not? He calls grafting anything from a wild olive tree into a cultivated olive tree 'contrary to nature" (verse 24). So at least he knows what he is saying. Some authors even use both of these arguments in order to help Paul out of his (imagined) difficulty, though it is hard to see how the apostle can receive help from those who on the one hand insist that the type of grafting he presupposes was in harmony with customary practice, be it only in Palestine, but who, on the other hand, point to Paul's admission that the grafting to which he refers was "contrary to nature." When two lines of argumentation clash, they cannot both be right. But even if the problem of grafting a wild shoot into a cultivated tree can be solved, how can we justify Paul's language when he speaks about grafting lopped off branches (back) into their own tree (verses 17, 19, 23, 24)?

The true solution is probably wholly different. To begin with, it is not true that in verse 24 Paul, in calling something "contrary to nature," is even indirectly referring to a method of horticultural grafting. See on that verse. And secondly, with respect to the first attempt to rescue Paul, those who endorse it seem to forget that Paul, in writing about grafting and regrafting

---

315. William M. Ramsay, *Pauline and Other Studies*, London, 1906, pp. 223, 224.

is under no obligation whatever to adhere to the rules and practices of Nature grafting. He is talking about grafting *in the spiritual realm*. How often did not Jesus, in his parables, draw pictures that departed strikingly from daily life customs and practices? Think especially of his parable of The Laborers in the Vineyard (Matt. 20:1-16).

What the apostle is saying, then, is clear. He is telling the typical Gentile member of the Roman church, who was tending to become somewhat arrogant, that he, that member, should never forget who he really is. He had come in from the outside and *had been spiritually grafted in among the Jews*. Only in this manner had he come to share "the nourishing sap from the olive root." To the proud Gentile member Paul is saying, "Consider how much you owe to the Jews!"

Was not Peter, whose possible connection with the founding of the church at Rome has been discussed earlier—see pp. 18, 19—a Jew? Was not Paul, who even before writing his present epistle seems to have been in contact with many prominent members of the Roman church (16:3-16), a Jew? Is it not true that the very gospel of *justification by faith* was based on the Jewish Scriptures? See 1:1, 2, 17; ch. 4. And, according to his human nature, was not even "the Author and Perfecter of faith" a Jew? Is it not true, therefore, that "salvation is from the Jews" (John 4:22)?

Must we not thank the Lord for the fact that the Holy Spirit so inspired Paul that, in addition to employing precious, unembellished theoretical arguments, he also made use of many vivid illustrations, the present grafting symbolism being one of them?

C. *What is its content?*

Paul warns the Gentile that he should not gloat over the fact that, while some of the natural branches—unbelieving Jews—have been lopped off, he, this Gentile, has been grafted in among the remaining (Jewish) branches, with all this implies with reference to partaking of "the nourishing sap from the olive root," the blessings promised to the patriarchs and realized in their lives and in the lives of their God-fearing children.

The Gentile, inclined to look down with a degree of contempt on his fellow-members, the Jews, is warned not to deem himself better than they. Let him bear in mind that it is not he, this boastful Gentile, who supports the root. How would it even have been possible for him to contribute anything to the blessings flowing forth from God's eternal decree, and from the promises, and imparted to the patriarchs, the all-inclusive promise being, "I will be your (or y o u r) God"? No, it was not the Gentile who supported the root, but the root that supported the Gentile.

The possible counter-remark made by the typical Gentile was, "Branches were lopped off so that *I*—with tremendous emphasis on this pronoun[316]—

316. Note how in the original this *I* is not merely included in the verb, as often, but is spelled out in full! It is ἐγώ.

might be grafted in" (verse 19). Paul answers, "True." Historically speaking as verse 11 has shown, that was indeed true. But there was another, even more important side to the answer. It was this: "it was for lack of faith that they were lopped off, and it is by faith that you stand." This *faith*, by virtue of its very essence, excludes all boasting, all arrogance or self-esteem. It includes godly *fear*, the kind of fear that is wholesome. See Prov. 3:7; Phil. 2:12, 13; Heb. 4:1; I Peter 1:17. Such fear leans wholly on God and his sovereign grace, and claims no merit of its own. The conclusion follows very naturally, "For if God has not spared the natural branches—the Jews to whom the promise was first made but who in large numbers had turned away from God—neither will he spare you."

22-24. Consider then the kindness and the severity of God: toward those who have fallen there is severity, but toward you God's kindness, if you remain in his kindness. Otherwise you also will be cut off. But they, if they do not persist in their unbelief, will be grafted in, for God has the power to graft them in again. For if you were cut out of an olive tree that was wild by nature, and, contrary to nature, were grafted into a cultivated olive tree, how much more readily will these, the natural olive branches, be grafted (back) into their own olive tree?

In preceding passages Paul has been speaking about the disobedience and rejection of many of the Jews (9:27, 31; 10:21; 11:7-10, 15), the "lopping off of branches" (11:17, 19, 20, 21). He has also commented on the salvation, riches, and grafting in of Gentiles (11:11, 12, 17, 19). It is God who rejects. It is also God who saves. Accordingly, Paul now rivets the attention of those addressed on the *kindness and the severity of God*. Not just on *one* of these qualities, namely kindness, as is the habit of some preachers, who overemphasize the love of God at the expense of his wrath, but on both. For those who have fallen—in the present context the Jews—there is severity, the rigor of the divine judgment. See 1:18, where God's *wrath* is directed especially against the unbelieving world of the Gentiles; but turn from there immediately to 3:19 where "the entire world is exposed to the judgment of God." That includes the Jews. So also here, in 11:22, God's severity of sternness[317] is directed against "those who have fallen," namely, the Jews, as the context clearly indicates.

"But toward you God's kindness." Note that the object of this kindness is still being described as the typical or representative Gentile Christian. Paul, who is himself "the apostle to the Gentiles," delights in calling attention to the salvation and riches God is imparting to the Gentiles (11:11, 12). On the concept of divine kindness see also 2:4; Eph. 2:7; Titus 3:4.

---

317. ἀποτομία, from ἀποτέμνω, to cut off; hence abruptness, rigor, severity, sternness. In the New Testament this noun is found only here. The adverb ἀποτόμως, sharply, harshly, occurs in II Cor. 13:10 and in Titus 1:13.

The manifestation of this kindness is, however, not unconditional. It requires genuine faith on man's part. Says Paul, "toward you God's kindness, if you remain in his kindness. Otherwise you also will be cut off."

This must not be understood in the sense that God will supply the kindness, man the faith. Salvation is ever God's gift. It is never a 50-50 affair. From start to finish it is the work of God. But this does not remove human responsibility. God does not exercise faith for man or in his place. It is and remains man who reposes his trust in God, but it is God who both imparts this faith to him and enables him to use it. For the interrelation between God's activity and man's, see Phil. 2:12, 13; II Thess. 2:13.

There is a sound, biblical sense, therefore, in which we can speak about salvation as being *conditional*. Its reception is conditioned on the life of trust in the Triune God who has revealed himself in Jesus Christ unto salvation and ultimately unto his own glory. This "if" character of salvation is very important. It is expressed beautifully in Felix Mendelssohn's *Elijah*. Note the words, "If with all y o u r hearts ye truly seek me, ye will ever surely find me" (based on Deut. 4:29). Note a similar "if" in such passages as Deut. 30:10; I Kings 8:47-50; Jer. 18:5-10; Col. 1:21-23; Heb. 3:6, 14. And is not a similar "if" *implied* in many other passages, including Matt. 11:28-30; John 3:16; Rev. 22:17? Absolute, unconditional promises, guaranteeing salvation to either Gentiles or Jews, *no matter how they live* exist only in people's imaginations, not in Scripture. Even if the condition is not always mentioned, for every responsible, thinking, individual it is always implied.

What happens when the condition remains unfulfilled? Ultimate rejection follows; and this, as Paul says in so many words, not only with respect to the Jew but also with respect to the Gentile.

Let not the Gentile believer imagine that God is through with the Jews; that, under no circumstances is salvation in store for them. The apostle states, "But they, if—there is that *if* again—they do not persist in their unbelief, will be grafted in, for God has the power to graft them in again." That the door of opportunity for the entrance of Jews—even for initially hardened Jews—is standing open, Paul is now going to demonstrate.

He starts out by saying, "For if you were cut out of an olive tree that was wild by nature, and, contrary to nature, were grafted into a cultivated olive tree . . ." In this part of the sentence what does Paul mean by "contrary to nature"? Does he mean "contrary to customary horticultural practice"? Would not such a statement, if at all deemed necessary, have been made much earlier; for example, in connection with verse 17? Is it not far more in harmony with the present context to interpret Paul's words as follows: "You, being a Gentile, belong by nature to the realm of unbelief. You are, as it were, part of a wild olive tree. Nevertheless, you were grafted into a cultivated olive tree, meaning: you were brought into the domain of grace, promise, and faith, the realm of Abraham, Isaac, and Jacob (cf. Gal. 3:9). For you this was an enormous change. It was contrary to nature, for not only did you have to be delivered from the pit of paganism, with all its vices (cf. 1:24-32); but, in addition, you had to be transplanted into the sphere of God's covenant, the realm of sovereign grace, holiness, light, and love. Accordingly, if, contrary to nature, *you* were grafted into a cultivated olive tree, how much more readily, then, will *the natural branches*, the children of the covenant, who were never immersed in paganism, and who, in addition, were in possession of all the remarkable privileges mentioned in 9:4, 5, be grafted back into their own olive tree; that is, be restored to their native stock"?

Note that the apostle does not say or imply that one day all unbelieving Jews are going to be grafted back into their own olive tree, are going to be saved. He carefully avoids saying anything of the kind. He states that the regrafting will take place "*if* they do not persist in their unbelief." Undoubtedly what he means is, "Some will persist; others will not." This interpretation is in line with previous statements about the hardened majority and the saved minority or remnant. See especially on 9:27 and on 11:5 (pp. 321, 322 and 362, 363).

In reading what Paul says about the olive tree there is one very important point that must not be overlooked. The apostle recognizes *only one (cultivated) olive tree*! In other words, the church is *one* living organism. For Jew and Gentile salvation is the same. It is obtained on the basis of Christ's atonement, by grace, through faith. The notion according to which God recognizes two objects on which he bestows his everlasting, saving love, namely, the Jews and the church, is contrary to Scripture. Here in Romans Paul has expressed himself on this subject again and again (3:29, 30; 4:11, 16; 5:18, 19; 9:22 f., 10:12, 13). *One olive tree* represents *all* the saved, regardless of their origin. And, as the result of the operation of God's saving grace, all the reborn are headed for the same everlasting home. Remember: *ONE OLIVE TREE.*

---

25 For I do not want y o u to be unaware of this mystery, brothers, so that y o u may not be conceited, that a hardening has come upon part of Israel (and will last) until the fulness of the Gentiles has come in. 26 And so all Israel will be saved, as it is written:

"Out of Zion will come the Deliverer;
he will turn godlessness away from Jacob.
27 And this is my covenant with them
whenever I shall take away their sins."

28 As far as the gospel is concerned, they are enemies for y o u r sake; but as far as election is concerned, they are beloved for the sake of the fathers, 29 for irrevocable are God's gracious gifts and his calling. 30 For just as at one time y o u were disobedient to God but now have received mercy as a result of their disobedience, 31 so they too have now become disobedient in order that, as a result of the mercy shown to y o u, they too may now[318] receive mercy. 32 For God has locked up all in the prison of disobedience in order that he may have mercy on them all.

---

318. Some MSS. omit this "now," but support for it is by no means weak.

God's Mercy on "the Fulness of the Gentiles" and on "All Israel"
"For God has locked up all in the prison of disobedience
in order that he may have mercy on all"
11:25-32

25. For I do not want y o u to be unaware of this mystery, brothers, so that y o u may not be conceited, that a hardening has come upon part of Israel (and will last) until the fulness of the Gentiles has come in.

Resuming use of the plural,[319] Paul directly addresses the entire congregation. Nevertheless, it is clear that even now he is thinking especially of those Gentile believers who stood in need of being warned against anti-Semitism. In no uncertain terms he has just told them that for the Jews, even for those who had become delinquent, and initially hardened, the door of opportunity to be saved was standing open at least as widely as it did for the Gentiles (verse 24). It is in connection with this thought that he now continues by using the explanatory conjunction *For*.

The words, "I do not want y o u to be unaware" signify, "I want y o u to take to heart." Note also here the word of tender affection "brothers." On both of these points (a. not unaware, and b. brothers) see 1:13.

". . . of this mystery." In referring to a mystery Paul is not using this term in the pagan sense of an esoteric doctrine for the initiated, but as indicating *a truth which would not have been known if God had not revealed it*.[320]

As appears from the very wording of verse 25—note "that a hardening has come upon part of Israel" (literally, "that a hardening in part has come on Israel"), this petrifaction is not absolute and unqualified; there is always a saved remnant, called into being in a marvelous manner:

a. Carnal Israel stumbles and is rejected because of its unbelief. Result:

b. The gospel is proclaimed to the Gentiles. The elect Gentiles are saved. Result:

c. God uses this salvation of Gentiles in order to arouse the envy of the Jews. Result:

d. The Jewish remnant accepts Christ, in accordance with God's eternal plan. In connection with each item it is God himself who brings about these results. But let us quote Paul's own words (verses 11, 12, 31):

a. "Because of their trespass

b. salvation (has come) to the Gentiles

---

319. Note change from σύ in verse 24 to ὑμᾶς in verse 25.

320. The word μυστήριον occurs also in Rom. 16:25 and six times in I Cor., six times also in Ephesians, four times in Colossians, once in II Thessalonians, and twice in I Timothy.

It is also found in the book of Revelation (1:20; 10:7; 17:5, 7). As there used it is perhaps best explained as "the symbolical meaning" of that which required explanation. In the LXX of Dan. 2, where the word occurs no less than 8 times (as a singular in verses 18, 19, 27, 30, and 47b; as a plural in verses 28, 29, and 47a) it refers to a "secret" that must be revealed, a riddle that needs to be interpreted. The meaning "divinely revealed truth" fits very well into the context of Luke 8:10 and its parallels (Matt. 13:11; Mark 4:11), the only Gospel instances of its use.

c. to make Israel envious, so that,
d. as a result of the mercy shown to y o u [Gentiles], they [Israel] too may now receive mercy."

Now is not that just too wonderful for words? Moreover, the blessed interaction Paul has in mind must not be given too limited a scope. It even reaches beyond that which is enclosed in these four items. For example, we may be sure that saved Gentiles (item b.) do not sit still, but, in turn, become witnesses for Christ; and so do saved Jews (item d.). This interdependence between the salvation of the Gentiles and that of Israel is the substance of the divine "mystery."[321]

In harmony, then, with the substance of this mystery, here in verse 25 the apostle states that the hardening has come *upon part of Israel*. That was true in the past, is true now, will still be a fact in the future. Is not this the same as to state that a remnant of Israel, *in every age*, is saved (see 9:27; 11:1-5)?

Israel's rejection is not absolute and unqualified, nor necessarily final. It is partial. Paul feels the need of stressing this fact because certain Gentiles seemed to have harbored contrary thoughts, as was pointed out in connection with verses 17-24. So he tells them, "I do not want y o u to be unaware of this mystery, brothers, *so that y o u may not be conceited*."

Not only is it true, however, that the divine hardening (in punishment for human hardening) affects part of the people in any period of history, but it is also a fact, as the apostle states here in verse 25, that a definite time-span has been assigned to this hardening. For the people as a whole it will last "until the fulness of the Gentiles has come in." In connection with verse 12, where the same word *fulness* (pleroma) occurs, it has been shown that by "fulness" the apostle means "full number." What Paul is saying, then, here in verse 25, is that Israel's partial hardening—the hardening of part of the people of Israel—will last until the full number of elect Gentiles has been gathered into God's fold.

And when will that full number have been brought to salvation in Christ? Scripture is very clear on this point. It will be on the day of Christ's glorious Return. Once he has returned, there is no longer any opportunity for accepting the gospel call. See Luke 17:26-37; II Peter 3:3-9. Cf. Belgic Confession, Article XXXVII:

"Finally we believe, according to the Word of God, when the time appointed by the Lord (which is unknown to all creatures) is come *and the number of the elect complete* (italics added), that our Lord Jesus Christ will come from heaven, corporally and visibly, as he ascended, with great glory and majesty to declare himself Judge of the living and the dead, burning this old world with fire and flame to cleanse it."

It has become clear, therefore, that the hardening of part of Israel and the gathering of Gentiles occur side by side. With respect to Israel this partial

---

321. So also Ridderbos, *op. cit.*, p. 263.

hardening began already during the days of the old dispensation (Rom. 9:27; 10:16, 21; 11:3), was taking place in Paul's own day, and will continue until the close of the new dispensation. Side by side with this hardening process, the gospel is being proclaimed to the Gentiles. Some reject it; some, by God's sovereign grace, accept it.

Returning now to Israel, it is obvious that if, in every age, some Israelites are hardened, it must also be true that in every age some are saved. Paul expresses this thought in words that have given rise to much controversy, namely, **26a. And so all Israel will be saved.**

THREE INTERPRETATIONS

A. *The Most Popular Theory*

"All Israel" indicates the mass of Jews living on earth in the end-time. The full number of elect Gentiles will be gathered in. After that the mass of the Jews—Israel on a large scale—will be saved. This will happen just previous to, or at the very moment of, Christ's Return.

For the names of some of the advocates of this theory see p. 306.

Evaluation

a. The Greek word οὕτως does not mean *then* or *after that*. The rendering "*Then* all Israel will be saved" is wrong. In none of the other occurrences of this word in Romans, or anywhere else in the New Testament, does this word have that meaning. It means *so, in this manner, thus.*

b. This theory also fails to do justice to the word *all* in "all Israel." Does not "all Israel" sound very strange as a description of the (comparatively) tiny fraction of Jews who will still be living on earth just before, or at the moment of, Christ's Return?

c. The context clearly indicates that in writing about the salvation of Israelites and Gentiles Paul is not limiting his thoughts to what will take place in the future. He very definitely includes what is happening *now*. See especially verses 30, 31.

d. Would it not be strange for God to single out for a very special favor—nothing less than salvation full and free—exactly that generation of Jews which will have hardened its heart against the testimony of the longest train of Christian witnesses, a train extending all the way from the days of Christ's sojourn on earth—in fact, in a sense, all the way from Abraham—to the close of the new dispensation?

e. The reader has not been prepared for the idea of a mass conversion of Israelites. All along Paul stresses the very opposite, namely, the salvation, in any age (past, present, future) of *a remnant*. See the passages listed under 11:5, p. 363. If Rom. 11:26 actually teaches a mass conversion of Jews, would it not seem as if Paul is saying, "Forget what I told y o u previously"?

f. If Paul is here predicting such a future mass conversion of Jews, is he not contradicting, if not the letter, at least the spirit, of his earlier statement found in I Thess. 2:14b-16:

". . . the Jews, who killed the Lord Jesus and the prophets, and drove us out, and do not please God, and are hostile to all men, in that they try to prevent us from speaking to the Gentiles that they may be saved, so as always to fill up the measure of their sins. But upon them the wrath [of God] has come to the uttermost"[322]?

g. The immediately following context (11:26b, 27) refers to a coming of "the Deliverer" who will turn away godlessness and remove sin from Jacob. Was not that the purpose of Christ's *first* coming? But the popular interpretation of Rom. 11:26 predicts a mass conversion of Jews in connection with Christ's *second* coming. That theory is, accordingly, not in harmony with the context.

For these several reasons Interpretation A. should be rejected.

B. *John Calvin's Theory*

"All Israel" refers to the total number of the elect throughout history, all those who are ultimately saved, both Jews and Gentiles. In his Commentary on this passage Calvin expresses himself as follows:

"I extend the word *Israel* to all the people of God, according to this meaning: when the Gentiles shall come in, the Jews also will return from their defection to the obedience of faith, and thus will be completed the salvation of the whole Israel of God, which must be gathered from both . . ."

The same view is defended by J. A. C. Van Leeuwen and D. Jacobs, *op. cit.*, p. 227; and, in a sense, by Karl Barth, *Der Römerbrief*, Zürich, 1954, p. 401; English tr., p. 416.

Evaluation.

Inasfar as Calvin interprets the term *Israel* spiritually—"Israel" refers to the elect—his theory must be considered correct. Cf. Rom. 9:6. Also his claim that the section, verses 25-32 (considered as a unit), describes *the one people of God* cannot be successfully refuted. On the other hand, Calvin's application of the term "Israel," in verse 26, to all the people of God, both Jews and Gentiles, is wrong. In the preceding context the words *Israel, Israelite(s)* occur no less than eleven times: 9:4; 9:6 (twice); 9:27; 9:31; 10:19; 10:21; 11:1; 11:2; 11:7; and 11:25. In each case the reference is clearly to Jews, never to Gentiles. What compelling reason can there be, therefore, to adopt a different meaning for the term *Israel* as used here in 11:26? To be sure, at the close of verse 25 the apostle makes mention of the Gentiles, but only in order to indicate that the partial hardening of the Jews will not cease until every elect Gentile will have been brought into the kingdom. Accordingly, Paul is still talking about the Jews. He does so also in verse 26b. Even verse 28 contains a clear reference to Jews. Not until verses 30-32 are reached does the apostle cause the entire body of the elect, both Jews and Gentiles, to pass in review together.

---

322. Or: at last; or, to the end.

Therefore, while appreciating the good elements in Calvin's explanation, we cannot agree with him in interpreting the term "all Israel" in 11:26 as referring to all the elect, both Jews and Gentiles. A passage should be interpreted in light of its context. In the present case the context points to Jews, not to Gentiles, nor in verses 26-29 to a combination of Jews and Gentiles.

C. *A Third Theory*

The term "All Israel" means *the total number of elect Jews, the sum of all Israel's "remnants."* "All Israel" parallels "the fulness of the Gentiles." Verses 25, 26 make it very clear that God is dealing with both groups, has been saving them, is saving them, and is going to save them. And if "All Israel" indicates, as it does, that not a single elect Israelite will be lacking "when the roll is called up yonder," then "the fulness of the Gentiles" similarly shows that when the attendance is checked every elect Gentile will answer "Present."

For the meaning of "will be saved" see on 1:16, p. 60. For Jew and Gentile the way of salvation is the same. In fact, their paths run side by side. Opportunity to be saved will have ended for both when Christ returns. As indicated previously, the two—"the fulness of the Gentiles" and "All Israel"—constitute *one* organism, symbolized by a single olive tree. It should be clear that if, in the present connection, *fulness* must be interpreted in its unlimited sense, the same holds for *all* in "All Israel."

The words "And so" are explained by Paul himself. They indicate, "In such a marvelous manner," a manner no one could have guessed. If God had not revealed this "mystery" to Paul, he would not have known it. It was, in fact, astonishing. The very rejection of the majority of Israelites, throughout history recurring again and again, was, is, and will be, a link in the effectuation of Israel's salvation. For details, see above, p. 366, 367, 377, 378 (Rom. 11:11, 12, 25).

Although, to be sure, this interpretation is not nearly as popular as is theory A, among its defenders are men of recognized scholarship (as holds also, of course, for theories A and B). Let me mention but a few.

One of the propositions successfully defended by S. Volbeda, when he received his summa cum laude doctor of theology degree from the Free University of Amsterdam was: "The term 'all Israel' in Rom. 11:26a must be understood as indicating the collective elect out of Israel."[323]

H. Bavinck, author of the four-volume work *Gereformeerde Dogmatiek* [Reformed Dogmatics], states, " 'All Israel' in 11:26, is not the people of Israel, destined to be converted collectively, neither is it the church consisting of united Jews and Gentiles; but it is the full number which during the course of the centuries is gathered out of Israel."[324] Cf. H. Hoeksema, *God's Eternal Good Pleasure*, Grand Rapids, 1950, p. 465.

323. Quoted from *De Intuitieve Philosophie Van James McCosh*, Grand Rapids, n.d., p. 415.

324. Vol. IV, p. 744. This is my translation from the Dutch. So also for the quotation from Volbeda.

And L. Berkhof states, " 'All Israel' is to be understood as a designation not of the whole nation but of the whole number of the elect out of the ancient covenant people . . . and the adverb οὕτως cannot mean 'after that,' but only 'in this manner.' "[325]

For a similar interpretation see H. Ridderbos, *op. cit.*, p. 263.

Not only scholars of *Reformed persuasion and Dutch nationality or lineage* have adopted this interpretation, but so have many others, as is clear from a glance at Lenski's commentary on Romans, pp. 714, 726, 727. See also O. Palmer Robertson, "Is There a Distinctive Future for Ethnic Israel in Romans 11?," in *Perspectives on Evangelical Theology*, Grand Rapids, 1979, pp. 81-94. These interpreters are convinced that this is the only interpretation that suits the text and context.

Objections Stated and Refuted

Objection No. 1. This interpretation destroys the contrast between the *remnant* mentioned in 11:5, on the one hand, and *the mass of Israel*, on the other.

Answer. Our interpretation does not destroy a contrast but defines it more accurately. The real contrast is that between single remnants (see, for example, 11:5), on the one hand, and "all Israel," that is, the sum of all the remnants throughout history (verse 26), on the other.

Objection No. 2. According to this interpretation the "mystery" mentioned by Paul amounts to no more than that all Israel's elect will be saved. But that is a truth so obvious that it fails to do justice to the implications of the term "mystery."

Answer. Not so! The mystery of which Paul speaks has reference to the marvelous chain of events that results in Israel's salvation. It points to seemingly contradictory factors which in God's loving and overruling providence are so directed that ultimate salvation for "all Israel" is effected. See above, pp. 377, 378.

* * * *

26b, 27. . . . as it is written:
"Out of Zion will come the Deliverer;
he will turn godlessness away from Jacob.
And this is my covenant with them
whenever I shall take away their sins."

Note the following:

a. It is logical to connect "And so all Israel will be saved" with "Out of Zion will come the Deliverer," and to interpret this divine deliverance as *rescue from sin* and *bestowment of salvation*, which blessings Jehovah brought about through the person and work of the Mediator, Jesus Christ.

b. As the words "as it is written" indicate, what immediately follows upon "And so all Israel will be saved" is material quoted from the Old Testament.

---

325. *Systematic Theology*, pp. 699, 670.

It does not consist, however, in a quotation of this or that single passage, but rather in a skillful symposium of several passages; such as, Isa. 59:20; 27:9; 59:21, in *that* order, with reminders of Micah 5:2 (or a similar verse) and probably Jer. 31:31 f.

In addition, it should be borne in mind that Paul is conversant with the LXX (Greek) translation of the Old Testament as well as with the original Hebrew text. What is to be admired is that he is able to weave these various strands into one beautiful, consistent pattern.

c. The words "Out of Zion will come the Deliverer" are quoted from LXX Isa. 59:20, except for the fact that LXX has "for the sake of Zion," the original Hebrew "to Zion," and Paul "out of Zion."

This presents no real difficulty, for all three are true. Did not the Deliverer come "for the sake of Zion," that is, to rescue Zion? And did he not also come "to Zion"? How else could he have saved it? And is it not also true that according to his human nature he came "out of Zion"? Think of Mic. 5:2.[326] In connection with "out of," "from" or "from among," see also Deut. 18:15, 18; Ps. 14:7; 53:6; and Isa. 2:3.

d. The task which, according to prophecy, the Deliverer was to perform, consisted, according to the LXX of Isa. 27:9, in this: to turn away godlessness or lawlessness from Jacob, that is, from Israel. Naturally it would be turned away only from the elect of Israel. We now understand why Paul has a right to quote these very passages to prove that "all Israel" would be saved; for, in order to save Israel it must be delivered not from this or that earthly foe but from godlessness, from sin.

e. Returning again to Isa. 59, this time to verse 21, the apostle continues (quoting the Lord as saying), "As for me, this is my covenant with them." He then quickly turns his attention to another precious passage in which *that divine covenant* is mentioned in connection with *the removal of sins*, namely, Jer. 31:31 f. There we read, "This is the covenant that I will make with the house of Israel and with the house of Judah . . . I will forgive their iniquity, and their sin will I remember no more." So he writes, ". . . whenever I shall take away their sins."

f. It is clear that in this entire passage (11:26b, 27) *Paul is not thinking of what Jesus will do at his second coming, when he will come not "out of Zion," but "from heaven" (I Thess. 4:16), and when forgiveness of sin will no longer be possible.* Paul is thinking of Christ's first coming when, by means of his vicarious death, he established the basis for the forgiveness of sins, and therefore also for the salvation of "the fulness of the Gentiles" and of "all Israel."

g. Paul is not deviating from his central theme. Is not the removal of sin one of the main ingredients of *justification by faith*? See Rom. 4:25; 5:8, 9, 19; 8:1-3. The promise of the covenant goes into effect "whenever" in the life of any Israelite sin is removed. Romans 9-11 shows that this doctrine is

326. As here used *Zion* in all probability represents Israel, viewed as "the people of God." See G. Fohrer's article on this subject in Th.D.N.T., Vol. VII, p. 309.

historical, indicating what happens again and again during history's course.

28-31. As far as the gospel is concerned, they are enemies for y o u r sake; but as far as election is concerned, they are beloved for the sake of the fathers, for irrevocable are God's gracious gifts and his calling. For just as at one time y o u were disobedient to God but now have received mercy as a result of their disobedience, so they too have now become disobedient in order that, as a result of the mercy shown to y o u, they too may now receive mercy.

In harmony with verses 25, 26, which speak first of a hardening of part of Israel and then about "all Israel" which will be saved, so here too the apostle first reminds us of those Israelites who, as far as the gospel is concerned, are enemies, and then of those who, as far as election is concerned, are beloved for the sake of the fathers. In reading on (see verses 30, 31), however, we soon become aware of the fact that these "enemies" and these "beloved ones" are the same people, namely, the elect. At first they were hostile to the gospel, but later on, because of the wonderful manifestation of God's mercy (see verse 25 f.) they become friends.

Note the following:

a. "As far as the gospel is concerned . . . enemies for y o u r sake." Note "for y o u r sake."

The explanation is found in verse 11: "Because of their trespass salvation (has come) to the Gentiles."

b. ". . . as far as election is concerned, they are beloved."

The same Jews who at one time had been enemies of the gospel had become friends, beloved of God and fellow-believers. This great change had been brought about because of the fact that these former enemies had been designed by God, in his eternal decree, to become friends.

c. "for the sake of the fathers."

Not because of any innate goodness or merit pertaining to Abraham, Isaac, and Jacob, but because of God's promise to the fathers, "I will . . . be y o u r God and the God of y o u r seed after y o u." See Gen. 17:7; cf. 26:23, 24; 28:12-15.

d. "for irrevocable are God's gracious gifts and his calling."

There are those who interpret this entire passage (verses 28-31) as a description of God's love for the people of Israel in general. The present clause shows that this interpretation is incorrect, for it refers to *God's irrevocable calling, a call that is not subject to change and is never withdrawn.* This is certainly the inner or effectual call, one that pertains only to the elect.[327]

e. This also proves that "God's gracious gifts" must not be identified, as often happens, with the special privileges granted to the Jews as a people (9:4, 5), but must refer to such products of God's special grace as faith, hope, love, peace that surpasses all understanding, life everlasting, etc., all of them being gifts bestowed on God's elect, *on them alone*.

---

327. So also L. Berkhof, *Systematic Theology*, p. 469, on Rom. 11:29.

f. The explanation of the words, "For just as at one time y o u were disobedient to God but now have received mercy as a result of their disobedience, so they too . . . may now receive mercy," is found in verse 11; note especially "to make Israel envious," and see the explanation of that verse on p. 367.

g. It is clear that the entire passage (verses 28-31), correctly explained, harmonizes with 11:26a, "And so all Israel will be saved." In both cases Paul is speaking about the true Israel. *They* are enemies (at first). *They* are beloved . . . have become disobedient in order that *they* too may now receive mercy. The apostle is telling the Romans, especially the Gentiles among them, who in all probability constituted the majority of the congregation, that, as a result of the mercy shown to them—that is, to this predominantly Gentile church—the Jews, stirred to envy, now receive God's *mercy*, his love to those in need.

h. The repetition of the word *now*, occurring either twice or three times in verses 30, 31, shows that all the while Paul is thinking not of something that will happen at, or just previous to, Christ's Return, but of events that are occurring right now, in fulfilment of God's plan from before the founding of the universe.

32. For God has locked up all in the prison of disobedience in order that he may have mercy on them all.

As the conjunction "For" shows, there is a close connection between verse 32 and the preceding passage. Therefore, although when verse 32 is lifted out of its context and applied to the whole human race, an intelligible meaning results (cf. 3:9-18), it is probably better to regard this verse as applying to "the fulness [=full number] of the Gentiles" and "all Israel."

What Paul is saying, then, is that God *has locked up* all these Israelites and the total number of these Gentiles. He has shut them all up as in a prison, "the prison of disobedience," for by nature all are disobedient to God's holy law. Cf. Gal. 3:22, 23.

Their situation is desperate: sin disturbs, the law condemns, conscience frightens, the final judgment threatens, and God has not accepted them. *By nature* such is their situation.

Suddenly the darkness is dispelled. It is God himself who opens the prison door and is letting the light shine in. The prisoners—every one of them without exception—walk out into freedom. God did it "in order that he may have mercy on them all."

The best commentary on these triumphant words is certainly Paul's own, "being justified freely by his grace through the redemption (accomplished) by Christ Jesus, whom God designed to be, by the shedding of his blood, a wrath-removing sacrifice (effective) through faith" (3:24). Hallelujah!

---

33 O the depth of the riches both of the wisdom and knowledge of God!
How unsearchable his judgments,
and untraceable his ways!

34 For who has known the mind of the Lord
Or who has been his counselor?
35 Or who has ever given (something) to God,
that God should repay him?
36 For from him and through him and to him are all things.
To him be the glory forever! Amen.

Doxology

"For from him and through him and to him are all things.
To him be the glory forever. Amen."
11:33-36

Reflecting on (a) what he has just now written (verse 32), on (b) "the mystery" introduced in verse 25 (the interdependence between the salvation of "the fulness of the Gentiles" and "all Israel," see pp. 377, 378, 381), and probably also on (c) all he has written so far on the glorious theme of *justification by faith*, it is not at all surprising that exuberant Paul, himself a marvelous product of God's sovereign grace, breaks out into a doxology.

All the more striking is this doxology when it is contrasted with the "great sorrow" which Paul expresses at the beginning of this large Section (see 9:1 f.).

33. O the depth of the riches both of the wisdom and knowledge of God!

How unsearchable his judgments,
and untraceable his ways!

When Paul reflects on the matters mentioned in connection with (a), (b), and (c) above—perhaps especially on (b)—his soul, filled with admiration, adoration, and awe, expresses itself in an exclamation, which can even be called a *song*, of praise to God. He has become aware of ocean-depths (cf. I Cor. 2:10) of riches (cf. Rom. 2:4; 9:23; 10:12) that cannot be plummeted, riches of God's wisdom and knowledge.

God's *wisdom* is his ability to select the best means for the attainment of the highest goal. One might call it the divine efficiency evident in all his works. The term *knowledge*, as applied to God, in the present connection (linked with wisdom), must not be understood in the sense of his eternal delight, a meaning which the word has at times, but rather as his insight into the very essence of things, people, ideas, etc., his omniscience.

The apostle adds, "How unsearchable are his *judgments*"; that is, God's sovereign decisions, decrees, disposals. In the present context the reference is especially to those judgments that are revealed in the divine plan of salvation and in the effectuation of that plan. The addition "and untraceable his ways," probably indicates, "and how impossible it is to trace or track down the means God uses to put his decisions into effect."[328]

34, 35. For who has known the mind of the Lord
Or who has been his counselor?
Or who has ever given (something) to God,
that God should repay him?

Still lifting up his heart in praise to God, Paul asks three questions. The first one is, "For who has known the mind of the Lord?"

This question is quoted, almost unchanged, from the LXX version of Isa. 40:13. It is quoted also in I Cor. 2:16. It immediately reminds us of Isa. 55:8, "For my thoughts are not y o u r thoughts, neither are y o u r ways my ways."

Of late more and more is becoming known about the mysteries of the human brain. The *real* men of science, pondering these new discoveries, are beginning to say, "How great is God!" But surely, if God is marvelous and incomprehensible in the work of creation, is he not at least equally astounding in his work of redemption? Who, indeed, has ever been able, even to a small extent, actually to probe God's mind?

The second question is, "Or who has been his counselor?"

This question too is quoted from Isa. 40:13.

We have all met people whom we correctly consider wise and knowledgeable, but they have not always been wise. There was a time when they lacked both wisdom and knowledge. How, then, did they obtain these qualities? To a certain extent, at least, by making good use of the counsel and information they received from parents, teachers, and friends.

But God never had any counselor to whom he could go for help!

The third question is, "Or who has ever given (something) to God, that God should repay him?" In other words, "Who has ever put God in debt to him?" As to its essence this question is quoted from Job 41:11 (Hebrew original).

What? God in debt to us? Impossible. In fact, our indebtedness to him is so great that our hearts are thrilled whenever we reflect on what he has done, is doing, and will do for us. An *adequate* response to God is simply impossible. So, we begin to respond in prayers of thanksgiving or of joyful exclamation. We copy Paul's words as recorded here in Rom. 11:35, or in II Cor. 8:9, or in II Cor. 9:15. Or, thrilled to the very depths of our soul, we sing Charles Wesley's song, ending with the words,

> Amazing love! how can it be
> That thou, my God, shouldst die for me?
>
> —Lines taken from
> "And Can It Be That I Should Gain?"

---

328. ἀνεξεραύνητα, note double prefix; hence the meaning of the compound is: *in*capable of being searched *out*; unsearchable, nom. pl. n. of ἀνεξεραύνητος. Originally the simple verb was ἐρευνάω, later changed to ἐραυνάω, to search (John 5:39; 7:52; Rom. 8:27; I Cor. 2:10; I Peter 1:11; Rev. 2:23). In the New Testament the *compound* is found only here.

ἀνεξιχνίαστοι, nom. pl. f. of ἀνεξιχνίαστος, also in Eph. 3:8; from ἀν plus ἐξιχνιάζω, to trace or track out. Cf. ἴχνος, footstep, track (Rom. 4:12; II Cor. 12:18; I Peter 2:21). The meaning of the compound is, therefore: incapable of being traced or explored, untraceable.

Or, with an equal thrill of amazement, we turn to the old, familiar *Amazing Grace* by John Newton.

36. For from him and through him and to him are all things. To him be the glory forever! Amen.

Interpreters have tried to discover the source of these words. Could Paul have borrowed them, perhaps, from this or that Greek poet or philosopher? Now although it is true that the apostle was acquainted with Epicurean and Stoic poetry and philosopy (Acts 17:18, 28), and therefore perhaps also with the saying, "All things come from thee [Nature], subsist in thee, and return to thee," he was by no means a pantheist. His song of praise is dedicated not to Nature or to the Universe but to God Triune who revealed himself in Jesus Christ unto salvation. The source of the apostle's saying, therefore, is Scripture, its teachings applied to his heart by the Holy Spirit.

What is the meaning of "all things"? Does this expression refer to all things in creation? Cf. John 1:3; I Cor. 8:6. Probably not. The immediate context (verse 25 f.) has to do with the gospel, and therefore with the realm of salvation.

Does the saying refer, then, to the Holy Trinity, so that the meaning would be: "The Father thought it; the Son bought it; the Holy Spirit wrought it"? Although there are those who favor an explanation of this kind, it should be immediately rejected. To assign the three separate elements (from him, through him, to him) respectively to the three persons is about as unreasonable as anything can be.

What then? In the immediately preceding quotations the reference was to Jehovah; that is, to God. So here too "from him" must mean "from the Triune God," and this holds also for the other two little phrases.

The correct interpretation, as I see it, is therefore this: God is the source of our salvation; it is through his grace and power that salvation becomes a reality in our lives; and to him, accordingly, all the glory is due. *He is the source, accomplisher, and goal of our salvation.*

It is certainly very logical that the apostle, nearing the conclusion of his doxology, writes, "To him be the glory forever." Since it was he who not only planned our salvation but who also caused it to become a reality, it follows that he—he *alone*—should receive all the glory.

Paul concludes this little paean of praise and thanksgiving, and therefore also chapters 9-11, and, in fact, the entire predominantly doctrinal Section of his book (chapters 1-11), by adding the word of solemn affirmation and enthusiastic personal approval, *Amen*.

Practical Lessons Derived from Romans 11

Verses 3, 4

"I have left for myself seven thousand men who have not bowed the knee to Baal."

Christian leaders—whether pastors or teachers, evangelists or missionaries—are prone to forget that the Christian work they are doing is in many cases receiving the constant but unheralded support of ever so many others who are not in their group. Every congregation has its devout members who by their prayers are supporting the work these leaders are doing. And let us not forget even the children. When a certain pastor's wife was seriously ill with a sickness that led to her death, he was being wonderfully supported by children who would come to him and say, "We are praying for you and your family." What a help this proved to be!

Verse 11

". . . because of their trespass salvation (has come) to the Gentiles to make Israel envious."

What an astounding statement! So wonderful is God that he is even able to use human trespasses in order to bring about salvation for Gentiles and Jews!

Verse 13

"I take pride in my ministry."

Humanly speaking, one important reason for Paul's success as a missionary was his joy in performing his task, the enthusiasm he was ever revealing. Study, for example, such passages as:

"Woe to me if I do not preach the gospel" (I Cor. 9:16)!

"I have become all things to all men in order that by any and all means I may save some" (I Cor. 9:22).

"Thanks be to God for his indescribably precious gift" (II Cor. 9:15)!

Such enthusiasm is catching. So is also the opposite frame of mind. A grumpy preacher—or any other person connected with religious work—who with a woebegone appearance and a hangdog disposition goes about his task, resembles a salesman who begs his customers not to buy his goods!

Verse 14

". . . in the hope that I may somehow arouse my own people to envy and save some of them."

In this connection see also Dan. 12:3, Rom. 10:1; I Cor. 9:22. In order to bring Jews to Christ, Paul was willing, if need be, even to make use of "envy," in the sense of a yearning, on the part of unbelieving Jews, to obtain the same precious blessings as those possessed by believing Gentiles.

We too should concentrate our attention on this great objective of being instruments in God's hand for the conversion of the Jews. To present a correct interpretation of Rom. 11:26 is important, but to be instrumental, even in some small way, in bringing a Jew to a saving knowledge of Christ is even far more important. We rejoice, of course, in the "Jews for Jesus movement" in the United States, and in the fact that through this and similar means a considerable number of the ancient covenant people have already been won for the Savior. It gladdens our heart to read the statement of Moishe Rosen, leader of the Jews for Jesus Mission, that "This past decade has seen more Jewish people making decisions for Jesus Christ than any other similar period of time since Apostolic Days." But we should remember that by far the most people who belong to this ethnic group have not been won over. Instead of confusing these people by telling them that they will all be saved if they can just remain healthy long enough to reach the day of Christ's Return, we should preach Christ to them, as their only Hope, and as the fulfilment of their need of *an atonement by blood*. Some Jews are keenly aware of this lack in their religion as now practiced.

None of this evangelistic work among the Jews will avail, however, unless it be accompanied by fervent prayer, and the power of Christ's resurrection be shown in our own lives. We should constantly bear in mind that for every Jew who reads *the New Testament* there are a hundred or more who read us!

The attempt to inspire the Jews with false hope, as if somehow, in spite of their rejection of Christ, they are still God's special favorites, is inexcusable. Our Lord wants the Jews to come to *him*. To be sure, everything that can possibly be done should be done in the present dispute between Jews and Arabs, in order, if possible, to reach a conclusion by means of which the needs of both parties are satisfied. But even if such a political solution should ever be reached, it would not, in and by itself, solve the deep-seated spiritual problem of the Jews. Salvation, to the glory of God Triune, is what the Jews stand in need of most of all, as is true with respect to us all. "For there is no distinction between Jew and Greek. For the same Lord (is Lord) of all and richly blesses all who call on him. For everyone who calls on the name of the Lord will be saved" (Rom. 10:12, 13).

Verse 18

"It is not you who support the root, but the root that supports you."

"We pay . . . thousand dollars annually in support of kingdom causes," said the boaster. He forgot to mention how much effort and pain these same kingdom institutions were expending to contribute to the spiritual welfare of himself and his family. It would have been a sum that cannot be expressed in monetary phraseology.

When through the mouth of Nathan the Lord told David, "I will establish a house for you. When your days are over . . . I will raise up your offspring . . . He is the one who will build a house for my name, and I will establish the throne of his kingdom forever," David, seeing from afar the dawn of the bright morning of glory which would culminate in the birth of Christ, poured out his heart in language of humble thanksgiving:

"Who am I, O Sovereign Lord, and what is my family, that thou has brought me this far?" He realized that it was basically not he who was supporting the root, but the root that was supporting him.

Religion without humility and gratitude does not deserve the name religion.

Verse 23

"But they, if they do not persist in their unbelief, will be grafted in, for God has the power to graft them in again."

But is not the idea of the regrafting of lopped off branches (the reincorporation into Christ's body of those who have become untrue to the faith) in conflict with the teaching of Heb. 6:4-6? A possible solution has been suggested by F. F. Bruce in his fine commentary on Hebrews (*The New International Commentary on the New Testament*, Grand Rapids, 1964, pp. 118, 119), namely, that as a matter of human experience the reclamation of such people is practically impossible; but also, that nothing of this sort is ultimately impossible for the grace of God.

Well, in the present passage (Rom. 11:23) we are told that "God has the power to graft them in again," that is, by his Spirit to regenerate them and reincorporate them into the organism of his church.

Summary of Chapter 11

Since chapter 10 closed with a description of Israel as disobedient and obstinate, it is not surprising that chapter 11 starts with the question, "Did God reject his people?" Did he in his wrath completely and irrevocably thrust Israel away from himself?

Paul answers, "God did not reject his people whom he foreknew," that is, on whom, from before the founding of the universe, he had set his love. "Look at me," says Paul, as it were. "I am an Israelite, and God did not reject me." He implies: there is always a remnant chosen by God. In fact, does not verse 5 suggest this thought?

This was true in the days of Elijah, as related in I Kings 19:1-18. When the disconsolate prophet complained that he alone had remained faithful and that his life too was in jeopardy, the Lord told him, "I have left for myself seven thousand men who have not bowed the knee to Baal."

As to those Israelites who did not respond favorably to God's gracious invitations but hardened their hearts against the gospel, God "gave them a spirit of stupor, eyes not to see, and ears not to hear, to this very day." Cf. Deut. 29:4; Isa. 6:9. To such people the words of David (see Ps. 69:22, 23) apply, "Let their table become a snare before them, a retribution and a stumbling block," etc.

All this is summarized in the words of Rom. 11:7, "What Israel is seeking so earnestly it has not obtained, but the elect have obtained it. The others were hardened" (verses 1-10).

Does this mean then that for these hardened ones, who as yet have not displayed any signs of having been elected from eternity, there is no hope? It does not.

We now learn that God gathers to himself a remnant even from this sin-hardened majority. Paul asks, "Did they stumble so as to fall?" He answers, "Of course not! Rather, because of their trespass salvation (has come) to the Gentiles to make Israel envious." This shows that it was not final, irrevocable doom God had in mind when he initially hardened the hearts of those who had hardened themselves. On the contrary, God was using even Israel's trespass in order to serve as a link in the chain of salvation, so as to save both Gentile and Jew.

"Because of their trespass salvation (has come) to the Gentiles." When the apostle wrote these words he must have vividly recalled how previously he and Barnabas had told the Jews in Pisidian Antioch, "Since y o u reject the word of God . . . we now turn to the Gentiles." Subsequently similar words were spoken and actions taken.

But that was not the end of the story. The salvation which thus came to the Gentiles filled some of the hardened Jews with envy. They began to yearn for the peace and joy that had come to the Gentiles who had yielded their hearts and lives to the Savior. Result: some of these Jews were now also gathered into the fold, thereby proving that they too had been elected from eternity. Now if even Israel's spiritual defeat had brought riches to the Gentiles, as had actually occurred, was occurring, and was going to occur, then surely Israel's arrival at full strength—the salvation, during the course of the centuries of the full number of Israelites destined for life everlasting—would progressively result in an abundance of blessings for the entire world.

That Paul, in saying these things, is not thinking of what will take place at history's close, but of what has been happening and is occurring right along, is clear from verses 13, 14, "Inasmuch as I am an apostle to (the) Gentiles, I take pride in my ministry, in the hope that I may somehow arouse my own people to envy and save some of them."

For the Israelites who had previously experienced God's punishment the consciousness that they are now accepted by God and are a blessing to mankind amounted to nothing less than "life from the dead."

They knew that they had been set apart to render service to God. In fact, of old the entire nation of Israel had been thus consecrated to God. Were they not all descendants of Abraham, Isaac, and Jacob with whom and with whose descendants God had established his covenant? Surely, if the cake offered as firstfruits is holy, then the whole batch is holy; if the root is holy, so are the branches. If the patriarchs had been set apart to render service to God, as was true, this held also with respect to their offspring.

But this did not mean that every Israelite was marked by inner holiness. Some of the "branches," that is, people, revealed the opposite character. They were branches that had to be, and were, lopped off the olive tree.

Such unfaithfulness seemed to give this or that rather arrogant Gentile church-member the excuse to say, "Branches were lopped off that *I* myself might be grafted in." Paul answers, "True! But it was for lack of faith that they were lopped off, and it is by faith that you stand. Don't be arrogant but fear! . . . For if you were cut out of an olive tree that was wild by nature, and, contrary to nature, were grafted into a cultivated olive tree, how much more readily will these, the natural olive branches, be grafted (back) into their own olive tree?" (verses 11-24).

Paul continues, "For I do not want y o u to be unaware of this mystery, brothers, so that y o u may not be conceited, that a hardening has come upon part of Israel (and will last) until the fulness of the Gentiles has come in." He means: throughout the ages a portion of the Jews is hardened, the others are saved. Reflecting on the marvelous manner in which God gathers the various remnants that constitute the collective body of those saved Israelites, he calls this chain of salvation, with its various links, "the mystery." It was indeed a mystery, for Paul could never have discovered it if God had not revealed it to him. For more on this mystery see Rom. 11:11, 12, 31, and pp. 366, 367, 377, 378, 384, 385. Paul adds, "*And so*—that is, in this manner—*all Israel*, the entire body of elect Jews, *will be saved*."

By referring to Old Testament passages—Isa. 59:20; 27:9; 59:21, in that order, and probably also Mic. 5:2; Jer. 31:31 f.—the apostle proves that the truth he is proclaiming is not a novelty but rests upon the solid foundation of Scripture. The coming and work of the Deliverer had assured sin's removal.

Those who previously had been enemies of the gospel had, accordingly, become friends, beloved ones. This had been brought about through the effectuation of the divine decree of election and the fulfillment of the promises made to the forefathers. Moreover, the state of being saved, once a reality, would never be lost; for "irrevocable are God's gracious gifts and his calling."

In verses 30, 31 Paul summarizes the mysterious ways of God, issuing in the salvation of the full number of Gentiles and of "all Israel." In verse 32 he adds, "For God has locked up all in the prison of disobedience in order that he may have mercy on them all" (verses 25-32).

Contemplation of God's wonderful plan of redemption causes the apostle to conclude this chapter with a meaningful doxology. It may be conveniently divided into three parts: (a) verse 33; (b) verses 34, 35; and (c) verse 36.

Verse 33 is an exclamation in praise of God's wisdom and knowledge. Paul is probably reflecting especially on these divine qualities as revealed in the plan of redemption and in the manner in which that plan is carried out. He is sure of the fact that the way of salvation decreed by God and the manner in which this salvation is realized in human lives surpasses anything mere human beings could ever have devised.

In verses 34 and 35 the author praises the divine self-sufficiency or independence. Who can compare with God? Who has ever imparted any wisdom or knowledge to him or helped him in any way in originating and/or carrying out the plan of salvation? No one, of course. Therefore the glory belongs to him alone.

Accordingly in verse 36 Paul ascribes glory to him who is the source, accomplisher, and goal of man's salvation.

To this sincere and thrilling doxology the writer attaches his very personal and enthusiastic word of solemn affirmation and approval: AMEN (verses 33-36).

Chapters 12—16

Practical Application

Outline of Chapters 12—16

Paul, having brought to completion his Exposition of the doctrine of Justification By Faith, now proceeds to its Practical Application. To be sure, there has been application right along, but every careful reader of this epistle will have to grant that whereas doctrine predominates in chapters 1—11, practical application to life in general and to concrete life situations holds sway in the remaining five chapters. Besides, as we shall see in a moment, the fact that the apostle himself so regards the connection between what he has said in chapters 1—11 and what he is about to say in chapters 12—16 is clear from 12:1.

PRACTICAL APPLICATION
Chapters 12—16
Outline
I. *Main Body of This Part of the Letter*

What Should Be the Attitude of the Justified Believer Toward:

Chapter	
12:1, 2	A. God "Offer yourselves as living sacrifices, holy and well-pleasing to God . . ."
12:3-13	B. Fellow-Christians
3-8	"We, who are many, are one body in Christ."
9-13	"Be devoted to one another in brotherly love."
12:14-21	C. Outsiders, including Enemies "Bless those who persecute y o u."
13:1-7	D. The Authorities "Let every person be subject to the governing authorities."
13:8-10	E. Everybody "Do not keep on owing anyone anything except to love one another."
13:11-14	F. The Lord Jesus Christ "The night is far advanced; the day is drawing near . . . Clothe yourselves with the Lord Jesus Christ, and make no provision for (the fulfillment of) the lusts of the flesh."
14:1-15:13	G. The Weak and the Strong
14:1-23	"Him who is weak in faith accept."
15:1-13	"We who are strong ought to bear the failings of the weak and not to please ourselves."

II. *Conclusion*

15:14-16 H. Closing Commendation and Explanation of Boldness in Writing
"I myself am convinced . . . that y o u yourselves are rich in goodness . . . I have written to y o u rather boldly . . . because of the charge God gave me to be a minister of Christ Jesus to the Gentiles . . ."

15:17-22 I. Review of the Past
"From Jerusalem all the way around to Illyricum, I have fully proclaimed the gospel of Christ."

15:23-29 J. Plan for the Future
"Now I am on my way to Jerusalem in the service of the saints . . . When I have completed this task . . . I will go to y o u on my way to Spain."

15:30-33 K. Prayer Request
"I exhort y o u, brothers, by our Lord Jesus Christ and by the love of the Spirit, to join me in my struggle by praying to God for me."

16:1-16 L. Commendation of Phoebe. Paul's Own Greetings and those of all the churches
"Greet Priscilla and Aquila, my fellow-workers in Christ Jesus."

16:17-20 M. Final Warning
"I exhort y o u, brothers, to watch out for those who cause divisions."

16:21-23 N. Greetings of Friends
"Timothy, my fellow-worker, greets y o u."

16:25-27 O. Doxology
"Now to him who is able to establish y o u in accordance with my gospel and the proclamation of Jesus Christ . . . be glory forever through Jesus Christ! Amen."

In most cases the paragraph heading covers the entire contents of the paragraph. In others it covers most, but not all, of the contents.

The Outline is intended as a useful tool to indicate, from the very beginning, what, on the whole, chapters 12 through 16 are all about.

Outline (continued)

Practical Application

A. *What Should Be the Attitude of the Justified Believer Toward God*

"Offer yourselves as sacrifices, living, holy, and well-pleasing to God"
12:1, 2

B. *What Should Be the Attitude of the Justified Believer Toward Fellow-Christians*

"We who are many, are one body in Christ"
12:3-8

"Be devoted to one another in brotherly love"
12:9-13

C. *What Should Be the Attitude of the Justified Believer Toward Outsiders, Including Enemies*

"Bless those who persecute you"
12:14-21

CHAPTER 12

ROMANS 12:1

12 1 I exhort y o u, therefore, brothers, in view of God's great mercy, to offer yourselves[329] as sacrifices, living, holy, and well-pleasing to God, (which is) y o u r spiritual worship. 2 And stop allowing yourselves to be fashioned after the pattern of
this (evil) age, but continue to let yourselves be transformed by the renewing of
y o u r mind, so that y o u may prove what is the will of God, namely, that which is good and
well-pleasing and perfect.

A. *What Should Be the Attitude of the Justified Believer Toward God*
"Offer yourselves as sacrifices, living, holy, and well-pleasing to God"
12:1, 2

1. I exhort y o u, therefore, brothers, in view of God's great mercy, to offer yourselves as sacrifices, living, holy, and well-pleasing to God, (which is) y o u r spiritual worship.

The very first expression, namely, "I exhort" (in the original *one word*) indicates the character not only of the opening paragraph but of the five final chapters of this epistle. Exhortation is not completely absent from the earlier chapters, but by and large it is *exposition* that is found in Rom. 1-11, while *exhortation* dominates Rom. 12-16.

It is as "a called apostle" (1:1), "a minister of Christ Jesus" (15:16), clothed with authority, that Paul, in the spirit of love and concern, exhorts his dearly beloved brothers in the church of Rome. On this word "brothers" see what has been said earlier (pp. 52, 214, 215). Literally Paul exhorts those addressed to offer their *bodies* as sacrifices[330] to God. However, that in such a context the word *body* refers to the entire personality is clear from 6:11-14; see also Phil. 1:20. Calvin states, "By *bodies* he means not only our skin and bones but the totality of which we are composed. He adopted this word that he might more fully designate all that we are, for the members of the body are the instruments by which we carry out our purposes."

---

329. Literally: y o u r bodies.
330. The apostle uses the sing. *sacrifice* where we would probably use the pl.

Paul states that these sacrifices must have the following characteristics: they must be "living," that is, must proceed from the new life within the believer; "holy," the product of the sanctifying influence of the Holy Spirit; and, accordingly, "well-pleasing" to God, not only accepted by, but most heartily welcome to, the One to whom believers dedicate themselves.

The apostle adds, "which is y o u r . . . worship."[331] What has been said earlier (see on 9:4, pp. 312, 313) about this word *worship* applies here also. Paul is thinking about the action of worshiping, the wholehearted consecration of heart, mind, will, words, and deeds, in fact of all one is, has, and does, to God. Nothing less!

Rendering such devotion will amount to y o u r logikēn worship, says Paul. The debate about *logikēn* (acc. sing. f. of *logikos*) is continuing. The word reminds us of *logical*. But the meaning of a word is not determined first of all by its etymology but by its use in given contexts. Nevertheless, in the present case *logical*, in the sense of *reasonable*, deserves consideration. Several translators have accepted "reasonable" or "rational."[332] As I am writing this, I am looking at the two volumes by W. à Brakel, a Dutch work on Dogmatics, to which he gave the title, based on Rom. 12:1, *Redelijke Godsdienst* (Leiden, 1893), that is, *Reasonable Religion* (or *Reasonable Worship of God*). What, according to this interpretation, Paul is saying is that rendering wholehearted devotion is the only logical or reasonable worship of God.

But though this interpretation of the Greek adjective makes sense, it is not the only possible one, perhaps not even the best. In the only other New Testament passage in which the adjective occurs, namely, I Peter 2:2, it means *spiritual*, as the context makes clear. Peter cannot have been referring to *logical* or *reasonable* milk! Moreover, in the context he mentions "a spiritual house" and "spiritual sacrifices."

It is not surprising, therefore, that also for Rom. 12:1 several English translators have accepted the rendering "spiritual worship."[333]

But even though "spiritual" may well be the best rendering of the adjective Paul uses, the meaning of 12:1, *considered as a unit*, is certainly this, that it is right and proper—hence logical, reasonable—that those who have been highly favored should offer themselves to God wholeheartedly, as sacrifices, living, holy, and well-pleasing to him. In fact, the emphasis in 12:1 is on the word "Therefore."

---

331. τὴν λογικὴν λατρείαν ὑμῶν is probably in apposition to παραστῆσαι . . . τῷ θεῷ.

332. A.V., Williams, Conybeare, Broadus, N.T. in Modern English. Similarly N.T. in Basic English points out that this is the worship "which it is right for you to give," and in a footnote N.E.B. offers a similar suggestion. At times—by no means always—Greek philosophers used the word in this sense. See Liddell and Scott's *Greek-English Lexicon*, Vol. I, p. 1056.

333. See, for example, A.R.V., R.S.V., N.I.V. See also G. Kittel, Th.D.N.T., Vol. IV, p. 142. The Amplified New Testament combines the two ideas: "reasonable and spiritual worship." The Berkeley Version, however, favors "worship with understanding," and Cranfield, similarly, "understanding worship."

What the apostle is saying is that in view of God's *mercy*,[334] a voluntary and enthusiastic response of gratitude is required. Accordingly, when in this connection he mentions "God's great mercy," he must be referring to the marvelous goodness of God described in the first eleven chapters of this letter: his *kindness* (2:4), *patience* (9:22; 11:22), *love* (5:5; 8:35, 39), and *grace* (1:7; 3:24; 4:16; 5:2, 15, 20, 21; 6:1, 14, 15, 17; 11:5, 6). Particularly, he must be reflecting on his great theme, namely, Justification by Faith, a justification based solely on the substitutionary self-sacrifice of Christ (3:24, 25). What he is saying, then, is that this sovereign divine mercy calls for *a life* of complete dedication and wholehearted commitment. *Animal* sacrifices will not do! Nothing less than thorough self-surrender out of gratitude is required.

What the apostle is teaching, therefore, is that Christian ethics is based on Christian doctrine. Accordingly, I Cor. 15:1-57 is followed by 15:58 f.; II Cor. 1:3, 4a, by 1:4b f.; 5:1-8 by 5:9 f.; Eph. 2 and 3 by Eph. 4; 4:32b by 5:1; Phil. 3:20, 21 by 4:1; Col. 2 by chapter 3; *and Rom. 1-11 by 12-16.*

Returning once more to the opening chapters of Paul's epistle to the Romans and from there quickly reviewing the remainder of this precious writing, one cannot help becoming aware of the fact that in 1:1—3:20 man's *sin and misery* are described; in 3:21—11:36 the way of *deliverance* is opened to him; and in 12:1—16:27 the rescued believer is shown how, by a life of *gratitude* to God and helpfulness toward God's children and, in fact, toward everybody, man should respond.

This reminds us of several passages in the Psalter, especially of Ps. 50:15, "Call upon me in the day of trouble, and I will deliver you, and you will glorify me"; and of Ps. 116:

MISERY

The cords of death had compassed me,
and the anguish of Sheol had overtaken me;
I was overcome by distress and sorrow.

DELIVERANCE

Then I called on the name of the Lord: O Lord, save me!
When I was in great misery he saved me.

GRATITUDE

I will lift up the cup of salvation and call on the name of the Lord.
I will fulfil my vows to the Lord in the presence of all his people.

This shows too how very appropriate is Q. and A. 2 of the Heidelberg Catechism:

Q. How many things are necessary for you to know, that you in this comfort may live and die happily?

---

334. The apostle uses the pl.: διὰ τῶν οἰκτιρμῶν, based upon the Hebrew pl. רַחֲמִים. See II Sam. 24:14; I Chron. 21:13; Ps. 25:6; 40:11 (Hebrew 40:12); cf. Phil. 2:1. This is an intensive pl., correctly rendered by the English sing. However, the intensive character of such a noun can be retained in the translation by prefixing an adjective; in the present case such as *tender, great, manifold.*

A. Three; the first, how great my sins and miseries are; the second, how I am delivered from all my sins and misery; the third, how I am to be thankful to God for such deliverance.

The division into these three parts is, however, not rigid or mechanical. Even in Ps. 116:1, 2 deliverance is clearly indicated, as is true also in Rom. 1:16, 17; and as to the Heidelberg Catechism, even its famous very first Q. and A. already implies all the "three things" that are necessary.

2. And stop allowing yourselves to be fashioned after the pattern of this (evil) age, but continue to let yourselves be transformed by the renewing of y o u r mind, so that y o u may prove what is the will of God, namely, that which is good and well-pleasing and perfect.

It is one thing to point out a goal to a person and to encourage him to try to reach it. Paul has done this in verse 1. It is a different matter to show him what he should do to reach that goal. The apostle does not fail us at this point. Here in verse 2 he shows the hearers and readers what *should be shunned* and what *should be done* in order to reach the goal.

First, what should be *shunned*!

The members of the Roman church were "saints," to be sure. But they had not as yet reached the pinnacle of sinlessness. They were saints but also still sinners, for on this side of heaven no mere human being ever attains to the condition of moral-spiritual perfection.

There is one more fact that should be added: the members of that church were imitators. Aren't we all to a certain extent? Or does this rule apply only to *children*? In a sense does it not apply to everybody? It holds especially in the realm of sin and evil. Did not even Juvenal say, "We are all easily taught to imitate what is base and depraved"?[335] "Bad company corrupts good character" (I Cor. 15:33), and in this present world it is well-nigh impossible completely to avoid "bad company" or even to steer clear of the bad habits which are still clinging to what, on the whole, can be called "good company." Therefore, unless we are on our guard, we are in great danger of falling prey to "the pattern of this evil age."

When Paul says, "And stop allowing yourselves to be fashioned after the pattern of *this (evil) age*"[336] (I Cor. 2:6, 8; Gal. 1:4), he is warning the membership then and now against yielding to the various manifestations of worldliness by which they are being constantly surrounded; such as the use of dirty or offensive language, the singing of scurrilous songs, the reading of filthy books, the wearing of tempting attire, engaging in questionable pastimes, associating, on intimate terms, with worldly companions, etc. There is hardly any end to the list.

Take the matter of amusements. It is possible to be guilty in this respect even though there is nothing wrong with the recreation of one's choice; for

---

335. *Satires* XIV.40.

336. τῷ αἰῶνι τούτῳ, associative instrumental case of ὁ αἰών οὗτος. See p. 265, footnote 226.

example, if a person sets his heart on it, becomes absorbed in it, depriving him of time and energy for involvement in necessary and noble causes (family, Christian education, church, charity, missions, etc.).

The main reason Paul warns against allowing oneself to be fashioned after the pattern of this (evil) age is that man's chief aim should never be to live only for himself. He should do everything to the glory of God (I Cor. 10:31).

A second reason is this: constant yielding to the temptation of becoming fashioned after the pattern of "this (evil) age" (I Cor. 2:6, 8; Gal. 1:4) ends in bitter disappointment; for, "The fashion[337] of this world is passing away" (I Cor. 7:31).

The experience of those who permit their lives to be frittered away in this manner resembles that of travelers in the desert. They are completely exhausted. Their lips are parched with thirst. Suddenly they see in the distance a sparkling spring surrounded by shady trees. With hope revived they hasten to this place . . . only to discover that they had been deceived by a mirage. "The world and its desires are passing away, but the person who does the will of God lives forever" (I John 2:17).

Secondly, what should be *done*!

"Let yourselves be transformed by the renewing of y o u r mind." Note the contrast: *not fashioned . . . but transformed*.[338]

---

337. Note similarity between συσχηματίζεσθε (Rom. 12:2) and τὸ σχῆμα (I Cor. 7:31).

338. Although this significant difference or contrast is admitted by most commentators, the admission is not unanimous. The reason for maintaining that in Rom. 12:2 a contrast is indeed pictured between (a) "Stop allowing yourselves to be *fashioned* (or conformed)" . . . and (b) "But continue to let yourselves be *transformed*," may be formulated as follows:

When elsewhere in the New Testament the verbs συσχηματίζω (in Phil. 3:21, μετασχηματίζω) and μεταμορφόω, or their respective cognates σχῆμα and μορφή (in Phil. 3:21, σύμμορφος), occur side by side, there is a significant distinction in meaning between the two.

Thus, in the Kenosis passage (Phil. 2:5-8) there is a distinction in meaning between μορφή and σχῆμα. See N.T.C. on Philippians, pp. 103-105.

So also in Phil. 3:21 Paul uses both a σχῆμα and a μορφή compound. We are told that, in connection with his glorious Return, Christ will refashion our lowly body so that it will have a form like his own glorious body. The new outward *fashion* or appearance will truly reflect the new and lasting inward *form*. The distinction in meaning is again clear.

Similarly we have every right to believe that when the two verbs συσχηματίζω and μεταμορφόω are used side by side here in Rom. 12:2 a significant difference in meaning is implied. In the present case, because of the context, that difference even amounts to a contrast. Note the strongly adversative particle ἀλλά.

There are those who deny this significant difference in meaning. In support of their view they point to the fact that the verb μεταμορφόω is used in the account of Christ's transfiguration (Matt. 17:2; Mark 9:2) even though there was no transformation of Christ's inner being.

In answering this argument I wish to point out two things: (a) the possibility must be allowed that the change in Christ's outward appearance was brought about by *the glory from within* irradiating his whole being; and (b) the transfiguration account in no way contradicts the *rule* mentioned above, for only *one* of the two verbs is used in that account.

The difference in meaning, here in Rom. 12:2, between the two verbs should accordingly be recognized. See also R. C. Trench, *Synonyms of the New Testament*, par. lxx.

This is my answer to the reasoning of Cranfield, *op. cit.*, second volume, pp. 605-607. He rejects the view which I share with most commentators. For the sake of fairness I urge the reader to read and study the indicated pages in Cranfield's excellent commentary.

Paul does not say, "Substitute one outward fashion for another." That would be no solution, for the trouble with those who allow themselves to be fashioned after the pattern of this present (evil) age is deep-seated. What is needed is *transformation*, inner change, the renewing of the mind, that is, not only of the organ of thinking and reasoning but of the inner disposition; better still, of the heart, the inner being. Cf. 1:28; 7:22-25.

It is important to pay close attention to the exact manner in which the apostle expresses himself in this exhortation. Note the following details.

a. He uses *the present tense*: "Continue to let yourselves be transformed." Accordingly, this transformation must not be a matter of impulse: on again, off again. It must be continuous.

b. The verb used is in *the passive voice*. Paul does not say, "Transform yourselves," but "Let yourselves be transformed." Transformation is basically the work of the Holy Spirit. It amounts to progressive sanctification. "And we all, with unveiled faces, reflecting the glory of the Lord, are being changed into his likeness from one degree of glory to another, which comes from the Lord, who is the Spirit" (II Cor. 3:18).

c. Nevertheless, the verb is in *the imperative mood*. Believers are not completely passive. Their responsibility is not canceled. They must allow the Spirit to do his work within their hearts and lives. Their duty is to co-operate to the full. See Phil. 2:12, 13; II Thess. 2:13.

Finally, the apostle describes the glorious result of this continuous transformation: "so that y o u may prove what is the will of God . . ." This is a very significant statement. It shows that in order to discern the will of God for their lives believers cannot just depend on their conscience. Conscience is indeed very important, but it must constantly be sent back to the school of Scripture to receive instruction from the Holy Spirit. It is in this manner that believers become and remain aware of God's will. Which will? Decretive or Preceptive? The latter, of course. See Deut. 29:29. In this way the will of God will become an increasingly well-established or proven component of the consciousness and lives of God's children. The more they live in accordance with that will and approve of it, the more also, through this experience, will they learn to know that will, and rejoice in that knowledge. They will exclaim, "Thy will is our delight."

And what is the contents of that preceptive will? In other words, what is it that God wants us to be and to do? The answer is: "that which is good and well-pleasing and perfect."[339]

Paul probably knew that adding these words was very necessary. He is as it were telling the Romans that what avails before God is not how *important* they are or deem themselves to be (cf. the immediate context, verse 3; see also 11:17-21), or how *charismatic* (verses 4-8), or how *strong* (cf. 15:1); but

339. The rendering "his good and well-pleasing and perfect will" is incorrect. The words τὸ ἀγαθὸν καὶ εὐάρεστον καὶ τέλειον indicate that what God wants his children to be and to do is to be and do what, *in his sight*, is good, well-pleasing, perfect.

rather how grateful, loving, outgoing they are. What matters is how obedient they are to the commandment, addressed to each one individually, "You shall love the Lord your God with all your heart and with all your soul and with all your mind. This is the great commandment. And a second like it is this: You shall love your neighbor as yourself." See Deut. 6:5; Lev. 19:18; Matt. 22:37, 39; Mark 12:30, 31; Luke 10:27; Rom. 13:8-10. In God's sight such a life is good and well-pleasing. The aim of such a life is nothing short of perfection. See Matt. 5:48 and add Phil. 3:7-11.

---

3 For, through the grace given me, I bid every one among y o u not to think of himself more highly than he ought to think, but so to think (of himself) as to think soberly, each person according to the measure of faith God has apportioned to him. 4 For, just as we have many members in one body, and these members do not all have the same function, 5 so we, who are many, are one body in Christ, and severally members of one another. 6 Moreover, having different gifts, according to the grace given us, if (a person's gift is) prophesying, (then let him exercise it) in accordance with the standard of faith; 7 or if (it is rendering) practical service, then let him use it in (rendering) such practical service; or if one is a teacher, (let him exercise his gift) in teaching; 8 or, if one is an exhorter (let him use his gift) in exhorting. Let him who contributes to the needs of others (do so) without ulterior motive. Let him who exercises leadership (do so) with diligence. Let him who shows mercy (do so) with cheerfulness.

B. *What Should Be the Attitude of the Justified Believer Toward Fellow-Christians*

"We, who are many, are one body in Christ"
12:3-8

In immediate thought-connection with verse 2 Paul continues:

3. For, through the grace given me, I bid every one among y o u not to think of himself more highly than he ought to think, but so to think (of himself) as to think soberly, each person according to the measure of faith God has apportioned to him.

Because of certain conditions existing in the Roman church, as we have seen, and perhaps also because of recent experiences in connection with the church at Corinth (I Cor. 12:14-31), Paul warns against the sin of exaggerated self-esteem. He issues a specific command ("I bid"; cf. Matt. 5:22, 28, 32, 34, 39, 44), appeals to his authority as an apostle ("according to the grace given me"; see on 1:5, pp. 44, 45), and addresses himself to everyone without exception ("everyone among y o u"). By means of a play on words, difficult to reproduce in English—something like "not to overestimate (himself) beyond a true estimate"—he urges everyone to be sober-minded, level-headed, sensible. To each member of the Roman church he says, as it were, "Don't fancy yourself to be Mr. BIG! The other person also has gifts. Each individual should evaluate himself not by measuring himself with his own yardstick but by the measure of faith God has apportioned to him."

The term *faith* is here used in the more usual sense of the trust in God by means of which an individual lays hold on God's promises. In the present context, however, the apostle is not thinking in quantitative terms (a large or a small amount of faith). He is thinking rather of the various ways in which each distinct individual is able to be a blessing to others and to the church in general by using the particular gift with which, *in association with faith*, God has endowed him or her. He is admonishing each of those addressed to recognize the diversity of gifts amid the unity of faith, and to ask himself, "How can I make the best use of my gift so as to benefit each and all?"

4, 5. For, just as we have many members in one body, and these members do not all have the same function, so we, who are many, are one body in Christ, and severally members of one another.

The comparison of the church and its members to the human body and its parts is a familiar one in the letters of Paul. *A little earlier* Paul had made use of this illustration in writing to the Corinthians. He had referred to this symbol in order to counteract sinful divisions (I Cor. 3:3, 4). He had written, "We who are many are one body" (I Cor. 10:17); and "Now y o u are the body of Christ, and each one of y o u is part of it" (12:27). *Later*—that is, after writing Romans—the apostle, in composing Colossians, with its theme, *Christ, the Pre-eminent One, the Only and All-Sufficient Savior*, was going to call the church "Christ's body" (1:24). He was going to describe Christ as "the Head, from whom the entire body, supported and held together by joints and ligaments, grows with a growth (that is) from God" (2:19). He was going to include the solemn and beautiful admonition, "And let the peace of Christ, for which y o u were called in one body, rule in y o u r hearts" (3:15). In his epistle to the Ephesians, also written during that first Roman imprisonment, with its theme, *The Unity of All Believers in Christ*, the description of the church as being one body in Christ, a body of which all believers are members, would occur again and again (1:23; 4:4, 12, 15, 16, 25).

Here, in Romans 12:4, 5, Paul emphasizes (a) *the organic unity of the body* ("many members in one body"), (b) *the purposeful diversity of the members and of their functions* ("and these members do not all have the same function"), and (c) *the mutual needs and benefits of these several members who are united in Christ* (". . . so we, who are many, are one body in Christ, and severally members of one another").

6-8. Moreover, having different gifts, according to the grace given us, if (a person's gift is) prophesying, (then let him exercise it) in accordance with the standard of faith; or if (it is rendering) practical service, then let him use it in (rendering) such practical service; or if one is a teacher, (let him exercise his gift) in teaching; or, if one is an exhorter (let him use his gift) in exhorting. Let him who contributes to the needs of others (do so) without ulterior motive. Let him who exercises leadership (do so) with diligence. Let him who shows mercy (do so) with cheerfulness.

Notes on This Summary of Gifts and Functions

1. It is marked by abbreviated style. The words implied but not expressed are numerous. See N.T.C. on John, Vol. I, p. 206, on Abbreviated Expression.

2. Paul is describing seven "gifts," distributed among individuals or groups of individuals who, making use of these gifts, exercise the corresponding functions.

3. The seven functions are:
   a. prophesying
   b. rendering practical service
   c. teaching
   d. exhorting
   e. contributing to the needs of people
   f. exercising leadership
   g. showing mercy.

4. Among commentators there is considerable difference of opinion with respect to the meaning of some of these functions.

5. Somewhat similar lists are found in I Cor. 12:8-10, where nine functions are mentioned; in I Cor. 12:28, 29 which mentions eight; and in Eph. 4:11 which lists four (as some see it five, but see N.T.C. on Ephesians, p. 197).

6. It is clear that Paul believes that not only ministers, elders, and deacons have gifts, but every believer has one or more divinely bestowed gifts or endowments. The apostle shows how these *charismata* should be used to benefit the church and, in fact, men in general.

Note "according to the grace given us." No one has the right to boast about his gift. Each member should bear in mind that his ability to serve others is a product of God's grace, his love for the undeserving.

a. *Prophesying*

So very important did Paul consider the gift and function of prophesying that both in I Cor. 12:28 and in Eph. 4:11 he mentions it immediately after that of the apostolate.

The question has been asked, "How is it that here in Romans 12, where Paul is describing how persons endowed with various gifts should conduct themselves in the performance of their respective duties, there is no mention at all of the function of *an apostle?*" Some answer: "This proves that no apostle had anything whatsoever to do with the founding of that church or with its early history." But such an argument is surely basing too much on too little. See also above, p. 19. Even the statement, "Paul is silent on the matter of telling another apostle how to conduct himself because it would have been very improper for one apostle to lay down the law for another apostle," is not absolutely true, as Gal. 2:11 f. proves, though in normal circumstances it is probably correct. What is true is that Paul had already alluded to his own apostolic office (in 12:3), and also that at this particular time there was no apostle in Rome. If there had been one, would his name not have been included in the list of greetings found in chapter 16?

Returning to the subject of the importance Paul attaches to the gift of prophecy, it is to be noted that in I Cor. 14:1 those addressed are told, ". . . eagerly desire spiritual gifts, especially the gift of prophecy." In verse 39 of that same chapter the writer adds, "Therefore, my brothers, be eager to prophesy."

One important reason for attaching such a high value to prophesying must have been that the message of the true prophet was the product not of his own intuition or even of his own study and research but of special revelation. The prophet received his message directly from the Holy Spirit (Acts 11:27, 28; note, "and through the Spirit predicted"). So also in Acts 21:11 Agabus, one of these prophets—there were others, both men and women (Acts 13:1; 21:9)—is quoted as follows, "*The Holy Spirit* says, In this way the Jews of Jerusalem will bind the owner of this belt . . ." (21:11).

Another reason why on Paul's list of spiritual gifts prophesying ranked so high was its comprehensive content. It was by no means restricted to the utterance of a prediction now and then. It included edification, exhortation, consolation, and instruction (I Cor. 14:3, 31).

However, not everyone who presented himself as a prophet was necessarily a genuine prophet. Not everything a "prophet" said was necessarily true. So in addition to supplying the church with prophets, God also saw to it that there were people who were able to distinguish between the true prophet and the false (I Cor. 12:10; 14:29) and between truth and falsehood. In line with this, here in Rom. 12:6 Paul writes, "If (a person's gift is) prophesying, (then let him exercise it) *in accordance with the standard of faith*." Here some interpreters interpret the word "faith" in the objective sense, as if the apostle was referring to God's revealed truth, the gospel. Others, however, accept the subjective sense, and view the word "faith" as indicating *trust* in God and in his promises.

Since just a moment ago (in verse 3) Paul has used this word in the latter sense, which, in the present connection, yields an excellent meaning, we need look no farther. The prophet must say nothing that is in conflict with his faith in Christ. For example, he might be tempted, for selfish reasons, to make startling statements which he himself did not believe. He is warned not to do so. He must be and remain God's mouth to the people.

b. *Rendering Practical Service*

The apostle uses the word *diakonia*, that is, practical service, ministry. Cf. I Cor. 12:5; Eph. 4:12. This service or ministry can be of various kinds. In the story concerning Martha and Mary (Luke 10:40) it amounted to whatever work was necessary in preparing a meal. "The diakonia" of *the word* is mentioned in Acts 6:4; that of *reconciliation* in II Cor. 5:18. Since in the present connection Paul is enumerating various functions pertaining to church life, it is natural here to connect the term with that particular type of work which we too ascribe to the *diaconate*, that is, to the office performed by the deacons. Accordingly, Paul is encouraging those who are qualified for this type of work to accept the opportunity to do so.

It may well be rather difficult for us to estimate the importance the apostle attached to the work of the deacon, the Church's ministry of mercy. We should bear in mind, however, that in the days of the apostle many believers were anything but wealthy. Some were slaves or freedmen. In fact, in this very epistle to the Romans (15:25) the apostle states the reason why he cannot travel straight to Rome but must first visit the saints in Jerusalem. Elsewhere he says, "I came to Jerusalem to bring my people gifts for the poor" (Acts 24:17). See also I Cor. 1:26 f., 16:1 f., II Cor. 8:1 f. It is worthy of special attention that the very man who insisted on purity in doctrine was at least equally interested in the cause of showing generosity in aiding the poor. In II Cor. 8:7, 8 he most strikingly connects the "grace" of giving to supply the needs of the poor with a central doctrine of the Christian religion, namely, that of Christ's voluntary humiliation in the interest of sinners. He says:

"But just as y o u excel in everything . . . see that y o u also excel in this grace (of giving) . . . For y o u know the grace of our Lord Jesus Christ, that though he was rich, yet for y o u r sake he became poor, that y o u through his poverty might become rich."

So also today the diaconate is no less important than the eldership. The cause of Christ is served equally by each. In each the love of Christ is reflected.

c. *Teaching*

The prophet received his message by direct revelation. The teacher derived his knowledge from the study of the Old Testament and of the teaching of Jesus, in whatever form this was accessible to him. Since *direct* revelations do not always occur, and besides, since the deposit of divine revelation found in Scripture—which, in Paul's day meant in the Old Testament—is of abiding and very important significance, it is clear that also for the teacher there is a very definite and important place in the life of the church. So, "if one is a teacher (let him exercise his gift) in teaching."

d. *Exhorting*

Acts 13:15 shows that in the synagogue, after a portion of the law and of the Prophets had been read, the rulers of the synagogue invited Paul and Barnabas to speak a word of exhortation. Such was the custom in those days. Here, in Rom. 12, those who have been blessed with the talent of exhorting are urged to make use of it for the benefit of all. Today *the minister* of the gospel is—at least should be—adequately equipped to take care of both teaching and exhorting. He not only teaches doctrine but also shows how doctrine should be applied to life so that all may be edified and encouraged. Among the laity, too, there may be excellent teachers and/or exhorters.

e. *Contributing to the Needs of People*

Paul writes, "Let him who contributes to the needs of others (do so) without ulterior motive."

The reasons why Paul devoted so much attention to pointing out the importance of the ministry of mercy (namely, great need and example of

Christ) have been given. See above, under b. So here, at first glance, we seem to detect a repetition of point b. Nevertheless, there is a difference. The *diaconate* has to do with the cause of *church benevolence*. By means of the deacons the entire church, functioning as a unit, engages in this important work. More, however, is needed. In addition to *collective* there must also be *private benevolence*. Let those who are able to function in this capacity by all means do so! Since the Lord has blessed them so abundantly let them, in turn, be a blessing to others.

But in so doing they must be sure to contribute "without ulterior motive."[340] Here the giving with ulterior motive, denounced by Malachi (1:13, 14), immediately occurs to the mind, and so does that of Ananias and Sapphira (Acts 5:1 f.). True givers are those who give wholeheartedly, all the while remembering what they themselves have received from their Lord and Savior Jesus Christ.

f. *Exercising Leadership*

There are those who believe that by placing f. between e. and g., both of which are, in a sense, concerned with benevolence, Paul, in f., must be referring to people who are in charge of church benevolence. However, e. does not seem to have anything to do with the diaconate, and g. does not necessarily refer to what is commonly meant by benevolence.

Besides, in other passages where the same word for leadership occurs as the one used here in Rom. 12:8 the reference is to overseers, elders (I Thess. 5:12; I Tim. 3:4; 5:17).[341] And even when one makes due allowance for the fact that it is not the apostle's intention to list every spiritual gift and function of church members, would it not seem strange if he were to include in his summary the ministry of the deacons, as he does (see point b.), but completely to omit from it that of the presbyters? With respect to their age and dignity these men were called presbyters or elders; with respect to the nature of their task they were called overseers or superintendents. Because a heavy burden rested on the shoulders of these men, and the temptation to shirk their responsibility was great, they are admonished to exercise their leadership "with diligence."

g. *Showing Mercy*

The sick, dying, and bereaved are in need of visits by someone who knows how to impart genuine Christian sympathy and understanding, someone who shows mercy *with cheerfulness*. "For as nothing gives more solace to the sick

---

340. Greek: ἐν ἁπλότητι. Basically the meaning of ἁπλοῦς, -ῆ, -οῦν is uncomplicated, uncompounded, simple; and, accordingly, ἐν ἁπλότητι would mean "in simplicity," and therefore: with a single goal in mind. This, by a very easy transition, becomes "without ulterior motive," though "without reserve," hence "generously" also deserves consideration. Cf. II Cor. 8:2; 9:11, 13. See also Eph. 6:5; Col. 3:22: with undivided mind, with singleness of heart.

341. Note prominence of the word προΐστημι, in participial form, in all these cases. Also, in I Tim. 3:1 the synonym "overseer" is used, and in 5:17 the synonym "presbyters" (elders).

or to anyone otherwise distressed, than to see those cheerful and prompt in assisting them, so to observe sadness in the countenance of those by whom assistance is given makes them feel themselves despised" (John Calvin on this passage). I would only add to this that a brief, cheering visit by a wise and sympathetic fellow-member, who is willing to help in every possible way, is certainly of far more benefit than the almost endless recital of all the horrendous details of the operation recently performed on the caller, namely, Mr. Sad. Truly, "A cheerful heart is good medicine, but a crushed spirit dries up the bones" (Prov. 17:22). This holds both for the patient and the visitor.

---

9 Love must be genuine. Abhor what is evil; cling to what is good. 10 Be devoted to one another in brotherly love. Prefer one another in honor. 11 Never come on behind in showing enthusiasm. Be aglow with the Spirit, serving the Lord. 12 Be joyful in hope, enduring in affliction, persistent in prayer. 13 Help to relieve the needs of the saints. Eagerly practice hospitality.

B. *What Should Be the Attitude of the Justified Believer Toward Fellow-Christians*
(continued)
"Be devoted to one another in brotherly love"
12:9-13

The connection between verses 8 and 9 is close: cheerfully showing mercy presupposes a love that is sincere. So Paul says:

9. Love must be genuine. Abhor what is evil; cling to what is good.

It is reasonable to believe that the "love" of which Paul speaks here is more wide-embracing than the "brotherly love" mentioned in verse 10. The apostle mentions the more inclusive concept first, then the more restricted one. What he emphasizes first of all is that love, taken in any sense—whether its object is God or fellow-believers or neighbors or even "enemies"—must be "unhypocritical," that is, unfeigned, sincere, genuine. It must not be faked, must not consist in empty words. Remember the saying, "Your deeds speak so loudly that I cannot hear your words."

In line with this is the exhortation, "Abhor what is evil." This does not refer only to insincerity in love, a mere show, which must be avoided. On the contrary, what Paul is saying amounts to this: "Avoid *whatever* is evil; cling to *whatever* is good." It should be clear that Paul's emphasis is on *agapē*, that is, love.[342]

---

342. According to Ridderbos, *op. cit.*, p. 281, the word ἀγάπη, when used by Paul, nearly always refers to the love of believers for one another.

As the Concordance shows, the apostle employs that term about 80 times. It is indeed true that in *very many* of these cases it refers to the believers' mutual love. However, when, in order to reach the number of times this agapē indicates the believers' love for each other, one subtracts the references to (a) agapē for the neighbor, (b) agapē with reference to God, and (c) agapē in general, without mention of subject or object, the resulting figure, though still *high*, is not so high that "nearly always mutual love among believers" is a justifiable characterization. In its 9 occurrences in Romans only 2 refer to the love of the saints for each other

10. Be devoted[343] to one another in brotherly love.

Whenever Paul thinks of believers he conceives of them as constituting (in the Lord) one family (Eph. 3:15). All have one Father (cf. Rom. 8:15; Gal. 4:5). This thought is entirely in line with the teaching of Jesus (Matt. 12:46-50 and parallels).

According to this teaching the bond that unites the members of this spiritual family are far more secure and lasting than those which bind together the members of a purely physical family (Luke 14:26). What the apostle is saying, therefore, is that the members of this spiritual family should do all in their power to be and remain devoted to each other in tender affection.

There is a sense in which believers should love everybody, including even those who hate and persecute them (see verse 14; add Luke 6:35). But tender, brotherly affection, implying intimacy, understanding, spiritual unity, is reserved for the inner circle. Believers have the right and the duty to discriminate between those who hate God and those who love him. As the apostle says elsewhere, "Let us do good to everybody, especially to those who are of the household of faith" (Gal. 6:10).

Paul adds: **Prefer one another in honor.**

What does this mean and how is this possible? Of the many interpretations offered note the following three:

a. The other person is the one in whom Christ is mysteriously present for me. Therefore I should honor him above myself.[344]

Evaluation. Must I assume, then, that Christ is not present in every believer, including even myself?

b. Do not wait for others to praise you but be the first to bestow praise whenever this can be done in harmony with the truth.

Evaluation. Though this is excellent advice, is it really what the passage means? Probably not. It seems to require that I regard my fellow-believer to be worthy of greater honor than I am, and that I, therefore, esteem him higher than myself.

(12:9; 14:15); 2 to love in inter-human relations (both in 13:10); the other 5 pertain to love proceeding from God (5:5; 5:8), from Christ (8:35), from God and described as "the love of God which is in Christ Jesus our Lord" (8:39), and from the Spirit (15:30). In II Thess. agapē refers to mutual love among believers only once (1:3). In the other 2 instances of its use one refers to love of the truth (2:10), the other to love of—i.e., proceeding from—God (3:5). Elsewhere in Paul's epistles, however, the love of the saints for each other is mentioned frequently: Gal. 5:13; Eph. 1:15; 4:2, 15, 16; etc.

The conclusion we arrive at is that in the New Testament the situation with respect to φιλία and ἀγάπη is somewhat similar to that between φιλέω and ἀγαπάω. Only once does φιλία occur in the New Testament (in the sense of friendship, James 4:4). There is, however, also φιλαδελφία (Rom. 12:10; I Thess. 4:9; Heb. 13:1; I Peter 1:22; and II Peter 1:7 twice). As to the cognate *verbs* see N.T.C. on John, Vol. II, pp. 494-501, footnote 306.

343. φιλόστοργοι = nom. pl. masc. of φιλόστοργος, devoted, tenderly affectionate. In the New Testament the word occurs only here.

344. Thus Cranfield, *op. cit.*, Vol. II, p. 633.

c. The exhortation does not demand of me that I deem every fellow-member to be in every respect wiser and abler than I am myself. But it asks that in humble-mindedness I count my fellow-member to be better than I am myself. See Phil. 2:3.

A Christian knows that his own motives are not always pure and holy (I Cor. 11:28, 31). This is a kind of knowledge which at times causes him to utter the prayer, "O Lord, forgive my good deeds." On the other hand, the Christian has no right to regard as evil the motives of his brothers and sisters in the Lord. Unless a consistently evil pattern is clearly evident in the lives of fellow-members, their outwardly good deeds must be ascribed to good, never to evil, motives. It follows that the child of God who has learned to know himself sufficiently so that at times he feels inclined to utter the cry of the publican (Luke 18:13) or of Paul (Rom. 7:24) will indeed regard others to be better than himself.

11. Never come on behind in showing enthusiasm. Be aglow with the Spirit, serving the Lord.

However, sinful human nature being what it is—and even saints are still sinners—it is not reasonable to expect that those whom Paul is addressing will, with enthusiasm, go about the business of preferring one another in honor. On the other hand, religion without enthusiasm hardly deserves the name *religion*.

Of course, the source of enthusiasm is not in man. If a person is going to be "set on fire," it is the Holy Spirit who must do this. So Paul says, "Never come on behind in showing enthusiasm." And he immediately adds, "Be aglow *with the Spirit*." Not only should the saints take care that they do not quench the Spirit, that they do not resist the Spirit, and even that they do not grieve the Spirit; they should earnestly ask the Holy Spirit to fill them with zeal, the enthusiasm needed for properly carrying out their Christian duties and attaining their goal. Only then will the command, "Be aglow with the Spirit" be fulfilled when, from the heart, they are able to sing:

> Teach me to love thee as thine angels love,
> One holy passion filling all my frame—
> The baptism of the heaven-descended Dove;
> My heart an altar, and thy love the flame.
>
> —Lines from "Spirit of God, Dwell Thou Within My Heart" by George Croly, 1854.

Then they will not be passive, but with joy and enthusiasm will address themselves to the task of actually and wholeheartedly *serving the Lord*. Observe that when the believer is really aglow with the Spirit, he does not show this by resorting to manifestations of religious (?) excitement, but by humbly carrying out his mandate of serving the Lord.

12. Be joyful in hope, enduring in affliction, persistent in prayer.

The hope of future salvation (cf. 5:2, 4, 5; 8:24, 25; 15:4, 13) stimulates present joy; in fact, to such an extent that God's children are even able patiently *to endure*[345] in the midst of affliction. This endurance indicates *strength to bear up under stress, plus the persistent application of this strength.* It is not the product of human wisdom or skill but of God's grace. Therefore Paul immediately adds "(Be) persistent in prayer."

Without constant prayer such joy and endurance would be impossible. The opposition coming from the side of the world and the doubts from within would prove too strong. In fact, without steadfastness in prayer obedience to none of the exhortations of chapter 12 or of other passages can be expected.

Paul continues:

13. Help to relieve the needs of the saints. Eagerly practice hospitality.

The urgent need for "relief" has already been explained. See verses 6-8, under the heading *Practical Service*, pp. 410, 411. Here, in verse 13, the apostle rivets our attention especially upon those saints who are in need of *lodging*. Finding a good and safe place to stay for the night, or perhaps even for several days, was by no means easy at that time. Besides, the apostle, himself a great traveler, understood this need. He wants those whom he addressed to become thoroughly involved in the business of supplying good lodging places. He wants them to practice hospitality gladly, not grudgingly, as seems to have happened at times (I Peter 4:9). Not only must the *overseer* be a hospitable person (I Tim. 3:2; Titus 1:8), but *every believer* should be. What should at all times be clearly taken to heart is that whatever is done for the person in need of hospitality is done for him who on the great Judgment Day is going to say, "I was a stranger, and y o u welcomed *me*" (Matt. 25:35). What the apostle is urging, therefore, is that believers will not only show hospitality when they are asked to do so, but will go out of their way to offer it. They should practice this grace . . . eagerly! See also Gen. 18:1-8; Heb. 6:10; 13:2.

---

14 Bless those who persecute y o u. Bless and do not curse. 15 Rejoice with those who rejoice; weep with those who weep. 16 Live in harmony with one another. Do not be snobbish, but readily associate with humble folk. Do not be conceited. 17 Do not return evil for evil to anyone. Always see to it that (y o u r affairs are) right in the sight of everybody. 18 If it is possible, as far as it depends on y o u, live at peace with everyone. 19 Do not take revenge, beloved, but leave room for the wrath (of God); for it is written, "Vengeance belongs to me; I will repay," says the Lord. 20 On the contrary:

"If your enemy is hungry, feed him;
if he is thirsty, give him something to drink;
for, by doing this, you will heap coals of fire on his head."

21 Do not be overcome by evil, but overcome evil by good.

C. *What Should Be the Attitude of the Justified Believer Toward Outsiders, Including Enemies*

"Bless those who persecute y o u"
12:14-21

---

345. See p. 273, footnote 235.

14. Bless those who persecute y o u.

The relation between the preceding paragraph (on brotherly love) and this one (on being persecuted) is not as remote as it may seem to be. In fact, there may be a twofold connection:

a. *material.*

Offering hospitality (verse 13) amounts to being engaged in a good work. According to I Peter 3:17 f. the anti-Christian world persecutes believers even for doing good!

b. *verbal.*

In the original the same verb,[346] used in verse 13, recurs in verse 14. The contextual meaning of the two forms used—one in verse 13, one in verse 14—though closely related, is not exactly the same. In English one obtains the identical result by rendering the two exhortations as follows:

Pursue hospitality (verse 13).

Bless those who *pursue* y o u (verse 14).

In the first instance *pursue* means *practice*. In the second it means *persecute*.

What we have in verse 14 is clearly an echo of the words of Jesus, "Love y o u r enemies and pray for those that persecute y o u (Matt. 5:44; cf. Luke 6:27 f.; I Cor. 4:12)." To bless, in this connection, means "to invoke God's blessing upon." See also Luke 2:34; Heb. 11:20.

Paul even adds: **Bless and do not curse.**

In other words, not the slightest desire for the outpouring of divine vengeance on our persecutors must be intermixed with our prayer that the Lord may bless them.

That this exhortation runs contrary to our sinful human nature is pointed out strikingly by Calvin who, in his comment on it, reveals keen psychological insight:

"I have said that this is more difficult than to let go revenge when anyone is injured; for though some restrain their hands and are not led away by the passion of doing harm, they yet wish that some calamity or loss would in some way happen to their enemies; and even when they are so pacified that they wish no evil, there is yet hardly one in a hundred who wishes well to him from whom he has received an injury; nay, most men daringly burst forth into imprecations. But God by his word not only restrains our hands from doing evil, but also subdues the bitter feelings within; and not only so, but he would have us be solicitous for the wellbeing of those who unjustly trouble us and seek our destruction."

A beginning of obedience to this command is possible for those who stop allowing themselves to be fashioned after the pattern of this (evil) age and continue to let themselves be transformed by the renewing of their mind (12:2).

15. Rejoice with those who rejoice; weep with those who weep.

---

346. διώκω, in verse 13 *nom.* pl. pres. participle; in verse 14 the same except *acc*.

One way of proving to ourselves that our hearts are in the right place is to identify with other persons, so that we not only weep with those who weep but even rejoice with those who rejoice; and this not only with fellow-believers but with all those with whom we enter into a relationship of relative closeness, be they believers or unbelievers. If we truly love our neighbor as we love ourselves (Luke 10:27), this should be possible. But never will it be possible for us truly to identify with the other person, whether believer or unbeliever, unless by God's sovereign grace the truth of Christ's taking upon himself our guilt and misery is by the Holy Spirit deeply impressed upon our heart and mind. The result will certainly be the advancement of the glory of God (Matt. 5:16), the entrance into our heart of the peace of God that surpasses all understanding (Phil. 4:7), and perhaps even the winning of the neighbor for Christ (I Peter 3:1).

The opposite of *rejoicing* is being filled with *envy* (Titus 3:3); and over against *weeping* stands *gloating* (over). Note sad result (Prov. 17:5).

16. Live in harmony with one another. Do not be snobbish, but readily associate with humble folk. Do not be conceited.

Believers are exhorted to agree among themselves, doubtlessly in order to exert a wholesome influence upon those who are still outside the kingdom (see context).

Now in order to live in harmony it is necessary that every manifestation of sinful pride be banished. So Paul says, "Do not lift up y o u r eyes to what is high," that is, "Do not be haughty" (cf. 11:20), or something on that order. That this is, indeed, the general sense of the passage follows also from the added exhortation, "Do not be conceited."

The A.V., however, reads, "Mind not high things but condescend to men of low estate." Today this rendering, especially because of the pejorative meaning attached to the word "condescend" (graciously descend to the level of inferiors!), will not do. Besides, it is hard to believe that Paul would be drawing a contrast between *things* and *people*. The A.R.V. rendering, "Set not your mind on high things but condescend to things that are lowly," is also unsatisfactory, especially because elsewhere the word used in the original refers not to things but to people who, in a sense, are lowly.[347] What Paul

---

347. The following translations of ταπεινός deserve consideration:

a. humble; (person or, if pl. people) of low degree (Luke 1:52; James 1:9; 4:6; I Peter 5:5).

b. lowly (Matt. 11:29).

c. downcast (II Cor. 7:6).

d. timid; according to some: ineffectual, inferior (II Cor. 10:1).

Here (Rom. 12:16) the meaning (*if n.*) could be "small and insignificant services"; (*if masc.*) humble people, humble folk.

Since the first part of the verse means, "Do not lift up y o u r eyes to what is high"; that is (something on the order of), "Do not be proud (or haughty)," and accordingly condemns an undesirable personal quality, and since the word ταπεινός elsewhere in the New Testament always expresses a personal trait, it is natural that also here in Rom. 12:16 it be so interpreted. The best translation of the words intervening between, "Live in harmony with one another," and "Do not be conceited," is probably, "Do not be snobbish (cf. Phillips, "Don't become snobbish"), but readily associate with humble folk." Although "haughty" will do, "snobbish" is saying is, "Do not be snobbish, but readily associate with humble folk." See also Luke 14:13.

Was he thinking, perhaps, of the beautiful words recorded in Prov. 3:6, 7? Here they are:

> In all your ways acknowledge him,
> And he will make your paths straight.
> Do not be wise in your own eyes.

In verse 14 Paul had issued the positive command, "Bless those who persecute y o u." After repeating the word "Bless" he had added the prohibition, "and do not curse." He now elaborates on this prohibition by saying:

17. Do not return evil for evil to anyone.

Two closely related wrongs are here combated:

a. *vindictiveness, the desire to get even with someone for a suffered wrong.* In this connection we are reminded of such earlier Pauline passages as:

> See to it that no one renders to anyone evil for evil. I Thess. 5:15.
>
> When we are cursed we bless; when we are persecuted we endure it; when we are slandered we answer kindly. I Cor. 4:12, 13
>
> Why not rather be wronged? Why not rather be cheated? I Cor. 6:7

Compare the words of another apostle:

"Do not repay evil with evil or insult with insult, but blessing with blessing" (I Peter 3:9).

The condemnation of vindictiveness is basic.

b. *assuming that private individuals have the right to take upon themselves the function of the civil magistrate in punishing crime.*

Even in the Old Testament the commandment "eye for eye . . . stripe for stripe" (Exod. 21:24, 25; cf. Lev. 24:20; Deut. 19:21) refers to the *public* administration of criminal law (see Lev. 24:14), and was issued in order that the practice of seeking *personal* revenge might be discouraged.

What (here in Rom. 12:17) Paul forbids—the yearning to retaliate—was the very sin against which Jesus warned (Matt. 5:38-42; cf. Luke 6:29, 35). And this teaching of our Lord can be considered a further development of such Old Testament instruction as is found in Lev. 19:18; Deut. 32:35; Prov. 20:22. See also S.BK. I, pp. 368-370; II, p. 299.

The manifestation of a vindictive spirit destroys Christian distinctiveness, the absolute prerequisite for success in winning people for Christ. It is this lack that causes outsiders to say, "Those Christians are no different than we are." Paul, the great missionary, wants believers to conduct themselves in such a manner that unbelievers will take note. It is for this reason that he continues as follows:

---

is perhaps even more precise because it refers to the character of those who look down on people whom they consider to be inferior. In the present context ("but readily associate with humble folk") that would seem to be the meaning the apostle intends to convey.

Cf. W. Grundmann, on ταπεινός, Th.D.N.T., Vol. VIII, pp. 1-26, especially pp. 19, 20.

17. Always see to it that (y o u r affairs are) right in the sight of everybody.

This reminds us of Prov. 3:3, 4:

> Let love and faithfulness never leave you;
> bind them around your neck,
> write them on the tablet of your heart.
> Then you will win favor and a good name
> in the sight of God and man.

Paul wants the addressed to live such lives of thorough consecration to God and genuine love for all, including even the persecutors, that outsiders will not be given a legitimate opportunity to complain or accuse (cf. I Tim. 5:14), and that slanderers will be put to shame (I Peter 3:16). He does not want the addressed to be a hindrance or stumblingblock, preventing the unconverted from accepting the gospel (I Cor. 10:32). Instead, he wants them so to conduct their affairs that the public conscience (cf. Rom. 2:15) will approve. His noble aim, as a lover of God, is that the devout lives of believers may be a means in God's hand for the conversion of sinners, to the glory of God (Matt. 5:16; I Peter 2:12).

Calvin has summarized the meaning of verse 17 as follows: "What is meant is that we ought diligently to labor, in order that all may be edified by our honest dealings . . . that they may, in a word, perceive the good and the sweet odor of our life, by which they may be allured to the love of God."

Proceeding along the same line Paul continues as follows:

18. If it is possible, as far as it depends on y o u, live at peace with everyone.

This exhortation to live at peace with everyone is in line with such other passages as, "Let there be no quarreling between you and me, or between your herdsmen and mine, for we are brothers" (Gen. 13:8); "Make every effort to live in peace with everybody" (Heb. 12:14); and "The wisdom that is from above is first pure, then peace-loving" (James 3:17). Jesus said, "Blessed (are) the peace-makers, for they shall be called sons of God" (Matt. 5:9).

In a world of peace-breaking this beatitude shows what a thoroughly relevant, vital, and dynamic force Christianity is. True peace-makers are all those whose Leader is the God of peace (I Cor. 14:33; Eph. 6:15; I Thess. 5:23), who aspire after peace with everyone (as here in Rom. 12:18), who proclaim the gospel of peace (Eph. 6:15), and pattern their lives after the Prince of Peace (Luke 19:10; John 3:12-15; cf. Matt. 10:8).

Nevertheless, the charge to live at peace with everyone is not presented in an unqualified form. There are two qualifications:

a. "If it is possible." There are circumstances under which the establishment or maintenance of peace is impossible. Heb. 12:14 not only advocates peace but also sanctification. The latter must not be sacrificed in order to maintain the former, for a peace without sanctification (or holiness) is not worthy of the name. If the maintenance of peace means the sacrifice of truth and/or honor, then peace must be abandoned. Cf. Matt. 10:34-36; Luke 12:51-53.

b. ". . . as far as it depends on y o u." There are situations that require the sacrifice of peace. But we must be sure that it is not we who are to blame for such exigencies. We have done everything in our power to establish and maintain peace. The other person (or persons) was (were) not willing to have peace except on conditions we, as Christians, were unable to accept. In such cases God does not hold us accountable for the lack of peace.

19. Do not take revenge, beloved, but leave room for the wrath (of God); for it is written, "Vengeance belongs to me; I will repay," says the Lord.

The tender appeal—note the word "beloved" here in verse 19—reminds us of the similarly affectionate appellative "brothers" in verse 1. In this connection see also 1:7; 16:5, 9, 12; I Cor. 4:14, 17; 10:14; 15:58; II Cor. 7:1; 12:19; Eph. 5:1; 6:21; Phil. 2:12; 4:1; Col. 1:7; 4:7, 9, 14; I Thess. 2:8; II Tim. 1:2; and Philem. 1 and 16.

Striking is the repetition of basically the same exhortation, namely, in slightly varying forms, "Do not take revenge." See verses 14, 17, 19, and 21. There must have been a reason for this, although exactly what it was has not been revealed. A suggestion would be that it resulted from (a) the fact that the members of the Roman church, or at least some of them, were greatly in need of this admonition; and (b) that the composer of this letter had been blessed, especially since his conversion, with an exceptionally sensitive and loving disposition. He was a man whose entire soul entered into the business of sympathizing and forgiving, in view of the pardon he had himself received from God.

After "Do not take revenge, beloved," Paul continues, "but leave room for the wrath . . ." The words, "of God" are not in the original. Accordingly, some commentators have suggested that what the apostle meant was, "Leave room for the adversaries' wrath." Others would fill in the lacuna with the phrase "y o u r wrath," and still others with "the civil magistrate's wrath."

However, it is not necessary to deal separately with each of these guesses, and to show why it cannot be correct. One solid reason will do for all three, namely, in the other cases where, in the New Testament, the word "wrath" occurs without a modifier showing whose wrath is being referred to, we are dealing with *God's* wrath. Moreover, it makes no difference whether the article ("the") is used (hence "the wrath") or is omitted (hence simply "wrath").[348] So it is altogether reasonable to believe, with most commentators, that also here, in Rom. 12:19, it is the wrath *of God* to which Paul refers.

---

348. *With* the article: Rom. 3:5; 5:9; 9:22; 13:5 (yes, also Rom. 13:5, though some deny this; see on that passage); *without* the article: Rom. 2:5, 8; Eph. 2:3; I Thess. 5:9).

When Paul says that those addressed—and ultimately all of us—must "leave room" for the wrath of God, he, in harmony with the entire context, is again emphasizing that we ourselves should not "play God," should abstain from attempting to usurp the divine prerogative of pouring out wrath, of wreaking vengeance.

In substantiation of this charge the apostle, as so often previously, appeals to the Old Testament, this time to Deut. 32:35; really to that passage in light of its context; see especially verses 20, 34, 36-43.

Did not Jesus himself, though he was the object of deeper and far more agonizing suffering, *unjustly* laid upon him by sinners—from *their* side it was certainly unjust!—instead of taking vengeance, commit himself to the One who judges righteously? See I Peter 2:23. Cf. the similarly beautiful words of Ps. 37:1-17.

In view of the fact that our Lord Jesus Christ, by his vicarious suffering, removed God's wrath from us, should we not be happy to refrain from taking revenge? What, then, is our duty when we are being unjustly treated? Is it, perhaps, to ask God to pour out his wrath upon those terrible people who have been so cruel to us? Is that what Paul means when he says, "Leave room for the wrath (of God)"? Is it not rather that we ask God to grant to the persecutors the grace of true repentance and faith? Should we not leave any notion of retributive righteousness entirely to the all-wise and sovereign God? And will not every true child of God, who has experienced the love of God in his own life, respond in this manner?

Instead of wreaking vengeance it is the Christian's duty and joy to return good for evil. The day of divine retribution has not yet arrived. Moreover, as indicated previously, the injured person has no right to assume the functions of an official magistrate.

The one who has suffered wrong should treat the one who hates him (not with concealed resentment or with a feeling of wrath but) *with kindness*.

So, after saying, "Do not take revenge . . . ," Paul continues:

20. On the contrary:

"If your enemy is hungry, feed him;
if he is thirsty, give him something to drink;
for, by doing this, you will heap coals of fire on his head."

The quotation is taken from Prov. 25:21, 22. If the enemy is hungry, the injured person should give him something to eat.[349] He should give him something to drink if he is thirsty. In other words, he should treat the enemy as did Elisha (II Kings 6:20-23).

In words that have given rise to many different interpretations, the apos-

---

349. ψώμιζε, 2nd per. s. pres. imperat. of ψωμίζω, to feed, to give something to eat. A ψωμίον is a small piece of bread. See John 13:26, 27, 30.

tle, still quoting from Proverbs, continues, "for by doing this, you will heap[350] coals of fire on his head."

Four different views. Heaping coals of fire on his head symbolizes

a. a form of self-inflicted torment,

b. a deed of benevolence (giving live coals to those in need),

c. a gesture of sorrow for sin,

d. a way of making the enemy ashamed of himself.

Explanation a. contradicts the present context, according to which one should treat an enemy with kindness. Both a. and c. describe the enemy's sorrow for sin rather than what the one whom he injured should do to him. The most widely accepted interpretation is d. The coals of fire in that view symbolize the burning pangs of shame and contrition resulting from the unexpected kindness received. The wronged person's magnanimous behavior, returning good for evil, has this effect.

As to meaning b.—an interpretation mentioned by Ridderbos, and in an interesting article revived (without definite endorsement) by E. J. Masselink—when the phrase "to those in need" is interpreted to mean, "*even though they are enemies*," resulting in the sense, "Overpower the enemy with your kindness" (E. J. Masselink), would not the effect be the same as that indicated in d.?

In stating a preference for d., therefore, I am not rejecting b.

Reasons for accepting this view (that of d. and possibly b.):

1. The words, "overcome evil by good" (verse 21) point in this direction.

2. So does I Peter 2:15, "For it is God's will that by doing good you should silence the ignorant talk of foolish people."

In the spirit of verse 20 Paul's concluding exhortation is:

21. Do not be overcome by evil, but overcome evil by good.

To be overcome by evil means (a) to allow the enemy to get you down, and (b) to plan and return evil for evil.

To overcome evil by good means (a) to continue living a life of faith in, and love for, God and for everyone, not excluding the person who has injured you, the kind of life marked by transformation into the image of Christ (verse 2), and therefore by humility (verses 3 and 16), helpfulness (verses 6-8), and peace (verse 16); and (b) to go out of your way, by word and deed, to show kindness to the one who has injured you.

---

350. σωρεύσεις, 2nd per. s. fut. act. indicat. of σωρεύω, to heap, pile up. In the New Testament this word occurs only here and in II Tim. 3:6.

For the different ways in which this saying is interpreted I have received help from the following sources:

C. E. B. Cranfield, *op. cit.*, Vol. II, pp. 648-650.

W. H. Gispen, *De Spreuken van Salomo (Korte Verklaring)*, Kampen, 1954, Vol. II, p. 234 f.

F. Lang, on πῦρ, Th.D.N.T., Vol. VI, p. 945.

E. J. Masselink, article in *Christian Cynosure*, Winter 1979, p. 21.

H. Ridderbos, *op. cit.*, p. 286.

This is the victorious life. But the victory cannot be obtained by human effort or exertion but only by faith. It is given to all those, and only to those, who, having been justified by faith, on the basis of Christ's vicarious sacrifice, derive all their power from the indwelling Holy Spirit.

Practical Lessons Derived from Romans 12

Verse 2

". . . Continue to let yourselves be transformed . . ." Certain suggestions showing how progress can be made toward this goal:

a. *Study the Word*. If possible not only on Sunday but even during the week, by means of the midweek Bible class, young people's group, or similar get-together.

b. Become involved in God-glorifying causes by contributing financially to them, and/or becoming a volunteer worker.

c. With the help of the minister or the church librarian post a list of the best literature, arranging the titles in various categories, to suit age-groups. For adults and adolescents be sure to include the books by Francis A. Schaeffer and C. Everett Koop (*How Should We Then Live?* and *Whatever Happened to the Human Race?*).

d. All of this—and much more—in conjunction with constant prayer for God's blessing.

Verses 3 and 16

". . . I bid every one among y o u not to think of himself more highly than he ought to think . . ." "Do not be conceited." Was it not the wish to be like God that caused the fall of Satan and his demonic followers? See Isa. 14:13, 14. And was it not a similar sinful desire that brought about man's fall? See Gen. 3:1-6.

Therefore, though it is true that "the love of money is *a* root of all kinds evil" (I Tim. 6:10), sinful pride is THE root of all evil. See also I Cor. 8:1-3.

Verses 4, 5

"For, just as we have many members in one body, and these members do not all have the same function, so we, who are many, are one body in Christ, and severally members of one another."

Diversity without unity spells confusion. Unity without diversity means monotony. As it is in the human body, so also in the church: both unity and diversity are needed and have been provided.

Imagine, for a moment, a marriage characterized by undiversified unity. In selecting garments to wear the bridegroom prefers blue. So does the bride for herself. In going out to eat, she gives the waiter her order. He says, "Make mine the same." The two even use the same dental cream, wear the same kind of glasses, talk with the same accent, etc., etc. How stale and monotonous such a marriage! Happy is the Christian marriage in which there is unity with respect to basic religious and moral beliefs and practices, but variety in tastes and talents. As long as this variety is made a servant of unity, and this unity a friend of diversity, all will be well. And this holds too for the human body and for the church, of which it is a symbol.

Verse 8

". . . without ulterior motive." This is indeed a very important restriction, for the person who contributes to the needs of others, but does this "with an ulterior motive," for example, merely to win public approval, is a hypocrite. He is "making as if . . ." On no class of people did Jesus pronounce such severe judgments as on the hypocrites of his day. See Matt. 23. The person who gives "with an ulterior motive" is leading a double life. He is generous only on the outside.

Therefore our prayer should always be, "Unite my heart to fear thy name," or, as this passage may also be rendered, "Give me an undivided heart, so that I may fear thy name" (Ps. 86:11).

Psalm 19 is ascribed to David. In rhyme its closing words, very appropriate in the present connection, are:

When thou dost search my life,
  May all my thoughts within
And all the words I speak
  Thy full approval win.
O Lord, thou art a rock to me,
  And my Redeemer thou shalt be.

Verses 14, 17, 19, 21

"Bless those who persecute y o u . . . Do not return evil for evil . . . Do not take revenge, beloved . . . overcome evil with good."

Why does Paul, with but slight variation, repeat this exhortation again and again?

Answer: (a) Because he himself, as a pastor was Kindness Personified (see I Thess. 2:7-10); (b) because he knew that returning good for evil was something against which sinful human nature violently rebels; and (c) because he knew that, nevertheless, if anything would succeed in filling the heart of an opponent with shame and penitence, *this* method would do it.

There are those who, on reading these verses, have made the comment, "Paul's advice will not work." They have even added that the apostle's recommended method of winning the opponent shows how little he knew about human nature. They are wrong. Paul does not say that the method he urges upon the Romans will always have the desired effect, but he knows that it is, nevertheless, the most effective method, and above all, that it is the only *right* method. See Luke 23:34; Acts 7:60; I Cor. 13.

Example from life. It was "under a cloud" that the former pastor had left. With part of the congregation he was, however, still popular. So, when his successor arrived, one of the members told the latter, "I do not recognize you as my pastor." The person to whom these words were addressed received grace to remain calm. Afterward he took special pains to perform his pastoral duties when sickness entered the home of the disgruntled church member. Result: the day came when that man told the minister, "I now fully and gladly recognize you as *my pastor*."

Summary of Chapter 12

When we arrive at chapter 12 we have reached the beginning of this letter's Practical Application, covering chapters 12-16. Chapter 12 consists of three well-defined sections, the second of which readily divides itself into two parts.

In the first of the three sections the apostle lovingly—note the word "brothers"—exhorts those whom he addresses to offer themselves to God as sacrifices which, in his sight, are living, holy, and well-pleasing. This first section, accordingly describes what should be the attitude of believers *to God*. They should render the wholehearted *spiritual worship* that is due him in view of "the great mercy" he has bestowed on them. As chapters 1-11 have shown, solely on the basis of divine grace, that is, the unmerited divine favor manifested in Christ's substitutionary self-sacrifice, believers have been declared righteous before God.

In keeping with this need of responsive wholehearted devotion, to be rendered by those who had been so abundantly blessed, is the exhortation that the addressed—which includes us all—in their life-style must no longer allow themselves to be outwardly conformed or fashioned after the pattern of this (evil) age, but instead must permit themselves to undergo a progressive and positive inner change, so as to become more and more Christlike. The goal and result of this inner transformation will be that they will *prove*—that is, will perceive, experience, and delight in—that which in the sight of God is good, well-pleasing, and perfect; that is, that which is in accordance with his will (verses 1 and 2).

In the first part of the second section—the section in which Paul describes what should be the attitude of believers *to fellow-believers*—it is made clear that progressive transformation will be impossible for those who, in their arrogance, imagine that they have already arrived. "Be and remain humble," is the essence of the exhortation. The saints must realize that the church resembles the human body, in which each part has a distinct function and none is self-sufficient. Similar is the situation in the church: each member needs the others. Each member should use his divinely imparted gift or gifts for the advantage of all the others. A list of seven gifts-functions follows, namely, that of prophesying, rendering practical service (probably in the capacity of deacon), teaching, exhorting, contributing to those in need (private benevolence), exercising leadership (probably as an elder), and showing mercy (as a visitor to the sick, etc.).

These tasks should be performed in accordance with the standard of faith (mentioned in connection with prophesying), without ulterior motive (in contributing to the needs of others), with diligence (in this manner exercising leadership), and (in connection with showing mercy) with cheerfulness (verses 3-8).

In the second part of this same section Paul emphasizes the supreme importance of love, here especially "brotherly love." Believers should prefer one another in honor. For further light on this see Phil. 2:3. The exercise of this virtue is possible only when believers have learned to know themselves.

This exhortation is followed by a miscellaneous group of admonitions, urging the exercise of Spirit-imparted virtues; such as enthusiasm, joy, hope, endurance, and prayer. The necessity of helping to relieve the needs of the saints is again stressed (see what has been said on this subject in connection with verses 7 and 8). In view of the fact that Paul will soon be starting out on his journey to Jerusalem with gifts (collected from several churches) for the poor saints in that city (Rom. 15:25; Acts 24:17), this emphasis is not surprising. Moreover, when Paul thinks about traveling—not just his own but that of many gospel witnesses—the exhortation, "Eagerly practice hospitality," fits in very well at this point (verses 9-13).

The final section (verses 14-21) shows what should be the believers' attitude *to outsiders*, including even *enemies*. In the midst of his own people, and even of people in general, the Christian should rejoice with those who rejoice, weep with those who weep, remain humble, showing this by readily associating with humble folk, and, as far as consonant with Christian principles, should live in peace with everybody. He should see to it that his affairs are right, so that nobody can accuse him of wrong-doing, and all will be impressed by his lofty moral-spiritual idealism.

In this connection there is one virtue Paul praises above all else, and, in varying phraseology, mentions again and again (verses 14, 17, 19-21). It is *the virtue of never returning evil for evil but always good for evil.* One should invoke God's blessing on persecutors, and by means of kindness strive to "heap coals of fire upon the heads" of those who had made the saints the objects of their cruelty. Yes, one should try to make these bitter opponents ashamed of themselves, so that, as a result they, in sorrow, flee to God for refuge. In this connection study the example of Joseph (Gen. 45:1-15; 50:15-21); Elisha (II Kings 6:20-23); Stephen (Acts 7:59, 60), and, above all, Jesus (Luke 23:34).

Outline (continued)

Practical Application

D. *What Should Be the Attitude of the Justified Believer Toward the Authorities*
"Let every person be in subjection to the governing authorities"
13:1-7

E. *What Should Be the Attitude of the Justified Believer Toward Everybody*
"Do not keep on owing anyone anything except to love one another"
13:8-10

F. *What Should Be the Attitude of the Justified Believer Toward the Lord Jesus Christ*
"The night is far advanced; the day is drawing near . . . Clothe yourselves with the Lord Jesus Christ, and make no provision for (the fulfilment of) the lusts of the flesh"
13:11-14

CHAPTER 13

ROMANS

13 1 Let every person be in subjection to the governing authorities. For there is no
authority except from God, and those that exist have been ordained by
God. 2 Consequently, he who opposes the authority is resisting the ordinance of
God, and those who do that will bring judgment on themselves. 3 For rulers are
not a terror to good conduct but to bad. Do you want to be free from fear of the one in
authority? Then do what is right, and you will receive his approval. 4 For he is God's servant
to do you good. But if you do wrong, be afraid, for he does not bear the sword in vain. He
is God's servant, an avenger to bring (God's) wrath upon the one who practices evil. 5 That
is why it is necessary to be in subjection, not only to avoid (God's) wrath, but also for the sake
of conscience. 6 This is also why y o u pay taxes, for when (the authorities) faithfully devote
themselves to this end, they are God's ministers. 7 Pay to all whatever y o u owe (them): tax
to whom tax (is due), custom to whom custom, respect to whom respect, honor to whom
honor.

D. *What Should Be the Attitude of the Justified Believer Toward the Authorities*
"Let every person be in subjection to the governing authorities" 13:1-7

When one reaches 13:1-7 a problem arises, that of apparent discontinuity. As many see it, there is no connection between 13:1-7 and either the preceding or the following context. *Love*, so very prominent in 12:9-21 and again in 13:8 f., is absent from 13:1-7. What is present is "the sword" (13:4).[351]

Besides, the theme of the fear-inspiring civil authority, "an avenger" who brings (God's) wrath upon the evil-doer (13:4), is completely absent from the preceding context of 13:1-7, as well as from the succeeding one (13:8 f.). As some see it, the distinctly spiritual flavor which marks the rest of this epistle is absent from 13:1-7.

It is for this reason that, as some see it, no Christian motif is to be heard in 13:1-7.[352] In fact there are those who regard this section as an alien body in Paul's exhortation.[353] But the mere statement of such a negative position does not constitute proof.

Still different is the method of treating 13:1-7 favored by those who say

---

351. There is, however, a close connection between the preceding context (12:9-21) and the following (13:8 f.), as is clear from the fact that μηδενί occurs in both 12:17 and 13:8, and in both cases in a context manifesting the spirit of love.

352. See O. Michel, *Der Brief an die Römer*, Göttingen, 1966, p. 289.

353. E. Käsemann, *Commentary on Romans* (tr. of *An Die Römer*), Grand Rapids, 1980, p. 352.

that when Paul mentions "governing authorities" (13:1) he is referring not only to civil authorities but also to a group of angels. That this "solution" should be rejected is shown in the footnote.[354]

On the positive side—i.e., the side of those who maintain that 13:1-7 is not only a part of the word of God, and was composed by Paul, but that it also suits the present context—note the following:

a. The section is not nearly as foreign to the context—whether preceding or following—as some seem to think. As to *the preceding context*, in 12:1, 2 Paul has urged the addressees to sacrifice their lives to God. Grateful and complete self-surrender is the only proper answer to the marvelous mercy God has shown. This means, of course, that the new life must reveal itself in every sphere of Christian enterprise and endeavor. Consistent with this starting point the apostle has indicated what should be the relation of believers *to God* (12:1, 2), to *one another* (verses 3-14), and *to outsiders*, even including *enemies* (12:14-21). Is it, then, so strange that he now also comments on the proper attitude of believers to *the civil authorities*, and this all the more so because he, being himself a Roman citizen by birth, and one who has received many favors from the Roman government, is writing to a church located in the very capital of the Roman Empire, the heart and center of government?

b. The exhortation to obey those in authority begins to look even more reasonable when one considers the following facts: a considerable proportion—though probably not the majority—of the membership of the Roman church consisted of Jews. That many of the Jews of that day and age were looking for an opportunity to shake off the yoke of subjection to Rome, and

---

354. Oscar Cullmann, in his book *Christ and Time* (tr. of *Christus und die Zeit*, Zürich, 1948), London, 1962 (see especially pp. 192-196), proceeds from the supposition that the late Jewish teaching concerning angels belongs to the content of New Testament doctrine. According to him evil angels, having been overcome by Christ, lost their sinister character, and were recommissioned to render favorable service for Christ.

Further, he argues that since the term used in Rom. 13:1, namely, ἐξουσίαι (here dat. pl. -αις) occurs also in Eph. 1:21; 6:12, where it refers to angels, it must indicate angels too in Rom. 13:1. But, as the context shows, in Rom. 13:1 it also signifies civil authorities. Accordingly, as Cullmann sees it, the word has a double meaning, referring both to the civil authorities and to the angels who, as it were, stand behind them. Cullmann finds that double sense also in I Cor. 2:8, "None of the rulers of this age understood it, for if they had, they would not have crucified the Lord of glory"; and in I Cor. 6:3, "Do y o u not know that we will judge angels?" Here, as he sees it, the civil authorities are viewed as the executive agents of the angelic powers.

Criticism.

1. The belief that in one and the same context a term or a statement can have two different meanings, in the present instance referring both to human beings and angels, reminds us of the double rule of interpretation adopted by some of the religious leaders of the sub-apostolic age. As they saw it, all Scripture passages must be interpreted *literally and allegorically*. In course of time this principle developed into the fourfold rule of exegesis: historical, aetiological, analogical, and allegorical. If one sets out on that road, where will he land? See L. Berkhof, *Principles of Biblical Interpretation*, Grand Rapids, 1950, p. 22. It is only fair to state, however, that Cullmann's theory is far more limited in its application.

2. Nowhere does Scripture teach that certain angels lost their evil character and were recommissioned to render service for Christ.

3. As to I Cor. 2:8, nowhere does Scripture ascribe the crucifixion of the Lord of glory to angels, whether good or bad.

were eager to become politically independent once more, with a king of their own, is clear from Scripture (John 6:14; 8:33; Acts 5:36, 37), from the writings of Josephus, and from other sources. Even in the capital there had been disturbances, with the result that Emperor Claudius had expelled all the Jews from that city (Acts 18:2, and see above, p. 18). When this edict was no longer in force many exiles had returned to Rome. But in view of the fact that the basic attitude of some of these people had probably not undergone a complete change, it is understandable that the apostle would issue this warning.

c. This all the more because he does not want Rome to think that the gospel of salvation through Jesus Christ is in any sense antagonistic to a properly functioning Roman government. In this connection it must be borne in mind that the epistle to the Romans was written several years before the terrible days of A.D. 64 (see N.T.C. on Luke, p. 32).

d. The connection between 13:1-7 and the preceding context may well be even closer than indicated so far. In 12:14-21 Paul had emphasized the principle of non-retaliation. Is it not possible that a believer might respond by saying, "With the help of God I will indeed return love for hatred. I will continue, by his grace, to do so even if my opponent remains hostile. I will invoke God's blessing on him and I will continue to be kind to him.—However, does this mean, then, that cruel, hardened criminals must be allowed to triumph? Is that in the best interest of the people as a whole, and would that really serve the cause of the gospel?" If his thinking was along this line,

---

4. With respect to I Cor. 6:3, how this passage can be interpreted to mean that people will be the executive agents of angelic powers is difficult to fathom. The real meaning of the passage is: If we are going to judge angels, how much more should we be able to settle disputes pertaining to the present life?

5. Here in Rom. 13:1-7 everything points to an earthly ruler, not to an angel or to angels. Note such items as the following: the ruler does not bear the sword "in vain." He punished the wrong-doer and commends the well-doer.

6. Reference to the necessity of paying taxes (13:6) also proves that the passage has nothing to do with angels or with the celestial realm.

7. A parallel to Rom. 13:1-7 is I Peter 2:13-17. But Peter describes the rule of the king and of governors as being "a human institution," probably indicating an institution established among human beings but deriving its authority from God. There is no hint here of any connection with angels. In fact, according to apostolic teaching, Satan and his underlings are never described as standing behind and supporting the good work carried on by civil authorities. On the contrary, the influence exerted by evil spirits is and remains evil, and their authors are doomed. See Rom. 16:20; II Cor. 4:4; Eph. 6:10-12; I Peter 5:8; II Peter 2:4.

Cullmann was by no means the only defender of the double meaning theory, as applied to Rom. 13:1-7. See for example, also M. Dibelius, *Die Geisterwelt im Glauben des Paulus*, Göttingen, 1909. Others who, for a while at least, defended it in one form or another, were K. L. Schmidt, K. Barth, G. Dehn, etc. Even Cranfield for a while felt attracted to it. It is only fair to state, however, that among those who upon further study abandoned this theory, were Dibelius, Barth, and Cranfield. See the latter's admission, *op. cit.*, p. 659.

Lekkerkerker, in his very interesting summary (*op. cit.*, Vol. II, pp. 129-136) traces the essence of this theory back to some second century A.D. gnostics, and shows how it gave rise to the persuasion, among many, that governments were able to yield themselves to demonic powers; example, Germany during Hitler's reign. In other words, people began to see a close link between Rom. 13:1-7 and Rev. 13, as interpreted by them.

It is probably fair to state that by now the double-meaning theory has lost much of its earlier fascination.

the apostle supplies the answer in 13:1-7: *the ruler does not bear the sword in vain*!

e. To all this should be added the fact that what Paul is saying here in 13:1-7 corresponds with the very teaching of Jesus Christ himself (Mark 12:13-17), unless, with some, we adopt the position of certain redactionists, namely, that Mark's report is nothing but a fabrication. With such a position one cannot argue. The debate ends, and believer and non-believer each goes his way.

Paul does not, within the compass of these few verses, give us a complete treatise on the respective rights of church and state. He does not give us *explicit* answers to such questions as, "If the government orders me to do one thing, and God, through his Word, tells me to do the opposite, what must I do?" and "Does the moment ever arrive when, because of continued governmental oppression and corruption, the citizens have the right, and perhaps even the duty, to overthrow such a government and to establish another in its place?" Though the answers may well be *implied* in the statement that "the one in authority . . . is *God's servant to do you good*," and though the answer to the first question has been clearly stated by Peter (Acts 5:29), inquiries into such matters lie beyond the sphere of Paul's immediate interest. See, however, also under verse 2.

Being, except for Jesus Christ himself, the greatest missionary who ever walked the earth, Paul is interested in the preservation of good order so that the cause of gospel proclamation to the glory of God may go forward.

With respect to the connection between 13:1-7 and *the immediately following context*, this can be indicated in a few words, for it is very clear. Verse 7 reads, "Pay to all whatever y o u *owe* them . . ." And verse 8 (the first verse of the new section) begins with, "Do not *keep on owing* anyone anything except to love one another."

1. Let every person be in subjection to the governing authorities.

Literally Paul says, "Let every *soul* . . . ," but the word "soul," as here used, means person, human being.[355] The apostle, writing by inspiration, wants

355. In the New Testament as a whole ψυχή occurs about 100 times, πνεῦμα more than 370 times. It is entirely impossible to draw a sharp distinction—as is often done—between these two words, as if in the New Testament ψυχή always has one meaning, πνεῦμα another. It is true that when *the apostle Paul* was thinking of man's invisible being in its relation to God, he generally used the word πνεῦμα. However, in the New Testament as a whole there is considerable overlapping of meanings. One should never say, "In the New Testament ψυχή is man's invisible part considered as that which animates his body; πνεῦμα is that same immaterial entity viewed in its relation to God." The subject is far more complicated than this generalization indicates. For example, the Greek equivalent for *breath* can be either ψυχή (Acts 20:10) or πνεῦμα (II Thess. 2:8). Similarly, the concept *life*, with emphasis on the physical, can be expressed either by πνεῦμα (Luke 8:55) or by ψυχή (Matt. 2:20). Not only is it possible for the πνεῦμα to be provoked (Acts 17:16), the ψυχή too can be stirred up (Acts 14:2). The πνεῦμα rejoices in God, to be sure (Luke 1:47), but the ψυχή too is said to magnify the Lord (Luke 1:46). An incorporeal being may be a πνεῦμα (Heb. 12:23), but may also be a ψυχή (Rev. 6:9). On the other hand, when the reference is to the Holy Spirit the word used is always πνεῦμα, with or without modifier (Mark 1:8-12; 3:29; 12:36; 13:11; Luke 1:15, etc.). An *unclean spirit* is πνεῦμα ἀκάθαρτον (Mark 1:23, 26, etc.). At times a synonym is used (Mark 9:17, 25). The word πνεῦμα can even indicate a disposition (I Cor. 4:21, "a spirit of gentle-

everyone to subject himself voluntarily to the then existing governing authorities.[356] In the divine providence the Roman government of Paul's day was such that within its boundaries compliance with the will of God and wholehearted consecration to him were possible. As Paul puts it:

For there is no authority except from God, and those that exist have been ordained by God.

The civil magistrates to whom Paul refers, from the emperor down to the rulers of the lowest rank, in the final analysis owed their appointment and right to govern to God. It was by his will and in his providence that they had been appointed to maintain order, encourage well-doing, and punish wrong-doing.

2. Consequently, he who opposes the authority is resisting the ordinance of God . . .

Does this mean, then, that the apostle was urging unlimited compliance, a subjection so absolute that even when the command of the magistrate should be in direct conflict with God's revealed will, it must nevertheless be obeyed? Of course not!

We should not forget that Paul was a Jew, well-versed in the Old Testament, as he proves again and again in his epistles. Therefore he also knew about, and heartily approved of, the courage shown by Daniel and/or his three friends when they disobeyed royal edicts and ordinances that were manifestly contrary to God's will as revealed in his law. See chapters 1, 3, and 6 of the book of Daniel. These chapters show that God rewards those who, in extremely difficult circumstances, remain faithful to himself, and who therefore deliberately disobey their earthly ruler.

---

ness"). On the other hand, when the reference is to the entire *self* or *person*, so that in a parallel passage a personal pronoun is used, or so that such a pronoun might have been substituted, this *self* is always ψυχή (Mark 10:45; cf. I Tim. 2:6). Here belong also Rom. 2:9, where the expression "for every soul of man" means "for every person (or human being)," and Rom. 11:3 where "my soul" or "my life" means "me." The word ψυχή also indicates the personal pronoun in Matt. 12:18; Luke 12:19; Acts 2:27, 41, 43; 3:23; 7:14; Heb. 10:38, 39; James 1:21; 5:20; I Peter 1:9; 3:20; Rev. 16:2. And so also here in Rom. 13:1 "every soul" amounts to "every person." This meaning of ψυχή is probably influenced by Hebrew usage.

Since there are these distinctions but also many areas of overlapping, it is impossible to lay down rigid rules. One can perhaps say that in general πνεῦμα stresses mental activity, ψυχή emotional. It is the πνεῦμα that perceives (Mark 2:8), plans (Acts 19:21), and knows (I Cor. 2:11). It is the ψυχή that is sorrowful (Matt. 26:38). The πνεῦμα prays (I Cor. 14:14), the ψυχή loves (Mark 12:30). Also ψυχή is often broader in scope, indicating the sum-total of life that rises above the physical; while πνεῦμα is more restricted. Often (especially in Paul's epistles), *but by no means always*, πνεῦμα indicates the human spirit in its relation to God, man's self-consciousness or personality viewed as the subject in acts of worship or in acts related to worship, such as praying, bearing witness, etc. But again, no hard and fast rule can be laid down. Every occurrence of either word will have to be interpreted in the light of the origin of the particular passage in which it occurs, and in the light of its specific context and of parallel passages.

356. Note the word ὑπερεχούσαις, dat. pl. f. pres. participle of ὑπερέχω, to hold (power) over. The sense "being" or "holding" over, being supreme, being better (than), shines through in every instance of the word's use in the New Testament: counting the other person *better* than himself (Phil. 2:3); all-*surpassing* excellence (Phil. 3:8); the peace of God *surpassing* all understanding (Phil. 4:7); *supreme* authority (I Peter 2:13).

It is clear, then, that, in writing as he does here in Rom. 13:2, the apostle is thinking of the ruler who is performing his duty of preserving order, approving good behavior, and punishing evil. In *that* case he who opposes the authority is, indeed, resisting the divine ordinance. Paul adds:

. . . and those who do that will bring judgment [not necessarily *damnation*, A.V.] **on themselves.**

The apostle is not establishing a universally valid principle that opposing the authority and disobeying a command issued by a civil magistrate is always wrong. In reading Paul's letters, filled with instructions and exhortations, one must be sure to make allowance for restrictions or qualifications, whether expressed or implied. Sèe, for example, I Cor. 5:9, 10, where the apostle is, as it were, saying, "Please do not interpret this exhortation as if there were no limits to its application."

That the apostle was referring to normal, and not to outrageous or mistaken, governmental functioning is clear from verse

3. For rulers are not a terror to good conduct but to bad.

In these verses Paul refutes the exclusively negative attitude toward civil authorities, as if they were always intent on doing evil, and as if one should be afraid of them. To be sure, the magistrates punish, but under normal circumstances those who receive punishment have only themselves to blame. "Rulers," says Paul, "are not a terror to good conduct but to bad." It is clear that in saying this he is personifying these two kinds of conduct. He means, of course, that rulers are not a terror to those who conduct themselves properly but to those who conduct themselves badly. It is the latter who have reason to fear.

It has been said that it is strange that Paul would speak so favorably about rulers. Had he not himself been treated cruelly by the civil authorities? See Acts 16:19-24. Cf. II Cor. 11:25: "thrice was I beaten with rods." And was it not the Roman "governor" Pontius Pilate who had unjustly condemned Jesus to death?

The answer generally given is, "These were the exceptions that prove the rule." Though there may well be some merit in this answer, is it not possible to add something to it, which will bring out even more clearly that the apostle was right when he said what he did here in Rom. 13:3?

In the case of Paul's experience at Philippi the authorities had been led astray by the mob, so that *they thought* that they were actually punishing wrongdoers. Subsequently, when they became aware of their mistake, they tried to make up (Acts 16:38, 39).

And as to Pilate, again and again he refused to condemn Jesus to death (Luke 23:4, 13-16, 20, 22). Finally, for selfish reasons, he succumbed to the demands of the Jews (23:24). In this connection note also the significant words, "*Y o u* handed him over to be killed, and *y o u* disowned him before Pilate, though *he* had decided to release him" (Acts 3:13).

Paul's statement that, in the normal run of events, rulers are not a terror to good conduct but to bad, stands therefore.

Turning now to the individual believer—note change from plural (those who) to singular (*you* instead of *y o u*)—the apostle continues:

Do you want to be free from fear of the one in authority? Then do what is right, and you will receive his approval.

This does not necessarily mean that the person who does what is right is going to receive a merit badge, ribbon, medal of honor, or—speaking in terms of Paul's own day—that a monument will be erected for him. It does mean, however, that the one in authority will form a favorable opinion of that well-behaved person, and will, whether only in his heart or even by means of an openly expressed commendation, approve of him. Cf. Rom. 2:29; I Peter 2:14.

4. For he is God's servant to do you good.

The civil magistrate is indeed God's servant, for, as verses 1 and 2 have shown, he was, in the final analysis, appointed by God and received his authority from God. Under normal conditions and circumstances the ruler, in the sphere of civil government, represents the divine will with respect to the people's conduct as citizens.

Moreover, the basic aim of the one in authority is not to hurt but to help, "to do you good." As the result of the work and watchfulness of these governmental representatives the believer is able to lead "a tranquil and quiet life in all gravity and godliness" (I Tim. 2:2).

But if you do wrong, be afraid, for he does not bear the sword in vain.

The *wrong-doer* better be afraid. First of all, he should have been afraid to do wrong. Having done wrong, he better be afraid, for punishment will not stay away. He should realize that the magistrate does not bear the sword "in vain," that is, "to no purpose," "for nothing," or, in colloquial language, "just for fun." The ruler bears that sword in order to instill fear of doing wrong; and, in order to inflict punishment when wrong has been done. The opinion according to which Paul simply means that the emperor and those who represent him wield military power merely to enable them to quell the forces of rebellion, hardly does justice to the present context, which refers to wrong-doers in general, not only to rebels. By means of the sword wrong-doing is punished. In fact, the vicious, dangerous criminal may even be put to death.

The fact that in the New Testament the use of the sword is often connected with the idea of putting to death is clear from such passages as Luke 21:24; Acts 12:2; 16:27; Rev. 13:10. See also Heb. 11:34, where "escaped the edge of the sword" means "escaped death." It should be clear, therefore, that the argument in favor of executing dangerous criminals, who have committed horrible crimes, is based not only on Gen. 9:6 but also on Rom. 13:4.

He—that is, the one in authority—**is God's servant, an avenger to bring (God's) wrath upon the one who practices evil.**

The fact that the authority is "*God's servant*" is repeated here. See verses 1, 2 and the beginning of verse 4. The apostle adds, ". . . an avenger to bring (God's) wrath," etc. The question has been asked, "Whose wrath? His own or God's?" The answer, however, is clear, for the sentence begins with the words, "He is *God's* servant to bring wrath," *God's* wrath, therefore. For further proof see on 12:19, p. 421.

In his infinite kindness God, through Paul, caused this message to be delivered to the Roman church, in order that its members—and further all, throughout the ages, who would read this letter or to whom it would be read and/or explained—might be kept from practicing evil, and might, by the grace of God and the power of the Holy Spirit, turn to God for pardon and for strength to live orderly and sanctified lives.

5. That is why it is necessary to be in subjection, not only to avoid (God's) wrath, but also for the sake of conscience.

Now a Christian's political conduct must not be motivated or regulated *only* by fear of incurring God's wrath. On the contrary, subjecting oneself to the divinely authorized civil authority has something to do with the believer's relation to *God*. The Christian knows that it is God's will that he subject himself to the authorities which God, in his providence, has placed over him for his (the subject's) good. Accordingly, failure to subject himself results in the accusing voice of conscience. Therefore, for both of these reasons, namely, to avoid God's wrath and to satisfy his conscience, one should voluntarily subject himself to the ruling authority.

This matter of conscience must not be passed over lightly. It should be borne in mind that a Christian's enlightened conscience is his sense of obligation *to God*. Note the words, "Submit yourselves *for the Lord's sake* to every authority instituted among men" (I Peter 2:13).

On *conscience* see also pp. 97, 98 (on Rom. 2:15), p. 310 (on 9:1); further: Acts 23:1; 24:16; I Cor. 8:7, 10, 12; 10:25-29; II Cor. 1:12; 4:2; 5:11; I Tim. 1:5, 19; 3:9; 4:2; II Tim. 1:3; Titus 1:15.

6. This is also why y o u[357] pay taxes, for when (the authorities) faithfully devote themselves to this end, they are God's ministers.

The nearest antecedent to the word "this" is "for the sake of conscience." It was because their conscience told them that it was right to pay taxes that they paid them. It was right, since it was in harmony with God's purpose for their lives. The collection of taxes must not be considered a disgraceful, tyrannical imposition. No, it is necessary for the maintenance of conditions that make normal living possible. Therefore those who faithfully discharge their duty of collecting taxes are doing so in their capacity as God's *ministers*.

For the word "ministers" Paul here uses a word (pl. of *leitourgos*; cf. *liturgy*) which generally has religious implications. Thus angels are God's *ministers* (Heb. 1:7) and *ministering* spirits (Heb. 1:14). Very properly the word is used with reference to *priests*, and in Heb. 8:2 Christ, in his capacity as highpriest, is called "a minister *(leitourgos)* of the sanctuary, the true tabernacle . . ." Also very properly Paul calls himself "a minister *(leitourgos)* of Christ Jesus to the

357. Note return to plural.

Gentiles" (Rom. 15:16). Nevertheless, here in Rom. 13:6 Paul, instead of using the more common word (pl. of *diakonos*, cf. deacon), as a designation of these *servants* who collect taxes, calls them *leitourgoi*; i.e., *ministers*; in fact, "*God's* ministers."

Is not the implication this, that, in the final analysis, the governing authorities owe their authority not to people but to God to whom they are responsible for all their actions; and that the citizens should so regard them; and, when these officials faithfully carry out their duty, even that of collecting taxes, should so honor them?[358]

Of course, this very principle has implications also for the officials, as Calvin correctly observes when he states, "It behooves them to remember that whatever they receive from the people is, as it were, public property, and not to be spent in gratification of private indulgence."

In close connection with the immediately preceding passage ("This is also why y o u pay taxes," etc.), Paul continues:

7. Pay to all whatever y o u owe (them): tax to whom tax (is due), custom to whom custom, respect to whom respect, honor to whom honor.

In connection with monetary obligations owed to the government the addressed—which includes us all—are exhorted that whatever is due should be paid to the proper persons: "tax," levied on persons and property (Luke 20:22-25), should be paid to whom tax is due; "custom," levied on imported and exported goods, similarly, to whom custom is due.

On the next expression ("respect to whom respect") opinions differ widely. The word here rendered "respect"[359] at times indicates "terror" (see verse 3 above), or "fear" (for example, "of the Jews," John 7:13; 19:38; 20:19), or "reverence" with God as object (Phil. 2:12). The same word can, however, also mean "respect" (of a slave for his master, I Peter 2:18; and cf. Eph. 5:33, where the cognate verb is used to indicate the *respect* a wife owes her husband). Since Paul is here (in Rom. 13:7) exhorting the Romans to render to *the officials* their due, the rendering "respect" would appear to be best.[360]

What Paul probably means is something on this order: "Simply paying y o u r taxes is not enough. Telling the officials, 'Here's the money, and now get out,' will never do. Y o u should *respect* these men for the sake of their

358. Considered ideally, that is, as God sees them and as they should be regarded, the spiritual and the political spheres are not nearly as widely separated as we generally view them. Note how in the New Testament the same terminology is applied to both spheres:

		Spiritual Sphere	*Political Sphere*
ὑποτάσσω	to be subject to	Rom. 8:7	Rom. 13:1
ἐξουσία	authority	Rev. 22:14	Rom. 13:1
διάκονος	servant	Col. 1:7	Rom. 13:4
λειτουργός	minister	Rom. 15:16	Rom. 13:6

359. φόβος (here acc. s. - ν).

360. The arguments of Cranfield in defense of the theory that the apostle is referring to the debt, namely fear, owed to *God* have not convinced me. Reference to Mark 12:17, where the word does not even occur, does not rescue this theory. But for the sake of fairness by all means read Cranfield's lengthy argument in substantiation of his view, *op. cit.*, pp. 670-673.

office, and *honor* them in view of their faithful devotion to their task (see verse 6). Remember: they are *God's ministers*! And by means of what is done with this money not only the people in general, including y o u yourselves, are benefited, but so is the cause of the gospel."

---

8 Do not keep on owing anyone anything except to love one another, for he who loves his neighbor has fulfilled the law. 9 For this, "You shall not commit adultery, you shall not murder, you shall not steal, you shall not covet," and whatever other commandment there may be, is summed up in the saying, "You shall love your neighbor as yourself." 10 Love does no harm to the neighbor. Therefore the fulfilment of (the) law is love.

E. *What Should Be the Attitude of the Justified Believer Toward Everybody*

"Do not keep on owing anyone anything except to love one another"
13:8-10

8. Do not keep on owing anyone anything except to love one another . . .

Other translations:

a. "Y o u owe no man anything . . ."[361] Although grammatically this translation is indeed possible, it would be out of line with the context, for Paul has just now been telling those addressed that they should pay to all whatever they owed them; hence, all their debts (verse 7). So not the indicative but the imperative mood must be meant here in verse 8.

b. "Owe no man anything . . ." This rendering would create the impression that Paul calls all borrowing wrong, a position that is clearly contrary to Scripture. See Exod. 22:25; Ps. 37:26; Matt. 5:42; Luke 6:35.

c. "Owe no man anything; only do love one another." This is perhaps even worse. It changes the one beautiful thought of the original into two separate ideas: not only are the readers-hearers told never to owe anything to anybody, but in addition they are exhorted to love one another! The original clause of eight words cannot be made to convey all this.[362]

d. "Let no debt remain outstanding, except the continuing debt to love one another . . . ," N.I.V., and somewhat similar: N.E.B., Weymouth. I can find no fault whatever with this excellent rendering. It is completely true to the original. On the other hand, if one wishes to show most clearly the close connection between verses 7 and 8, where the original uses words based on the same stem,[363] the rendering "Pay to all whatever *y o u owe* . . ." (verse 7), followed by "*Do not keep on owing* anyone anything except to love one another . . ." (verse 8) would seem to be required.

---

361. The word used in the original can be interpreted either as a second per. pl. present indicative or imperative. The original would use the same form for either: ὀφείλετε.

362. I cannot agree, therefore, with Murray's interpretation, *op. cit.*, pp. 158, 159; instead I am in accord with Cranfield's reasoning on this point, *op. cit.*, p. 674.

363. ὀφειλάς . . . ὀφείλετε.

Three thoughts are clearly implied here:

First of all, this is a condemnation of the practice of some, who are ever ready to borrow but very slow to repay the borrowed sum. In this connection see Ps. 37:21, "The wicked person borrows but does not repay . . ."

Secondly, this is clearly a eulogy of love, composed by an author who, somewhat earlier, had written I Cor. 13. He is saying that among all the debts a person may have incurred there is one that can never be repaid in full, namely, the debt of love. Moreover, in the present connection Paul is thinking not, first of all, of the debt we owe to God, but, *as the context indicates*, of the debt we owe to our fellowmen. So,

Thirdly, it is a love "for one another." But this "one another," does not, in this instance, merely mean "for all fellow-believers." These, to be sure, are included. One can even say, they are included *in a special way* (see 12:10, 13; Gal. 6:10), but by adding **"for he who loves his neighbor has fulfilled the law"** it is made clear that all those with whom the believer comes into contact—and of course particularly those with special needs—are included. In fact, in a sense no one is excluded from this all-embracing love.

God's holy law, to be sure, does not save anyone. See Rom. 8:3. Nevertheless, once a person has been justified by faith, he, out of gratitude, motivated and enabled by the Holy Spirit, desires to do what God wants him to do. And this is found in the law of the Ten Commandments, as summarized in Lev. 19:18, and later in the words of Jesus as recorded in Matt. 22:39; Mark 12:31; Luke 10:27b.

9. For this, "You shall not commit adultery, you shall not murder, you shall not steal, you shall not covet," and whatever other commandment there may be, is summed up in the saying, "You shall love your neighbor as yourself."

The very fact that Paul mentions these commandments in the order Nos. 7, 6, 8, 10 (cf. Exod. 20:1-17), not even mentioning the fifth and the ninth, but covering these with the summarizing expression "and whatever other commandment there may be," shows that it is not his main intention to enter into the substance of each separate "Thou shalt not." Rather he wishes to emphasize the one great truth, namely, that all these commandments touching the believer's attitude toward his fellowmen "are brought together under one head" in the one, great summarizing rule, "You shall love your neighbor as yourself."

This proves that every negative command ("You shall not") is at bottom a positive command. The meaning, therefore is: "You shall love, and therefore not commit adultery but preserve the sacredness of the marriage-bond. You shall love, and therefore not murder but help your neighbor keep alive and well. You shall love, and accordingly not steal anything that belongs to your neighbor but rather protect his possessions. You shall love, and as a result not covet what belongs to your neighbor but rejoice in the fact that it is his."

The expression, "You shall love your neighbor *as yourself*" merits a word of explanation. What Paul—and before him Jesus—actually means must at least include this thought: it is a certain thing that a person will love himself, and it is also certain that he will do so in spite of the fact that the self he loves has many faults. So, then, also he should most certainly love his neighbor. He may not *like* him, but he should *love* him, and should do so regardless of that neighbor's faults.

10. Love does no harm to the neighbor. Therefore the fulfilment of (the) law is love.

In the words, "Love does no harm to the neighbor," we have an example of a figure of speech called *litotes*. This means that a negative expression of this type implies a strong affirmative. So, "He's no fool" may mean, "He is very shrewd." And similarly "Love does no harm to the neighbor" means "Love greatly benefits the neighbor." ". . . does no harm" is an understatement for "greatly benefits." The reason that this truth is here expressed negatively may well have been to make it coincide with the law's prohibitions.

Notice how beautiful is the style of verse 10: the verse begins and ends with the word *love*. The apostle is indeed very consistent, for if *the fulfilment* of the law does no harm to the neighbor but benefits him, and if love—and only love—does exactly that, then the fulfilment of the law must be love.

It is exactly Spirit-wrought love, this alone, that is sufficiently powerful to cause a person to remove all obstacles and to love his neighbor even though that neighbor is perhaps not a pleasant person! It is *love* that "is not easily angered, keeps no record of wrongs, always protects and always hopes" (I Cor. 13:5, 7). Such human love has its origin in God, for "God is love" (I John 4:8). It was Jesus who, a few hours before his crucifixion told his disciples, "A new precept I give y o u, that y o u keep on loving one another; just as I have loved y o u, that y o u also keep on loving one another" (John 13:34).

---

11 And (do this) especially because y o u know how critical the time is. The hour has arrived for y o u to wake up from (y o u r) slumber, for our salvation is nearer now than when we (first) believed. 12 The night is far advanced; the day is drawing near. So let us put aside the deeds of darkness and put on the armor of light. 13 Let us walk honorably, as in the daytime, not in orgies and drinking bouts, not in sexual excesses and debaucheries, not in dissension and jealousy. 14 Rather, clothe yourselves with the Lord Jesus Christ, and make no provision for (the fulfilment of) the lusts of the flesh.

F. *What Should Be the Attitude of the Justified Believer Toward the Lord Jesus Christ*

"The night is far advanced; the day is drawing near . . . clothe yourselves with the Lord Jesus Christ, and make no provision for (the fulfilment of) the lusts of the flesh"

13:11-14

The discussion of this section will follow this outline:

a. Exegesis of verses 11, 12a; of verses 12b, 13; and of verse 14.

b. Statement of the problem that arises in connection with this section (verses 11-14).

c. Discussion of proposed solutions.

That there is a close connection between verses 11, 12a and that which precedes is evident from the very opening words:

11, 12a. And (do this) especially because y o u know how critical the time is. The hour has arrived for y o u to wake up from (y o u r) slumber, for our salvation is nearer now than when we (first) believed. The night is far advanced; the day is drawing near.[364]

When Paul says, "And (do this)," he is referring at least to what is found in the immediately preceding verses. Therefore, he is now saying, " 'Love your neighbor as yourself,' but do it not only because the law demands this, but *especially also* because y o u know how very critical is the time in which we are now living." It is possible, however, that in saying "And (do this)" he is referring to the broader context, extending all the way back to 12:1 f.

By saying, "especially because y o u know how critical the time is," and immediately adding, "The hour has arrived for y o u to wake up from y o u r slumber, for our salvation is nearer now than when we first believed," he is exhorting the membership of the Roman church—and us all—to lay aside their (our) sinful practices and, with the help of the Holy Spirit, to advance in sanctification. "Our salvation is nearer now than when we (first) believed" means "The culmination of our salvation is closer to us in time now than it was at the moment when we first confessed our faith in the Lord Jesus Christ and were baptized."

It is clear that the apostle is making an appeal to eschatology; that is, to the doctrine of the Lord's Return. He is using this as an incentive to holy living. One finds a similar exhortation and argument in Phil. 4:4-7; I Thess. 5:1-11, 23; Heb. 10:24 f.; James 5:7-11; I Peter 4:7-11; and, of course, also already in the teaching of Jesus (Matt. 25:31-46; Mark 13:33-37 etc.).

Such an appeal is especially understandable when we consider that the Lord is coming "to reward his servants." Cf. the parable of *The Watchful Servants* (Luke 12:35-48); that of *The Five Foolish and The Five Sensible Girls* (Matt. 25:1-13); and, in fact, also the rest of Matt. 25. Add Rom. 14:10; II Cor. 5:10; II Tim. 4:1; James 5:9; I Peter 4:5; cf. Eccl. 12:14.

---

364. καὶ τοῦτο, and at that; or and that too; and especially. See I Cor. 6:6, 8.

εἰδότες, 2nd perf. masc. act. nom. pl. participle of οἶδα, with sense of present.

The principal verb has to be supplied, perhaps ποιήσατε, 2nd per. pl. aor. act. imperat. of ποιέω, to do.

καιρόν, acc. s. of καιρός, here probably the critical time, decisive moment, moment of destiny. In 5:6 and 9:9 the word means appointed time; in 8:18 and 11:5 present time. The word καιρός should be distinguished from χρόνος, which indicates time as progression from past into present into future, progression of moments.

ὕπνου, gen. s. of ὕπνος, sleep, slumber. Cf. *hypnotism*.

ἐγερθῆναι, aor. mid. and pass. infin. of ἐγείρω, to awaken; in mid. to rouse oneself; hence, to wake up; here used symbolically, to a life of greater sanctification.

προέκοψεν, 3rd per. s. aor. indicat. of προκόπτω, to go forward; here: to be (far) advanced.

ἤγγικεν, 3rd per. s. perf. indicat. of ἐγγίζω, to approach, draw near.

The words, "The night is far advanced; the day is drawing near" indicate that for God's people the present era of darkness, sin, and sadness is rapidly coming to an end; and the never-ending age of light, holiness, and gladness is near. Paul, as it were, hears the cry of the night watchman, "Wake up, for the morning is dawning."

Here we must be careful, however. Paul cannot have meant, "Christ will return tomorrow. He will come back immediately." Such teaching would have amounted to a refutation of his own earlier statement, namely, that the Return would be preceded by the coming of the apostasy and the arrival of "the man of lawlessness, the son of perdition" (II Thess. 2:1-5). Compare with this the similar teaching of Jesus himself (Matt. 24:21, 29; 25:5). What the apostle is saying, therefore, is this, "*The day* will be here very soon."

12b, 13. So let us put aside the deeds of darkness and put on the armor of light. Let us walk honorably, as in the daytime, not in orgies and drinking bouts, not in sexual excesses and debaucheries, not in dissension and jealousy.[365]

Because of the critical time in which Paul and his contemporaries were living, and because of the tremendous issues at stake—nothing less than to glorify God forever in heaven or to suffer forever with Satan and all the lost in hell—Paul urges all—including even himself (note "Let us")—to put aside the deeds of darkness and to put on the armor of light.

He summarizes the deeds of darkness in verse 13. Though the six vices mentioned do not constitute a complete list, they are sufficiently representative to indicate what the apostle has in mind. Besides, we are permitted,

---

365. ἀποθώμεθα, let us put aside; and ἐνδυσώμεθα, let us put on, are 1st per. pl. aor. middle subjunctives; respectively, of ἀποτίθημι and ἐνδύω. Of the latter verb the 2nd per. aor. imperat. mid. occurs in verse 14 ("Put on," or "Clothe yourselves with").

τὰ ὅπλα, weapons, armor; see also on Rom. 6:13, p. 202, including footnote 174.

ὡς, as, meaning: as is actually the case.

εὐσχημόνως, lit. in good form; hence, in a becoming manner, gracefully, honorably. Cf. I Cor. 14:40; I Thess. 4:12.

The following six nouns (three pairs of two each) are all in the dative. In the original the first four nouns are in the pl., the last two in the sing.

κῶμος (see also Gal. 5:21; I Peter 4:3), boisterous merrymaking, carousing, orgy.

μέθη (Luke 21:34; Gal. 5:21), drinking bout.

For the meaning of κοίτη see above, on Rom. 9:10, p. 319. Here (in Rom. 13:13) indecency, sexual excess.

ἀσέλγεια, debauchery, licentiousness; so also in Mark 7:22; II Cor. 12:21; Gal. 5:19; Eph. 4:19; I Peter 4:3; II Peter 2:2; Jude 4.

ἔρις (Rom. 1:29; see p. 81), strife, dissension. Besides its occurrence in Rom. 1:29 and 13:13 it is also found in I Cor. 1:11; 3:3; II Cor. 12:20; Gal. 5:20; Phil. 1:15; I Tim. 6:4; and Titus 3:9.

ζῆλος, depending on the context, can mean zeal, enthusiasm, ardor (Rom. 10:2; II Cor. 9:2; Phil. 3:6; but can also mean jealousy, as here in Rom. 13:13 and in I Cor. 3:3; II Cor. 11:2; 12:20; Gal. 5:20. In II Cor. 7:7, 11 it seems to refer to *ardent concern*. The πυρὸς ζῆλος of Heb. 10:27 is a raging, devouring fire; and the ζῆλος of James 3:14, 16 spells *envy*. The word also occurs in John 2:17 in the sense of *zeal*, and twice in the book of Acts (5:17; 13:45) in that of *jealousy*.

of course, to add "and the like" to the list, as in a similar but lengthier list found in Gal. 5:19-21.

These vices comprise the deeds of darkness, often even performed in the dark, but certainly always encouraged by "the prince of darkness."

Though it is not necessary to suppose that either Jews or Gentiles were exempt from these evil deeds and dispositions, some of those that are mentioned remind us especially of the sins pertaining to the world of the Gentiles (cf. Rom. 1:28 f.). As has been shown—see pp. 20-23—most of the members of the Roman church had probably been gathered out of the world of the Gentiles. For more information on the individual vices here mentioned see footnote 365.

Living as we do, in an age in which all the emphasis is on the positive, so that we are constantly being warned never to say "Don't" but always "Do," we note that Paul is not afraid to say, "Do not . . . not . . . not."

However, he also knows that the only way to overcome evil is by means of goodness. So, between two negatives—"let us put aside" and "not in orgies," etc., he places, "Let us put on the armor of light." Now if *darkness* indicates (spiritual) dullness, depravity, and despair, *light* certainly spells (spiritual) learning, love, and laughter (the joy inexpressible and full of glory mentioned in I Peter 1:8), though in the present context the emphasis is on *love* (13:8-10).

Note that here again Paul uses military language ("armor of light,") as he does often (Rom. 6:13; 13:2; I Cor. 9:7; II Cor. 6:7; 10:4; Eph. 6:10-20; I Thess 5:8; II Tim. 2:3). There must be a reason for this. A good soldier does not lie down on the job, exerts himself to the full, has a definite goal in mind, uses effective armor, obeys rules. Does not all this apply also to soldiers for Christ?

14. Rather, clothe yourselves with the Lord Jesus Christ, and make no provision for (the fulfilment of) the lusts of the flesh.[366]

This closing admonition is a most apt and beautiful summary of what the apostle has been saying in 12:1-13:13. It touches on both justification and sanctification. It means that, having accepted Christ and having been baptized, believers should now not rest on their laurels, but should continue to do in practice what they have already done in principle (Gal. 3:27). Paul is, as it were, saying, "Having laid aside the garment of sin, now deck yourselves more and more with the robe of Christ's righteousness, so that whenever

---

366. For ἐνδύσασθε see above, footnote 365.

σαρκός, "for the flesh" (objective gen.). Literally the final clause reads: "and for the flesh do not make (or: stop making) provision for lusts." Another instance of abbreviated expression. On the meaning of σάρξ see footnote 187, p. 217. Meaning h. (sinful human nature) applies here.

πρόνοια, in the New Testament only here (in the sense of *provision*) and in Acts 24:2 (*foresight*).

ἐπιθυμίας, acc. pl. of ἐπιθυμία, here meaning lust, sinful desire. For a more detailed study of this word see N.T.C. on II Tim. 2:22, footnote 147, pp. 271, 272.

Satan reminds y o u of y o u r sinfulness, y o u immediately remind him and yourselves of y o u r new standing with God.

"*Become more and more spiritually united with Christ*, so that he will be the Light of y o u r light, the Life of y o u r life, the Joy of y o u r joy, and the Strength of y o u r strength."

The person who, by virtue of the enabling power of the Holy Spirit, does this is able to sing

Jesus is all the world to me. . . .

—Will L. Thompson

Such a person must make no provision for the satisfaction of the urges of his sinful human nature. To be sure, there will be these temptations, for the believer remains a sinner even when he becomes a saint (Rom. 7:14 f.). But if he is truly a child of God he must and will learn more and more to control and subdue these enticements in the realm of *Pleasure* (inordinate craving for the satisfaction of physical appetites), *Power* (lust to shine and be dominant), and *Possessions* (uncontrolled yearning for material possessions and for the prestige that accompanies them). With Christ as his Sovereign Lord, the victory is assured!

* * * * *

It was toward the end of the summer of the year A.D. 386. In the garden of a villa near Milan, Northern Italy, sat Augustine, born Nov. 13 of the year 354. Beside him, on a bench, there was lying a copy of Paul's epistles. But he seemed not to be particularly interested in it. He was experiencing an intense spiritual struggle, a violent agitation of heart and mind. Getting up from the bench he flung himself down on the grass beneath a fig tree.

As he is lying there he hears the voice of a child, boy or girl he could not tell. That voice was repeating again and again, "Tolle, lege; tolle, lege" ("Take up and read; take up and read").

He gets up, returns to the bench, and, having picked up the copy of Paul's epistles, reads the first passage on which his eye lights, a Latin version of Rom. 13:13b, 14, "Not in orgies and drinking bouts, not in sexual excesses and debaucheries, not in dissension and jealousy. Rather, clothe yourselves with the Lord Jesus Christ, and make no provision for the (fulfilment of) the lusts of the flesh."

It was this passage plus the love and constant prayers of devout mother Monica that led to the conversion of Augustine, who became one of the greatest leaders of the church. See *Conf.* VIII,xii.28,29.

* * * * *

The Problem

Paul wrote, "Our salvation is nearer now than when we (first) believed. The night is far advanced; the day is drawing near" (13:11, 12). But more than nineteen centuries have gone by since the apostle wrote this. Did he commit an error?

By no means all commentators attempt to solve this problem. Several do not even mention it. By those who tackle it the following solutions have been proposed:

Proposed Solutions

I

Paul is not necessarily thinking—or is not thinking only—of the day of Christ's Return. He may have been thinking of, or at least including, the moment when a person dies. It is then that for the child of God darkness turns into day.[367]

This solution will not do, for when Paul, in the present connection, refers to future salvation, he must have been thinking about salvation's culmination for body and soul. This great blessing will be bestowed not on individual believers, one by one, but on all God's children simultaneously, at Christ's Return. Moreover, the "day" to which he refers in verse 12 is best interpreted as is the same term in I Cor. 3:13; I Thess. 5:4; Heb. 10:25; and II Peter 1:19. In all these cases the reference is to the day of Christ's Return and the final judgment.

II

The words "Our salvation is nearer now than when we (first) believed. The night is far advanced; the day is drawing near" mean that in the unfolding of God's redemptive plan there is *only one great event* that must still take place, namely, Christ's Return to judge the living and the dead.[368]

This suggestion is very helpful. We might summarize the course of redemptive history as follows:

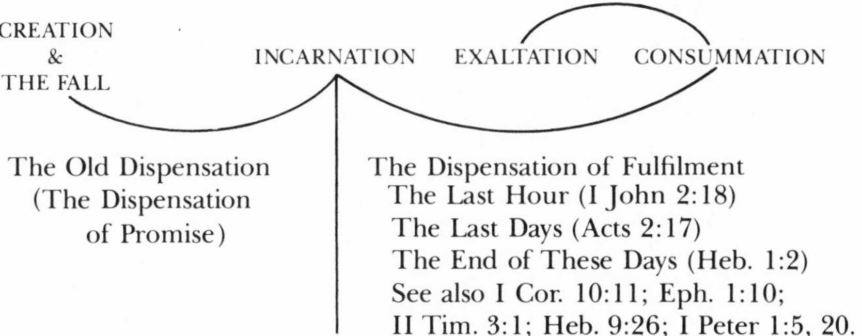

367. Thus Sanday and Headlam, *op. cit.*, p. 378; Greijdanus, *Kommentaar*, Vol. II, pp. 578, 579; A. T. Robertson, *Word Pictures* IV, p. 410; Cranfield, *op. cit.*, p. 682.

368. Murray, *op. cit.*, Vol. II, p. 168; and several others.

In this diagram INCARNATION implies crucifixion (II Cor. 8:9). We are now living in the very last part of the period that extends from INCARNATION to CONSUMMATION; that is, in the part extending from EXALTATION (resurrection, ascension, coronation, outpouring of the Holy Spirit) to CONSUMMATION (Second Coming, resurrection of the dead, final judgment).

This answer, accordingly, goes a long way in explaining the language Paul uses here in Rom. 13:11, 12. But it may not go quite far enough. It hardly explains what the apostle meant when he said, "for our salvation is nearer now than when we (first) believed," for the objection might still be raised, "If the time intervening between the composition of Romans and the arrival (at Christ's Return) of full salvation is still not less than nineteen centuries, then what difference does the interval between (a) first believing and (b) 'now' (the date of the composition of Romans), make?" In view of the very lengthy time period of more than nineteen centuries it is hard to understand why Paul would say, "for our salvation is nearer now than when we (first) believed." We feel like saying, "Yes, nearer, Paul, but by a very, very small fraction, indeed!"

Besides, we still experience some difficulty with the expression "the day *is drawing near*," when more than nineteen centuries have gone by, and the prediction remains unfulfilled.

III

Perhaps we should refer, first of all, to II Peter 3:8. Thorough interpretation of that passage belongs to commentaries on II Peter. One observation can be made, however. The unbelievers and scoffers of Peter's day were told that *their time calculation was faulty*.

For a different reason, the time calculation adopted by those who have difficulty with Rom. 13:11, 12 is probably also wrong. The error is committed not by Paul but by us *when we apply earth's chronology to heaven's mode of life*. We really have no right to say that the saints to whom Paul was addressing this letter had to wait at least another nineteen centuries before the night of darkness would for them be changed into the daylight of full salvation.

What happens when a person dies and his soul goes to heaven? Does that soul then become timeless? Does it adopt one of God's incommunicable (!) attributes, that of *eternity*, ex-temporal existence? Of course not. Not then, nor ever. The oft-quoted passage (Rev. 10:6) proves nothing of the kind. Neither do some of our popular hymns that are based upon the wrong translation of Rev. 10:6. "No more time" should be "no more delay."

What is true, however, is that the computation of time will be different on the other side of the grave. Sorrow spells slow time, but joy inexpressible and full of glory indicates fast-flying time. Rev. 6:11 tells us that for the redeemed souls "under the altar" the period between their martyrdom and the final judgment would amount to "a little while." We will, as it were, be geared to a different kind of time-scale.[369]

So, we arrive at the conclusion that what Paul wrote here in Rom. 13:13, namely, "Our salvation is nearer now than when we (first) believed" makes sense, after all. And so does, "The night is far advanced; the day is drawing near."

We should not forget, however, that the main lesson taught in Rom. 13:11-14 is, "let us put aside the deeds of darkness and put on the garment of light." In other words, "Clothe yourselves with the Lord Jesus Christ."

Practical Lessons Derived from Romans 13

Verse 1

"Let every person be in subjection to the governing authorities." A presidential election year has arrived. In a newspaper someone wrote an article which could be summarized as follows: "The minister, in his preaching, should not discuss the implications of the gospel for the exercise of Christian citizenship, for Church and State must remain separate." Right or Wrong?

Verses 2, 3, 4

". . . he who opposes the authority is resisting the ordinance of God . . . rulers are not a terror to good conduct but to bad . . . he [the magistrate] is God's servant to do you good."

If the church wishes to exert an influence for good upon the State, it should not take recourse to separation but should try spiritual infiltration. It is not surprising that some time later Paul was able to write, ". . . it has become clear throughout the whole praetorian guard and to all the rest that my bonds are for Christ" (Phil. 1:13); and "All the saints greet y o u, especially those of Caesar's household" (4:22).

Verse 6

"This is also why y o u pay taxes, for when (the authorities) faithfully devote themselves to this end, they are God's ministers." Does not this thought make paying taxes somewhat less burdensome?

Verse 8

"Do not keep on owing anyone anything except to love one another . . ."

The attempt to pay a continuing debt may seem to be a very disappointing task. Yet, in the present case this is not really true, for during the process of paying this debt one receives at least the following blessings: (a) the satisfaction of knowing that we are helping the neighbor; (b) assurance of salvation (I John 3:18, 19); and (c) the conviction that we are doing what God wants us to do; that is, that out of gratitude we, with the help of the Holy Spirit, are fulfilling his law.

---

369. For a more complete discussion of TIME in HEAVEN see W. Hendriksen, *The Bible on the Life Hereafter*, pp. 70-74.

Verse 12

"The night is far advanced; the day is drawing near."

Said the minister from the pulpit, "About the day and the hour of Christ's Return we know nothing (Matt. 24:36). In fact, about the life hereafter the Bible tells us almost nothing. So, let those who wish to indulge in wild speculations do so. I shall concentrate my attention on more important subjects." Is that the right approach?

Summary of Chapter 13

Having commented on the believers' proper attitude to God, to fellow-believers, and to outsiders (including enemies), Paul now describes how God's children should relate to *governing authorities.* He states that these rulers have been ordained by God, so that those who oppose them are resisting God's ordinance. Moreover, the addressed should bear in mind that magistrates have by God been appointed to promote the interests of the people over whom they were placed in charge. Therefore, in order to avoid God's wrath and also for the sake of conscience those for whom Paul's letter was written—believers in every age—should submit themselves to the civil authorities. Those who follow the opposite course better remember that they are opposing God himself; also, that the magistrate does not bear his sword in vain.

Taxes too, of whatever kind, should be paid, and those who judiciously and faithfully collect them should be respected. This section closes with the words, "Pay to all whatever y o u owe (them): tax to whom tax (is due), custom to whom custom, respect to whom respect, honor to whom honor" (verses 1-7).

Having just a moment ago stated, "Pay to all whatever y o u owe (them)," Paul now adds, "Do not keep on owing anyone anything except to love one another." Thus he condemns the practice of those who are ever ready to borrow and ever slow to repay; emphasizes that the debt of love we owe to others can never be repaid in full; and makes clear that in our loving embrace we should not only include fellow-believers but *anyone at all* whom God has placed in our path for help and protection of any kind. He says, "For this, 'You shall not commit adultery, you shall not murder, you shall not steal, you shall not covet,' and whatever other commandment there may be, is summed up in the saying, 'You shall love your neighbor as yourself.' " Paul closes this section with the striking understatement, "Love does no harm to the neighbor. Therefore the fulfilment of (the) law is love" (verses 8-10).

It is clear, therefore, that we should love our neighbor as we love ourselves because that is what God's holy law demands. The apostle now adds another reason why we should do this, and probably also why we should strive to live in accordance with all the exhortations found in 12:1 f. (thorough devotion to God, etc.). He writes, "And (do this) especially because y o u know how critical the time is. The hour has arrived for y o u to wake up from (y o u r) slumber, for our salvation is nearer now than when we (first) believed. The night is far advanced; the day is drawing near." He was undoubtedly referring to the day of Christ's Return in glory. That what he stated with reference to the imminent character of this great event and of full salvation for both body and soul, to be imparted to all who walk in the light, is true, has been indicated on pp. 445-447. Paul, accordingly, exhorts the addressed to abandon the kind of deeds associated with darkness (orgies, drinking bouts . . . dissension, jealousy), and, instead, to put on "the armor of light." In closing this section he states, "Clothe yourselves with the *Lord Jesus Christ* [i.e., strive to attain to full spiritual union with him], and make no provision for (the fulfilment of) the lusts of the flesh" (verses 11-14).

Outline (continued)

Practical Application

G. *What Should Be the Attitude of the Justified Believer Toward the Weak and the Strong*

"Him who is weak in faith accept"

14:1-23

"We who are strong ought to bear the failings of the weak and not to please ourselves"

15:1-13

CHAPTER 14:1—15:13

ROMANS

14 1 Him who is weak in faith accept, but not with the idea of passing judgment on
(his) opinions. 2 One person believes he may eat anything, but another, being
weak, eats (only) vegetables. 3 Let not him who eats look down on him who does
not, and let not him who does not eat judge him who does, for God has accepted
him. 4 Who are you that you dare pass judgment on someone else's servant? To his own
master he stands or falls. And he will stand, for the Lord is able to make him stand.

5 One person regards one day as being better than another; another regards every day as
being good. Let each one be fully convinced in his own mind. 6 He who regards one day
as being special, does so in honor of the Lord; and he who eats does so in honor of the Lord,
since he gives thanks to God. And he who abstains does so in honor of the Lord and gives
thanks to God. 7 For none of us lives to himself alone, and none of us dies to himself
alone. 8 If we live, we live to the Lord; and if we die, we die to the Lord. So then, whether
we live or whether we die, we are the Lord's. 9 For to this end Christ died and lived, that
he might be Lord of both the dead and the living.

10 But you, why do you pass judgment on your brother? Or why do you look down on
your brother? For we shall all stand before the judgment seat of God. 11 For it is written,

> " 'As surely as I live,' says the Lord,
> 'Before me will every knee bow down,
> And every tongue will acclaim God.' "

12 So then each of us will give an account of himself to God.

13 Therefore let us stop passing judgment on one another; but rather, let this be y o u r
judgment, namely, that y o u should not put any stumbling block or obstacle in y o u r brother's
way. 14 I know and am convinced in the Lord Jesus that nothing is unclean in itself; but if
anyone considers something to be unclean, then for him it is unclean. 15 For if your brother
is seriously upset because of what you eat, you are no longer walking in love. Do not by your
eating destroy your brother for whom Christ died. 16 Therefore do not allow that which
for you is a good thing to become an occasion for slanderous talk. 17 For the kingdom of
God is not eating and drinking but righteousness and peace and joy in the Holy Spirit; 18 for
anyone who serves Christ in this way is pleasing to God and respected among men.

19 Let us then pursue the things that lead to peace and to mutual edification. 20 Do not
tear down the work of God for the sake of food. Everything, indeed, is clean, but it is wrong
for a person to eat anything that causes (someone else) to stumble. 21 It is better not to eat
meat or drink wine or to do anything else that will cause your brother to stumble.

22 Whatever you believe (about these things) keep between yourself and God.[370] Blessed
is the person who does not need to condemn himself over what he approves. 23 But the

---

370. Literally: The faith which you have, have it to yourself before God.

one who has misgivings[371] when he eats is condemned, because (his eating does) not (spring) from faith; and everything (that does) not (spring) from faith is sin.

G. *What Should Be the Attitude of the Justified Believer Toward the Weak and the Strong*
"Him who is weak in faith accept"
14:1-23

As Paul is approaching the end of this epistle he is aware that there is one important problem on which he has not yet touched, namely, that of the relation between *the weak* and *the strong*. The strong were those who were able to grasp the significance of Christ's death for daily living; that is, for eating and drinking, etc., the weak were not.

1. *Origin of the problem*

God had laid down certain rules with respect to clean versus unclean animals. Only the clean were permitted to be used as food. See Lev. 11:1-45; Deut. 14:3-21. Cf. Dan. 1:8 f.; Tobit 1:10-12; I Macc. 1:62; II Macc. 7: Josephus, *Antiq.* IV.vi.8.

In connection with his teaching that whatever enters a person from the outside is undefiling, Jesus had pronounced all foods clean (Mark 7:15-19). But if even Peter was slow in taking to heart the full implications of this dominical pronouncement, as Acts 10:9-16; 11:1-18; Gal. 2:11-21 indicate, it is understandable that for other Jewish converts to Christianity the situation became even more difficult.

It has been suggested that in the church of Rome the clash between meat-eaters and abstainers became more explosive when Jews who had been expelled from the capital by Claudius (see p. 18) returned. During their absence the Roman church experienced no difficulty, but with their return to Rome a somewhat strained relation began to develop between the two ethnic groups. Whether this theory is correct cannot now be determined, but it may well be. The view according to which "the strong" consisted of the Gentile portion of the congregation, the majority (see pp. 21-23), while "the weak" consisted of the Jewish portion, seems to be confirmed by 15:7 f. (See on that passage). However, this does not mean that only Gentiles belonged to the strong portion, and only Jews to the weak. A Hebrew of Hebrews was Paul; nevertheless, he included himself among the strong (15:1).

But had not Christ, by his death on the cross, fulfilled and thereby abolished, the Old Testament shadows? And if even the divinely established dietary regulations had lost their validity, was not the same true, in fact more decisively, with respect to all man-made rules that had been embroidered upon them?

---

371. Or: who wavers.

True indeed, but this legitimate inference was not drawn by every believer in Christ. Many, especially in Jerusalem and vicinity, but also in Rome and probably elsewhere, held fast to their "traditions."

Now as long as no saving significance or merit of any kind was ascribed to the perpetuation of such rules and regulations, and no offense was given, such persistence in clinging to the old could be tolerated. The adherents must be treated with love and patience. This was true especially during what might be called "the period of transition."

However, in mixed communities problems immediately presented themselves. Customs—Gentile versus Jewish—were bound to clash. The fact that the law of ordinances had been nailed to the cross, and along with it all man-made regulations had also become logically extinct, had not become clear to every believer in Christ. And the further and closely related fact that "in Christ" the wall of separation between Jew and Gentile had been broken down, never to be rebuilt, was frequently ignored, as it is even today in certain circles!

2. *What the two groups—the strong and the weak—had in common:*

a. The members of each group must be regarded as genuine believers (Rom. 14:1-4, 6, 10, 13).

b. Each group was critical of the other (14:3, 4, 13).

c. Each group will have to give an account of itself to the Lord (14:11).

3. *The points with respect to which the two groups differed:*

a. The strong believed that they were permitted to eat anything (meats as well as vegetables); the weak were vegetarians (14:2).

b. The strong regarded every day as being "good." The weak regarded one day as being better than another (14:5). The emphasis falls on a.

4. *Paul's attitude toward the two groups and his admonitions addressed to the groups and to the congregation in general:*

a. In at least one important point Paul agrees with the strong, namely, in believing that nothing (no food) is unclean in itself (14:14, 20; 15:1).

b. He admonishes each group not to look down on the other (14:3, 5, 19).

c. He is especially emphatic in denouncing the attitude of some strong people toward the weak (14:14-21), and he admonishes the strong lovingly to bear with the failings of the weak (15:1).

d. He stresses the fact that the matter of eating and drinking is not nearly as important as that of being a citizen of the kingdom of God, for the essence of that kingdom is not "eating and drinking but righteousness and peace and joy in the Holy Spirit" (14:17).

e. He admonishes both groups—*in fact, the entire congregation*—to pursue those things that lead to peace and mutual edification (14:19; 15:2, 3).

f. He points to the example of Christ, who did not please himself, and was willing for our sake, and to the glory of God, to suffer reproach (15:3-6).

g. He summarizes his exhortations by pleading: "Accept one another, then, just as Christ accepted y o u, to the glory of God" (15:7). He shows that, in Christ, Jews and Gentiles attain their unity. He states, "Christ has become a servant of 'the circumcision' (i.e., of the Jews) for the sake of God's *truth* . . . but the Gentiles glorify God for the sake of (his) *mercy*," quoting passages from the Old Testament to prove what he had just now said with respect to the Gentiles (15:8-12).

h. He closes this section—and in a sense, the entire letter up to this point—with the beautiful prayer-wish, "May the God of hope fill y o u with all joy and peace, in the exercise of (y o u r) faith, so that by the power of the Holy Spirit y o u may overflow with hope" (15:13).

5. *Similarities and differences between Paul's teaching (with respect to diets and days), a. in Romans, and b. in other epistles:*

There are resemblances and there are also differences between that which Paul says about this subject here in Romans, on the one hand, and what, on the other hand, he says about it in I Corinthians, Galatians, and Colossians; differences not in doctrine but in approach and style.

a. *Romans and I Corinthians*

Both here in Romans and in I Cor. 8:1-13; 10:14-33 Paul teaches that the church—and of course also believers individually—*should treat with consideration and tenderness* those who are *weak*; that is, who are, or seem to be, unable to grasp the significance of Christ's death on the cross for daily life. The strong and the weak should treat each other with kindness.

"Let not him who eats look down on him who does not, and let not him who does not eat judge him who does, for God has accepted him" (Rom. 14:3). "Be careful, however, that the exercise of y o u r freedom does not become a stumbling block to the weak" (I Cor. 8:9).

In the *Corinthian* passages Paul speaks about food that had been *offered to idols* (I Cor. 10:20, 28). This feature is not *mentioned* in Romans, though it may be implied. Also, in Romans (14:5 f.) there is a reference to the observance of *special days*. This item is absent from I Corinthians.

b. *Romans and Galatians*

Also between what Paul says here in Rom. 14:1-15:13 and what he says in *Gal.* 4:10, 11 there is a resemblance. In both letters reference is made to the observance of certain special *days*. But the manner in which the apostle refers to these days differs widely in these two epistles. In Galatians the reference is to sabbath-days, days of the new moon, festival seasons belonging to the Jewish cycle, and either (1) the sabbath and jubilee years, or (2) the New Year (Rosh Hashana) on the first day of the month Tishri. Paul is saying that strict observance of such days and festivals has nothing whatever to do with securing divine favor. As a foundation upon which to build one's hope of being justified in the sight of God such observance is merely a superstition. It is utterly futile, nothing but sinking sand. Paul, as it were, shakes his head in utter disgust when he reflects on the fact that rigid, painstaking adherence to the Mosaic law regarding stated days was actually being substituted for simple faith in Jesus Christ. He even states, "I am afraid about y o u, lest somehow I have labored among y o u in vain" (Gal. 4:11).

Here, in Rom. 14:5, Paul simply says, "One person regards one day as being better than another; another regards every day as being good. Let each one be fully convinced in his own mind." The sharply critical and denunciatory style that characterizes the Galatian passages is completely absent from Romans, the reason being that by the weak brothers in Rome the observance of certain days was not viewed as having anything to do with obtaining salvation. So in Rom. 14:1, 5, 19; 15:1, 7 the apostle expresses himself in a very gentle and subdued manner.

c. *Romans and Colossians*

There are also similarities and differences between Rom. 14:1-15:13 and *Colossians*. In Col. 2:16, 17 Paul writes, "Therefore allow no one to pass judgment on y o u by what y o u eat or drink, or with respect to a (religious) festival or a New Moon celebration or a sabbath day." And in 2:20, 21 he asks, "If with Christ y o u died to the rudiments [or: basic principles] of the world, why, as though y o u were still living in the world [or: as though y o u still belonged to the world], do y o u submit to its regulations 'Do not handle! Do not taste! Do not touch!' "?

It is clear that here, in Colossians, Paul again sharply rebukes those whom he addresses, the reason now being that these people were giving heed to false teachers who were telling them, "Faith in Christ will not give y o u fulness of knowledge, wisdom, power, salvation. Therefore y o u must follow our rules concerning days and diets." At bottom this was an attack on the supremacy and all-sufficiency of Christ, "in whom all the fulness of the godhead dwells bodily" (Col. 2:9).

As has been indicated, the treatment of the same general theme—days and diets—in *Romans* differs sharply, since the *weak* ones addressed in this epistle did not attach any saving significance to their eating, drinking, and abstaining, and to their observance of certain special days.

1. Him who is weak in faith accept, but not with the idea of passing judgment on (his) opinions.[372]

---

372. προσλαμβάνεσθε (14:1 and 15:7), 2nd per. pl. pres. mid. imperat. of προσλαμβάνω, to take to oneself; hence, to accept, welcome. Note the third per. s. aor. mid. indicat. of the same verb in 14:3 and again in 15:7.

διακρίσεις, nom. and acc. pl. (here acc. after εἰς) of διάκρισις, a distinguishing or judging. Cf. I Cor. 12:10 (ability to distinguish or judge between).

διαλογισμῶν, gen. pl. (here objective gen.) of διαλογισμός, opinion, thought, reasoning. On this word (s. and pl.) see also N.T.C. on Mark, pp. 282-286. In nearly every instance the deliberations or reasonings are of a sinful nature. See the following passages: Matt. 15:19; Mark 7:21; Luke 5:22; 6:8; 9:46, 47; 24:38; Rom. 1:21; I Cor. 3:20; Phil. 2:14; I Tim. 2:8; James 2:4.

Paul is telling the members of the Roman church, whom he regards as being "strong"—he evidently is thinking of the majority—that they must not commit the moral error of passing judgment upon those who are "weak" in faith, must not condemn them for refusing to eat any meat.

The "weak" members probably reasoned as follows: "In this pagan city how do we know whether any meat at all is really 'clean'? How do we know whether the animal from which it came was actually a 'clean' one? How do we know whether it was slaughtered in the prescribed manner? And how do we know whether it was not first of all offered to idols?"

The apostle reasoned that as long as the vegetarianism of these people did not result from the conviction, "By becoming vegetarians we are putting God in debt to ourselves," they must be viewed as believers, brothers and sisters in Christ. They must be fully "accepted," that is, not only should they be formally recognized as members in good and regular standing of the church but they must also be heartily welcomed into daily fellowship with all other believers. From every aspect the welcome extended to them must be warm and genuine. The very suggestion of "accepting" (?) them with the purpose of adversely criticizing them for their "opinions" (or "scruples") must not even occur to anyone.

2, 3. One person believes he may eat anything, but another, being weak, eats (only) vegetables. Let not him who eats look down on him who does not, and let not him who does not eat judge him who does, for God has accepted him.

One person, namely, the strong, is convinced that there is no valid restriction on the kinds of food he may eat and enjoy. Another person, being weak—for explanation of "strong" and "weak" see p. 453—eats only vegetables. The strong one, or eater, should not look down with contempt on the weak one, or abstainer.

Nevertheless, this is exactly what the strong one would be inclined to do. As was explained earlier (p. 452) the strong ones or eaters were mostly converts from the world of the Gentiles, and in the church of Rome constituted the majority (pp. 21-23). "Why bother with those few vegetarians?" might well be their contemptuous outcry—the Jerusalem Council had been far more conciliatory (Acts 15:20).

The weak or abstainers, on the other hand, might be tempted to derive satisfaction from the very fact that they were in the minority—is not *one* on God's side a majority?—and might therefore begin to pass judgment on the eaters.

The apostle condemns both attitudes, that of *contempt* and that of *condemnation*. Though he desires that the rights of the weak shall be fully respected and that the vegetarian shall be treated with sympathetic regard and genuine deference, he is no less insistent on demanding that the weak refrain from condeming the strong, the eater, stating as his reason "for God has accepted him." It should be clear that in the present context the pronoun "him" can refer only to the eater, the strong one.[373] This view receives further confirmation from the next verse:

4. Who are you that you dare pass judgment on someone else's servant? To his own master he stands or falls.

The form of the question reminds us of 9:20, "But who are you, O man, to talk back to God?" What Paul is saying is that the eater or strong one is answerable only to "his own master," namely, the Lord Jesus Christ; just as, by way of illustration, a servant or slave would be answerable only to his own master. The eater is certainly not obliged to give an account to the abstainer. The latter has no right to condemn him. Paul continues: **And he will stand, for the Lord is able to make him stand.**

It should be borne in mind that the "eater" or "strong one" is the person who has, by God's sovereign grace and the enlightening power of the Holy Spirit, gained an insight into the meaning of Christ's death for daily living. Better than the "weak" person or "abstainer" he has grasped the truth expressed so beautifully in Col. 2:14, namely, that Christ "blotted out the handwritten document that was against us, which by means of its requirements testified against us, and he took it out of the way by nailing it to the cross."

The question, then, is this, "When a person, by the grace of God, has taken this lesson to heart, will he surrender this precious jewel?" To be sure, he cannot remain standing in his own power. But he has a Savior who said, "My sheep listen to my voice, and I know them, and they follow me, and I give them everlasting life, and they shall certainly never perish, and no one shall snatch them out of my hand" (John 10:27, 28). Or, as Paul expresses the same truth here in Rom. 14:4, "And he will stand, for the Lord is able to make him stand." The further question, namely, whether the term "the Lord" refers, in the present instance, to Christ, or to God, is academic. A good answer might well be, "It refers to Christ, and therefore to God."

In the introduction to this chapter—see above, p. 453—we took note of the fact that in addition to a difference of opinion, between the strong and the weak, with respect to *eating*, there was also a difference with respect to the observance of *special days*. Turning now to this subject Paul says:

5. One person regards one day as being better than another; another regards every day as being good.[374]

What was the day which "one person," that is, this or that convert to Christianity, regarded as more sacred than another day? According to some

373. For the opposite view see Käsemann, *op. cit.*, p. 369. Unless there is a good reason to do otherwise, the pronoun (here αὐτόν) should be interpreted as referring to its nearest antecedent, which in the present case is τὸν ἐσθίοντα.

374. Though textual support for the conjunction γάρ at the beginning of this sentence, so that it would read ὃς μὲν γὰρ κρίνει, etc., is rather strong, the context makes clear that if this γάρ is authentic it cannot very well be interpreted as indicating cause but must be viewed as continuative. Whether it is regarded as continuative or as unauthentic, in either case it can be omitted in translation.

it must have been the seventh day of the week, the Jewish sabbath.[375] Even though such an individual would join with the other members of the church in worship on the first day of the week (cf. Acts 20:7), he would close shop and cease to work on Saturday. Other commentators, however, call attention to the fact that the law of Moses not only distinguished between meats as being either clean or unclean, but also prescribed the observance of certain specific days as religious festivals. So, these people would continue to adhere to the Mosaic legislation on this point.[376] Again, since the very subject of *foods*, to which Paul made reference in verses 2-4, brings up that of *fasting*, it has been suggested that the apostle is here referring to days of fasting, after the manner indicated in Luke 18:12.[377]

On the other hand, the idea that in the present context Paul was distinguishing between *lucky* and *unlucky* days[378] must be rejected. If that had been the case Paul would certainly have condemned such a practice in no uncertain terms. He would not have written, **Let each one be fully convinced in his own mind.**[379]

Also, since the New Testament does indeed ascribe very special significance to the first day of the week (Matt. 28:1; Mark 16:2, 9; Luke 24:1; John 20:1, 19; Acts 20:7; I Cor. 16:2; Rev. 1:10), it is indeed very doubtful that the apostle would have expressed himself in such moderate terms if the "weak" members of Rome's church had been indifferent about setting this day apart from all the others (as far as practical in those days) as a day of rest and worship.

We must admit that we cannot now determine in what sense the weak members of the Roman church regarded one day as being better than another, while they still observed and honored the Lord's Day, that is, the first day of the week. That this ignorance on our part is not very serious is shown by the fact that, after verses 5, 6, in this entire epistle the apostle never again refers to this difference about *days*. He does insist, however, that "each one be fully convinced in his own mind" that what he is doing is right. No one must do what is contrary to the dictates of his own conscience as illumined by the Word! Let not the weak condemn the strong; but also, let not the strong look down on the weak; for:

6. He who regards one day as being special, does so in honor of the Lord; and he who eats does so in honor of the Lord, since he gives thanks to God. And he who abstains does so in honor of the Lord and gives thanks to God.

As a comparison with verse 5 shows, "He who regards one day as being special" is the weak person. Now Paul states tht the person who makes this

---

375. So, for example, Lenski, on this passage.
376. C. Hodge, *op. cit.*, pp. 660, 661.
377. See Ridderbos, *op. cit.*, p. 306.
378. A view favored by Käsemann, *op. cit.*, p. 370.
379. I fully agree, accordingly, with Cranfield (*op. cit.*, p. 705) on this point.

distinction between days, a distinction which strong persons would not make, must not be looked down upon for doing so, for he does so with the purpose of honoring the Lord.[380] Similarly, the one who eats, paying no attention to the Mosaic distinction between clean and unclean, cannot be accused of being indifferent to the will of God. On the contrary, he too honors the Lord by doing what he does. Both the weak and the strong, in this matter of indifference, are honoring the Lord; the weak, by giving thanks to him for their vegetarian meal; the strong, by giving thanks for their meat, etc.

7-9. For none of us lives to himself alone, and none of us dies to himself alone. If we live, we live to the Lord; and if we die, we die to the Lord. So then, whether we live or whether we die, we are the Lord's. For to this end Christ died and lived, that he might be Lord of both the dead and the living.

Note the following:

a. "For none of us lives to himself alone," etc.

The fact that "we," both kinds of Christians, the strong and the weak, behave as we do, is because none of us lives a self-centered life. On the contrary, while still alive on earth we live for the Lord Jesus Christ. Cf. Phil. 1:21. Our basic aim is to please him. When we die we strive, even by means of our dying, to glorify the Lord.

b. "So then . . . we are the Lord's."

It is, after all, this Lord whose servants we are, and to whom we belong. Did he not purchase us with his precious blood? (I Cor. 6:20).

c. "For to this end Christ died and lived . . ."

Not here "lived and died" (Phillips), as if "lived" referred to Christ's life on earth before his death by crucifixion, but "died and lived." He died, and afterward, having risen from the dead, he went to live in heaven. Note the parallel:

	Christ *died* and *lived*
that he might be Lord of both	the *dead* and *the living*.

As our Mediator, Christ secured the indisputable right to exercise lordship over both those believers who have already died and those who are still alive on earth. This mediatorial lordship was the reward for the price he paid, the death he died. By means of his substitutionary death, followed by his intercessory life in heaven (Heb. 7:25), he sees to it that whatever he has merited for us, his children, is bestowed on us. Cf. II Cor. 4:10, "We always carry around in our body the *death* of Jesus, so that the *life* of Jesus may be revealed in our bodies." Cf. Rom. 6:4; Phil. 3:10.[381]

---

380. Literally "to the Lord." Such a *dative* can be viewed as one *of advantage*.

381. First of all see above, p. 221, footnote 192. The textual tradition of Rom. 14:9 is by no means uniform, but ἀπέθανεν καὶ ἔζησεν has the strongest support. Someone has tried to change the text by substituting ἀνέστη for ἔζησεν. There is also a variant that substitutes ἀνέζησεν for ἔζησεν, and there are variants that have all three verbs. Sometimes the sequence in which ἀπέθανεν and ἔζησεν follow each other has been reversed. The logic of the passage favors the already indicated parallel: *died* and *lived* followed by *the dead* and *the living*. It is

10-12. But you, why do you pass judgment on your brother? Or why do you look down on your brother? For we shall all stand before the judgment seat of God. For it is written,

> **" 'As surely as I live,' says the Lord,**
> **'Before me will every knee bow down,**
> **And every tongue will acclaim God.' "**

So then each of us will give an account of himself to God.

In verse 3 Paul had warned the strong not to look down on the weak, and the weak not to condemn the strong. That this was nevertheless actually occurring and is an inexcusable sin he makes clear in verse 10, where, in reverse order (now referring to the weak first of all) the apostle accusingly asks why one church member is sinning against another. These critics should bear in mind that the one whom they condemn or despise is, after all, *a brother*. Note how this term of endearment, which has not been used since 12:1, indicates the seriousness of the sin that was being committed. See further on pp. 52, 214, 215.

Also, those who are passing judgment, or are looking down on a brother, must remember that not they are lords, but Christ is the Lord; and accordingly, that not they are the legitimate judges, but Christ is the Judge. They are therefore arrogating to themselves a prerogative that belongs to Christ and to God alone.

Says Paul, "We shall all stand before the judgment seat of God." In confirmation of this fact he quotes from the Old Testament. As happens frequently, so also here, the quotation is composite: the first part, " 'As surely as I live,' says the Lord," may be regarded as taken from Isa. 49:18 (cf. Num. 14:28; Deut. 32:40; Ezek. 33:11); the rest of the quotation, "Before me will every knee bow down, and every tongue will acclaim God," is from Isa. 45:23, according to the LXX text, with transposition of two words,[382] but without change in meaning.

The quoted words do indeed confirm the thought Paul has expressed, namely, that in the end every person, without exception, will pay homage to God (cf. Phil. 2:10, 11), recognizing him as Sovereign over all, and acclaiming him as being the righteous Judge of all.

That there will indeed be a universal judgment is the teaching of Scripture (Eccl. 12:14; Eph. 6:8; Rev. 20:11-15). That believers as well as unbelievers will stand before the throne of judgment is also clear from Acts 10:42; I Cor. 3:8-15; 4:5; II Cor. 5:10, and from the teaching of Jesus (Matt. 16:27; 25:31-46). That it is, indeed, God who through Christ will judge is taught in Matt. 16:27; 25:31-46; John 5:22; Acts 10:42; I Cor. 4:5; II Cor. 5:10. It

---

clear, of course, that the words "Christ lived" imply his resurrection. The possibility that ἔζησεν is an ingressive aorist, and means "became alive" or "began to live" must be granted. But the obvious parallel noted above seems to require "died and lived." It is because of Christ's death and because of his life in heaven that God's children are living to the glory of God.

382. LXX: ἐξομολογήσεται πᾶσα γλῶσσα; Paul: πᾶσα γλῶσσα ἐξομολογήσεται.

is as stated in Rom. 2:16 (see pp. 98, 99), "God, through Jesus Christ, will judge men's secrets."

Repeating the thought of verse 10 ("For we shall all stand before the judgment seat of God"), Paul concludes his reflection on this theme by stating, "So then each of us will give an account of himself to God." Note: *each* of us! Not a single one will be exempted. Also, the account will have to be given not to men but to *God*, the *Omniscient*, the *Holy* and *Righteous* One, who is also the God of *Love*.

Summarizing the main idea of verses 10-12—and in a sense even of 1-12 (see especially verses 1, 3, 4, 10-12)—Paul, addressing both the strong and the weak (note: "on one another"), but probably especially *the strong*, and drawing a conclusion, continues with the following exhortation:

13. Therefore let us stop passing judgment on one another; but rather, let this be y o u r judgment, namely, that y o u should not put any stumbling block or obstacle in y o u r brother's way.

Note the word-play: *passing judgment* . . . y o u r *judgment* or decision.[383]

Paul urges the weak to stop criticizing the strong, and the strong to cease finding fault with the weak. Both parties should decide not to place any hindrance in the way of their brothers. On the contrary—for the negative implies the positive—each group should help the other to become a more effective witness for Christ.[384]

In view of the fact that both parties love the Lord, repose their trust in him, and wish to walk in his way, it would be wrong to hurt one another's feelings by insisting that there be absolute unanimity with respect to every aspect of the practice of religion.

If, on a Sunday evening, perhaps after the church service, you invite six people to your home, but you happen to know that three of them have objections to the singing of a certain hymn, then, even though the other three plus yourself consider that hymn unobjectionable, you are not going to include that particular number in your evening social program. Instead, you are going to see to it that everybody receives a blessing and is happy. The same principle should be applied to ever so many similar situations. If an important religious principle is at stake, you are not going to be silent

---

383. Greek μηκέτι . . . κρίνωμεν, Let us pass judgment no more. ἀλλὰ τοῦτο κρίνατε, but decide this.

384. πρόσκομμα, in addition to its occurrence here in Rom. 14:13, is found also in Rom. 9:32, 33; 14:20; I Cor. 8:9; and I Peter 2:8. Meaning: (a) *literal*, a rock or other hard object against which a person may strike his foot, causing him to stumble or even to fall; (b) *figurative*, an occasion to take offense, an obstacle to the development of spiritual life or happiness, an incentive to sin.

σκάνδαλον, also in Matt. 13:41; 16:23; 18:7; Luke 17:1; Rom. 9:33; 11:9; 16:17; I Cor. 1:23; Gal. 5:11; I Peter 2:8; I John 2:10; Rev. 2:14.

Meaning: (a) *literal*, the bait-stick in a trap or snare; (b) *figurative* (about the same as πρόσκομμα), obstacle, that which causes opposition, resentment, offense, sin. On πρόσκομμα and σκάνδαλον see also G. Stählin, Th.D.N.T., respectively, Vol. VI, pp. 756, 757, and Vol. VII, pp. 352-358.

about your convictions, but in all circumstances you will observe the rule: "In things essential unity; in doubtful (or indifferent) liberty; in all things charity" (identity of the author of this motto not entirely certain). See also what has been said about Paul's flexibility (pp. 12, 13).

The substance of this exhortation is certainly entirely in line with, and may even have been induced by, the teaching of Christ (Matt. 18:1-9; Mark 9:42-48; Luke 17:1, 2).

14. I know and am convinced in the Lord Jesus that nothing is unclean in itself . . .

Paul's language is very emphatic.[385] His conviction is firm, deep, and unshakable Cf. Gal. 5:10; Phil. 2:24; II Thess. 3:4; II Tim. 1:5, 12. It amounts to a persuasion that is based not only on the teaching of Jesus but also on the apostle's spiritual closeness to his Lord and Savior. For the teaching of Jesus on this subject see Matt. 15:10, 11, 16-20; Mark 7:14-23. For Paul's similar teaching see also I Tim. 4:4 "Everything God created is excellent, and nothing is to be rejected if it is received with thanksgiving." Add Titus 1:15, "All things are pure to those who are pure."

Accordingly, the impurity pertains not to the food as such but to the person who questions whether or not he should eat it: **but if anyone considers something to be unclean, then for him it is unclean.** This does not mean that sin is wholly a matter of subjective opinion or of conscience. No, there are indeed many things that are definitely forbidden. No mere opinion on man's part, or even the silence of conscience, can make right what God has declared to be wrong. But it does mean that even a human activity—in the present case eating meat a person considers to be unclean—is wrong for those who consider it to be wrong.

By expressing himself as he does the apostle accomplishes two things: (a) He encourages the strong by clearly showing that he takes their side; see verse 14a; (b) he helps the weak by reminding the strong that the weak are right in refusing to eat that which *they* (the weak) consider to be unclean (verse 14b). Should not this consummate, exquisite tact be a lesson for everyone; especially also for every pastor? What a loving heart, this heart of Paul, and how wise a disposition! No wonder that he continues as follows:

15. For if your brother is seriously upset because of what you eat, you are no longer walking in love.

The word "For" shows that the clause it introduces links with verse 13b rather than with verse 14. (Verse 14 can best be regarded as a parenthesis.) So what Paul is saying is really, ". . . Do not put a stumbling block or obstacle in your brother's way, for if your brother is seriously upset,[386] you are no

385. πέπεισμαι, 1st perf. pass. indicat. of πείθω, to persuade. To add strength to the expression this verb is even preceded by οἶδα.

386. λυπεῖται, 3rd. per. s. pres. pass. indicat. of λυπέω, to cause serious grief or distress. This verb occurs also in Matt. 14:9; 17:23; 18:31; 19:22; 26:22, 37; Mark 10:22; 14:19; John 16:20; 21:17; Eph. 4:30; I Thess. 4:13; I Peter 1:6; and frequently in II Cor., beginning with 2:2.

longer walking in love." Paul now uses the 2nd per. sing., you, driving home this urgent lesson, impressing it upon each of the addressed, one by one. He returns to the very subject, *love for one another*, on which he had expatiated with such warmth and eloquence in 12:9, 10; 13:9, 10, and even earlier (I Cor. 13). Love was the theme close to the heart not only of Paul but also of Peter (I Peter 4:8) and of John (I John 4:8); of God (John 3:16) and of Christ (I John 3:16)!

Paul continues: **Do not by your eating destroy your brother for whom Christ died.** The apostle is, as it were, saying, "Consider what you are doing! So dear is that brother of yours to Christ that he died for him. Nevertheless, you, by means of your unbrotherly conduct, are treating him in a manner which, were it not for God's irresistible grace, would destroy him. Immediately stop doing what you are doing, and do the very opposite!"

16. Therefore do not allow that which for you is a good thing to become an occasion for slanderous talk.

Paul realizes that if in the presence of the weak a strong individual eats that which by the weak is considered "unclean," he will be hurting that weak person. This would be even more true if, due to the insistence of the strong, the weak fellow-Christian would finally surrender and do what his conscience forbids him to do. Moreover, open quarrels between the two groups would certainly result in slanderous talk on the part of outsiders.

So the apostle warns the strong that they should not allow that which for them is "a good thing" to become an occasion of slanderous talk. But what is meant by "a good thing"? Opinions differ widely, as the footnote shows.[387]

What, then, does Paul mean when he, addressing the strong, says, "that which for you is a good thing"? In view of the immediately preceding con-

---

387. See General Bibliography.
The references are to the *commentaries* written by the following:

Commentator	*Theory*
	1
Calvin, p. 506 Harrison, p. 148 Käsemann, p. 376 Murray, p. 193 Sanday and Headlam, p. 391	Christian liberty: freedom from ceremonial observance
Van Leeuwen & Jacobs, p. 263	2 the kingdom (or kingship) of God
Greijdanus (*Kommentaar*), Vol. II, p. 605 Lekkerkerker, Vol. II, p. 165 (mentions both salvation and evangelical freedom) Lenski, p. 839 (the whole Christian faith, our whole salvation, the gospel) Luther, *Works*, Vol. 25, p. 504 Ridderbos, p. 312	3 salvation
Cranfield, Vol. II, p. 717 Hodge, pp. 667, 668	4 the gospel

text, the natural answer might seem to be "your Christian liberty." The possibility that this answer is correct must be granted. Nevertheless, a good argument can be advanced for No. 4, the gospel. *Would an outsider not be more likely to slander the gospel itself than to take sides in this debate between the strong and the weak?* Besides, the apostle certainly regards the gospel as being a very good thing indeed. He uses the term "gospel" about 60 times in his epistles. He is so fond of it that he calls it "*my* gospel" (Rom. 2:16; 16:25), and even tells us that he is willing to put up with anything rather than hinder the gospel of Christ (I Cor. 9:12). What he considers a good thing for himself he must also have considered a good thing for others.

As to answers 2 (the kingdom or kingship of God) and 3 (salvation), if the correct answer is "the gospel," this surely is "the gospel of salvation," and if we look carefully at the meaning of the term "kingdom" or "kingship," as defined by Paul himself in verse 17, namely, "righteousness and peace and joy in the Holy Spirit," we will probably have to conclude that this description makes "kingdom" (or "kingship") of God equivalent to "salvation."

There is merit, therefore, in all four answers, though personally, if a choice must be made, I would still give a slight edge to "the gospel of salvation"; that is, of the realization of the kingship of God in the lives of God's children.

Having said, "Do not by your eating destroy your brother for whom Christ died. Therefore do not allow that which for you is a good thing to become an occasion for slanderous talk," the apostle continues,

17. For the kingdom of God is not eating and drinking but righteousness and peace and joy in the Holy Spirit;

The essence of God's royal reign, the evidence of that blessed reign in your midst, says Paul, as it were, is not affected by the kind of food a person consumes, whether ceremonially clean or unclean, whether only vegetables or also meats, but is attested by one's possession of the state of *righteousness* before God, consciousness of *peace* with God, a peace resulting from reconciliation with God (5:1, 10). It is characterized by the experience of Spirit-wrought *joy*, a joy inexpressible and full of glory (I Peter 1:8).

It is immediately apparent that this answer is in complete accord with the words of Jesus, "The kingdom of God does not come with outward display; nor will people say, 'Look, here (it is)!' or 'There (it is)!' for, note well, *the kingdom of God is within* y o u" (Luke 17:21).[388]

18. for anyone who serves Christ in this way is pleasing to God and respected among men.

Note: "serves Christ *in this way*"; that is (as the preceding verse makes clear), in the consciousness of having been justified by God, having peace with God, and experiencing the joy that was imparted to him by the Holy Spirit.

Such a person is, first of all, "pleasing to God." He is truly living for God, to God's honor and glory. See 14:6-8 and earlier, 6:22.

388. See also N.T.C. on Matthew, pp. 249, 250.

Note also the phrase, "and respected[389] among men." Those who say, "I don't care at all what people think of me," may be guilty of an other-worldliness that is not exactly pious. Paul had already written, "Always see to it that y o u r affairs are right in the sight of everybody" (12:17b). Calvin was certainly correct when, commenting on Rom. 14:18, he wrote, "That man is acceptable to God, because he obeys his will; he testifies that he is approved by men, because they cannot do otherwise than bear testimony to that excellence which they see with their eyes; not that the ungodly always favor the children of God; on the contrary, when there is no cause, they often pour forth against them many reproaches . . . but Paul speaks here of honest judgment, blended with no moroseness, no hatred, no superstition."

19. Let us then pursue the things that lead to peace and to mutual edification.[390]

Note the following:

a. *Peace* is a gift which God in Christ imparts to the church (John 14:27; 16:33; 20:19, 21, 26; Rom. 15:33; 16:20; II Cor. 13:11). He is "the God of peace" (Phil. 4:9; I Thess. 5:23; II Thess. 3:16). Therefore genuine peace is "the gift of God" (Phil. 4:7).

This does not mean, however, that we can take this peace for granted. On the contrary, here in 14:19 we are being reminded that it is our duty to "pursue the things that make for peace." This is in line with the thinking of Peter (I Peter 3:11), of the author of the epistle to the Hebrews (12:14), and, much earlier, of the Psalmist (34:14).

b. *Mutual edification.* This expression shows that Paul conceives of the church as being *an edifice*. This implies that it is a united body. However, this edifice or building must not be thought of as being finished. No, it is constantly rising (Eph. 4:16). Even the individual stones are anything but static. If matters are as they should be, the stones are in the process of being made more and more beautiful. Moreover, they are *living* stones! (I Peter 2:5).

The main building material is *love* (Eph. 4:16). This is even more important than *liberty*. "Be careful that the exercise of y o u r liberty does not become a stumbling block to the weak" (I Cor. 8:9). In fact, love is even better than *knowledge*. "Knowledge puffs up, but love builds up" (I Cor. 8:1).

20. Do not tear down the work of God for the sake of food. Everything, indeed, is clean, but it is wrong for a person to eat anything that causes (someone else) to stumble.

---

389. δόκιμος, approved, respected, esteemed. See also Rom. 16:10; I Cor. 11:19; II Cor. 10:18; 13:7; II Tim. 2:15; James 1:12.

390. Though the reading διώκομεν instead of διώκωμεν has strong support, it cannot be accepted. The transition from a conjectural, "We are pursuing the things that lead to peace . . ." (verse 19) to "Do not tear down the work . . ." (verse 20), would be very unnatural and abrupt. Besides, as it is true that didactic style predominates in the earlier part of the book of Romans, so hortatory style can be expected in the latter part. See, for example, 14:13. For the rest the reader's attention is called to footnote 140, p. 168.

We have already taken note of the fact that in verse 16 Paul was addressing the strong. There is no reason to believe that in the immediately following verses—including verse 20—he is directing his words of warning and exhortation to a different group. The first part of the passage causes no difficulty. Paul returns to the second person singular, last used in verse 15. This increases the forcefulness of his admonitions.

Having just a moment ago encouraged the work of *building up*, the apostle now warns against engaging in its very opposite, namely, *tearing down* or *destroying* (cf. Matt. 5:17; 24:2; 26:61; 27:40; II Cor. 5:1; Gal. 2:18). Such tearing down is all the more wicked because it concerns *the work of God* in the heart and life of the weak brother, and doing this for the sake merely of something material, namely, food!

And if someone objects that it is perfectly proper for the strong person to eat whatever he likes to eat, since everything in the line of food is clean, as Paul has himself admitted (14:14; cf. Mark 7:19-23; I Tim. 4:4), the answer is, "Everything, indeed, is clean, but it is wrong—or bad, evil—for a person to eat anything that causes (someone else) to stumble."

However, in the original this final clause of verse 20 is compressed into very few words: "but wrong for a person the eating with a stumbling block [or: with offense]."

The question arises, "Does Paul mean that the *strong* person should be on his guard lest by his eating he is giving offense to the weak brother?" Or is he saying, "It is wrong for the *weak* person to eat with a troubled conscience"?[391] For the first alternative see Robertson, *Word Pictures*, Vol. IV, p. 415; and Cranfield, Vol. II, pp. 723, 724. For the second, Murray, Vol. II, p. 195. Of these two, the first, as this interpreter sees it, deserves the preference. Reasons: (a) Not only in the immediately preceding but even in the immediately following context (verse 21) Paul is addressing the strong. It is natural, therefore, to assume that also here in verse 20 he does so. (b) This conclusion brings the present passage into harmony with verse 13b, where Paul admonishes the strong to cease finding fault with the weak. (c) Elsewhere, in a similar context, the apostle declares, "Therefore, if what I eat causes my brother to fall into sin, I will never eat meat again, so that I will not cause him to sin" (I Cor. 8:13).

After having stated what is *wrong*, a statement about what is *right* follows very naturally: **21. It is better[392] not to eat meat or drink wine or to do anything else that will cause your brother to stumble.**

It is not the apostle's intention to "lay down the law" with respect to eating and drinking. He is not issuing an order; rather, in a fatherly manner he is

---

391. The original reads, ἀλλὰ κακὸν τῷ ἀνθρώπῳ τῷ διὰ προσκόμματος ἐσθίοντι. Here the phrase διὰ πρ. expresses accompaniment or attendant circumstance.

392. That which is recommended as being "good" or "better" is expressed by means of an infinitive (in the present case articular), which forms the subject of the clause. Cf. I Cor. 7:1, 8, 26: Heb. 13:9.

urging the strong person voluntarily to curtail the use of his freedom, to do this out of regard for his weak brother in Christ. In the presence of that weak person let him forego the privilege of eating meat.[393] The same Paul who in verse 15 was saying, "For if your brother is seriously upset because of what you eat, you are no longer walking in love," is speaking here in verse 21.

There are three things from which, according to verse 21, the strong person is advised to refrain, out of consideration for those who are weak:

a. eating meat
b. drinking wine
c. doing anything else that will cause "your brother" to stumble.[394]

As to (a) refraining from eating meat, this follows naturally from the thought expressed in verses 2, 15, 16, 20.

As to (b), abstaining from wine, without additional information it is probably impossible to determine exactly why Paul adds this. According to some—see Cranfield, Vol. II, p. 725—this does not imply that the weak actually abstained from wine, but is simply mentioned because in verse 17 Paul made reference to eating *and drinking*. On the other hand, Murray's view (Vol. II, p. 195), shared by many other commentators, namely, that drinking wine was involved in the scruples of the weak, impresses me as being preferable. The reason for this abstinence is not given. Is it possible that the weak abstained from the use of wine because wine was used as a libation in animal sacrifices? We just do not know, but see also Dan. 1:8, 16.

As to (c), the apostle "is simply commending to others what has for some time been the rule for himself" (E. F. Harrison, *op. cit.*, p. 149). Cf. I Cor. 8:13.

The apostle was certainly giving excellent and inspired advice when he stated: **22. Whatever you believe (about these things) keep between yourself and God.** Note strong emphasis on the pronoun *you*, in the original occurring at the very beginning of the sentence. It is as if Paul, in his imagination, is listening to a "strong" believer; one, however, who delights in hearing himself talk. That loud talker is saying, "*I insist on my* freedom; and *I* say that *I* will not allow anyone to interfere with that unrestrained freedom of *mine*," etc. So Paul, as it were, answers, "*You* better keep between *yourself* and God that conviction *you* have!" He adds, **Blessed is the person who does not need to condemn himself over what he approves**; meaning, Inwardly happy is that person—namely, that "strong" believer—who *avoids* bringing God's judgment upon himself by insisting on the exercise of his

393. Here not the more general βρῶμα (verses 15, 20) or βρῶσις (verse 17), but κρέα, pl. of κρέας, "flesh-meat," as in I Cor. 8:13, the only other occurrence of this word in the New Testament. Cf. pan*crea*s; lit., all flesh.

394. On the assumption that the Nestle-Aland text is correct, something like ἄλλο τι ποιῆσαι (to do anything else) must be supplied in thought.

"liberty" even though such insistence results in harming his "weak" fellow-believer.

Over against the person who does not need to condemn himself stands the one who "has misgivings," and accordingly "is condemned." Says Paul: **23. But the one who has misgivings when he eats is condemned, because (his eating does) not (spring) from faith . . .** The "weak" believer—that is, the person who is not sure that he is doing the right thing but "wavers" (cf. 4:20) when he eats (meat)—stands condemned. This is true because his eating "does not spring from faith," that is, "is not in harmony with an *inner conviction that what he is doing is in line with his Christian faith.*"

This person is sinning because he is trying to silence the voice of his conscience. He is convinced that what he is about to do is wrong, yet he does it. Accordingly, he is sinning. Says Paul: **and everything (that does) not (spring) from faith is sin**; that is, whatever thought, word, action, etc. does not spring from the inner conviction that it is in harmony with a person's faith in God; or, stating it differently, whatever action is contradicted by one's Christian conscience, is sin. To be sure, a person's conscience is not the Final Judge of his actions, whether past, present, or contemplated. That Final Judge is God, or, if one prefers, the Word of God. But this does not alter the fact that even for that individual who may not have become fully informed about the will of God as revealed in his Word it is wrong by means of his actions to oppose the voice of his Christian conscience.

---

15 1 We who are strong ought to bear the failings of the weak and not to please
ourselves. 2 Let each of us please his neighbor for (his) good, with a view to (his)
edification. 3 For even Christ did not please himself but, as it is written,
"The reproaches of those reproaching thee fell on me."
4. For whatever was written in former times was written for our instruction, in order that,
through patient endurance and the encouragement of the Scriptures, we might have hope.
5 May the God (who is the Source) of patient endurance and of encouragement grant y o u
to live in harmony with one another, in accord with Christ Jesus, 6 so that with one heart
and mouth y o u may glorify the God and Father of our Lord Jesus Christ.
7 Accept one another, then, just as Christ accepted y o u, to the glory of God. 8 For I
declare that Christ has become a servant of the circumcised for the sake of God's *truth*, to
confirm the promises made to the fathers; 9 but the Gentiles glorify God for the sake of
(his) *mercy*; as it is written:

"Therefore I will praise thee among the Gentiles,
and sing hymns to thy name."

10 And again, it says,

"Rejoice, y o u Gentiles, together with his people."

11 And again,

"Praise the Lord, all y o u Gentiles,
let all the peoples praise him."

12 And again, Isaiah says,

"There will spring up the root of Jesse,
he who arises to rule over the Gentiles.
In him shall the Gentiles hope."

13 May the God of hope fill y o u with all joy and peace, in the exercise of (y o u r) faith, so
that by the power of the Holy Spirit y o u may overflow with hope.

G. *What Should Be the Attitude of the Justified Believer Toward the Weak and the Strong* (continued)

"We who are strong ought to bear the failings of the weak and not to please ourselves" 15:1-13

The opening of chapter 15 looks like a new beginning. Actually the apostle summarizes what he has been saying about the weak, and indicates what should be the attitude of the strong toward them. But the opening does not stop here. It soon broadens in scope and fixes the attention of the entire congregation—and of all who will subsequently be brought into contact with this letter—on Christ, whose example of self-sacrifice in the interest of others should be followed by weak and strong alike.

1. We who are strong ought to bear the failings of the weak and not to please ourselves.

When Paul says, "*We* who are strong," he classes himself with the strong. When he continues, "ought to bear the failings of the weak," he means, "A moral-spiritual obligation rests on us strong ones; namely, not to think only of ourselves but also of the needs of others, in the present case the needs of those who are weak." See I Cor. 10:33.

What Paul is saying here in Rom. 15:1 cannot be far removed from his exhortation found in Gal. 6:2, "Bear one another's burdens, and so fulfill the law of Christ." The expression, "*bear*" the failings, does not merely mean, "tolerate" or "put up with" those failings, or even "bear with" them and "exercise patience" with those who have them. It means, "*We should put our shoulders under* these failings, and meaningfully *help* our weak fellow-believers *to carry* them."[395]

Noblesse oblige! People of high birth should behave *nobly* toward others. This well-known motto, when applied to the present situation, would mean that those highly privileged people who are endowed with clear insight into the liberating significance of the death of Christ for daily living, so that they are correctly called "the strong," are under obligation to deport themselves in a manner that is in keeping with their high privilege. Hence, they should

---

395. The verb βαστάζω—here βαστάζειν, pres. act. infin.—occurs more than 25 times in the New Testament. It is especially common in the Gospels and in Acts. It means: *to carry* (a water-jar, Mark 14:13; Luke 22:10), stretcher (Luke 7:14), stones (John 10:31), money (i.e., carrying it away, stealing it, John 12:6); also *to carry* (a corpse, transferring it from one place to another, John 20:15), a yoke (Acts 15:10), a man, Paul (Acts 21:35), a woman (Rev. 17:7). In Gal. 6:2 and also here in Rom. 15:1 it can best be interpreted in the figurative sense *to bear* or *carry* the burdens, cares or scruples, griefs or failings, of another person or of other persons. For a somewhat different meaning see Gal. 5:10 (*to bear* a person's judgment = to pay the penalty); and Rev. 2:2 (*to tolerate*, put up with). In Matt. 20:12 the sense is: *to endure*; and in John 16:12 and Gal. 6:17, *to bear*.

ἀσθενήματα, pl. of ἀσθένημα, in the New Testament occurring only here, means weakness, failing. In the present context the word refers to the scruples of those whom Paul describes as being "weak." The literal meaning of ἀσθενής is "without strength."

vigorously, generously, and cheerfully help the (in a sense) less privileged persons, the "weak" individuals.

When Paul adds, "We who are strong ought . . . not to please ourselves," he does not mean, "We, the strong, should never do anything to promote our own interests." Pleasing God above all (Rom. 8:8), and, while doing so, also pleasing God's image-bearers, including even ourselves, is the very purpose for which God created and redeemed us (Matt. 22:37-39; Rom. 13:9; I Cor. 10:33; Titus 2:9). *It is the pleasing of ourselves regardless of how this pleasing affects others that is here condemned.*

However, the divine approval does not even necessarily rest upon every attempt to please the neighbor. As Gal. 1:10 indicates, there is an attempt to please the neighbor that is evil. One who, being "nice" with a selfish purpose, trims his sails to every breeze of opinion or bias is acting wickedly. The person who, "with ulterior motive" (cf. 12:8), strives to please others is condemned. A vivid example is that of Absolom:

"Whenever anyone came with a complaint to be placed before the king for a decision, Absalom would call out to him, 'From what town are you?' He would answer, 'Your servant is from this or that tribe of Israel.' Then Absalom would say to him, 'Your claims are valid and proper, but there is no representative of the king to hear you.' And Absalom would continue and say, 'O, if only I were appointed as judge in the land! Then any man with a complaint or a case would come to me, and I would see to it that he gets justice.' "

"Also, whenever anyone approached him to bow down before him, Absalom would reach out his hand, take hold of him and kiss him . . . And so he stole the hearts of the men of Israel" (II Sam. 15:2b-7).

As has now been indicated, it is not only *the deed* but *also*—perhaps even *more* so—*the motive and purpose* that count. It is for this reason that Paul states,

2. Let each of us please his neighbor for (his) good, with a view to (his) edification. In other words, *with a view to the spiritual advantage of that neighbor.*

Now doing good for the benefit of others immediately reminds Paul of Christ (II Cor. 8:9), whose example we should follow. Therefore he continues,

3. For even Christ did not please himself but, as it is written, "The reproaches of those reproaching thee fell on me." Ps. 69:9.

Meaning: Christ is addressing God, and is saying, "For the sake of my people I am taking upon myself the reproaches leveled against thee."

The main lesson Paul is conveying is this: *If Christ, the Holy One, was willing to take upon himself so much suffering, in the form of insults hurled at him by his enemies, then should not we be willing to sacrifice just a little eating-and-drinking pleasure for the sake of our fellow-believers?*

Now for the details:

a. As often—see I Cor. 11:1; II Cor. 8:9; 10:1; Eph. 5:1, 2; Phil. 2:5 f.; Col. 3:13—Paul directs the attention of the addressed to Christ. In doing this, was he not copying Christ? See Matt. 11:29; 16:24; 20:27, 28; Mark 10:42-45; John 13:15. For Christ, as our Example, see also Heb. 3:1; 12:2; I Peter 2:21.

In connection with this subject two extremes should be avoided: (1) that of denying the truth that *first and most of all* Christ is not our Example but *our Savior*; and (2) that of denying that there is a sense in which our Savior Jesus Christ is indeed also our Example. Of course, he cannot be our Example unless he is first of all our Savior!

b. The words "Christ did not please himself" are a remarkable litotes or understatement for his marvelous and wholehearted self-sacrifice in the interest of sinners. See especially Isa. 53; Matt. 20:28; Mark 10:45; II Cor. 8:9; Phil. 2:5 f.

c. When the question is asked, "Why did the apostle refer to the insults or reproaches that were heaped upon Christ by *men* rather than to the far more terrible wrath of *God* which he suffered?" the answer might be that in so doing Paul makes his argument all the more effective, because the insults flung at Christ by *men* were heard, discussed, and remembered, but the wrath of *God* remained unseen.[396]

d. Paul quotes Ps. 69:9b. The words quoted are found in that exact form in LXX Ps. 68:10.

Psalm 69 is one of six Psalms most often referred to in the New Testament, the others being Pss. 2, 22, 89, 110, and 118.[397]

e. According to Ps. 69:9b, interpreted in light of the immediately preceding context, namely verse 9a, it was "zeal" for God's house that consumed the Speaker, namely, Christ, as pictured in this Old Testament passage. The implied lesson is that also the "strong" believers of the new dispensation should be filled with zeal: they should be eager to make sacrifices for the sake not only of their "weak" fellow-believers, but also, and most of all, for God. They should strive to promote his glory.

f. The eyes of those who maintain that Ps. 69:9 simply records the outcry of a devout child of God, and has nothing to do with the Messiah, are covered with a veil (II Cor. 3:14). These people are forgetting two things: first, the unbreakable bond existing between the old and the new dispensation (Luke

396. For a different answer, one worthy of serious consideration, see Cranfield, *op. cit.*, Vol. II, pp. 733, 734.

397. Other New Testament quotations from Ps. 69 are as follows:

Psalm 69 Verse(s)	*New Testament*
4	John 15:25
9a	John 2:17
21	Matt. 27:34, 48; Mark 15:23, 36; Luke 23:36; John 19:28, 29
22, 23	Rom. 11:9, 10
24	Rev. 16:1
25	Acts 1:20
28	Phil. 4:3; Rev. 3:5; 13:8; 17:8; 20:12, 15; 21:27

24:27, 44; John 5:46; I Cor. 10:1-4); and secondly, the indissoluble tie between Christ and his true followers (Acts 9:4; 22:7; 26:14; Col. 1:24).

The propriety of appealing to Scripture, as Paul does frequently and has done just now, is based on the principle embodied in verse

4. For whatever was written in former times was written for our instruction, in order that, through patient endurance and the encouragement of the Scriptures, we might have hope.

A very practical and unforgettable passage! In brief it informs us that if religion is going to mean anything to us we must practice it. Whatever was written in the Scriptures—which for Paul meant what we now call The Old Testament—was written "for our instruction."

As often, so also here, that word "instruction" indicates far more than impartation of *intellectual* knowledge. The emphasis, in fact, is on *practical* knowledge, knowledge that can be, and should be, applied to living the life of a Christian.

Two things are necessary if the sacred writings are going to be of benefit to us:

a. *patient endurance.* Anyone who diligently studies Scripture, asking God to apply its teachings to his heart and life, will be hurt by it again and again, for he will become more and more conscious of the fact that the distance between his own conduct and the ideal held before him in Holy Writ is great indeed. Nevertheless, he must pray for *strength to persist* in this study, learning more and more how to apply it to his life.

b. *the encouragement of the Scriptures.* Those who by God's grace and power persist in such a practical study will discover that these sacred writings, written in former times, not only hurt but also heal. In fact, they are filled with *encouraging* promises, which, when accepted by God-given faith, result in the birth and growth, within men's hearts, of firmly rooted Christian *hope*. See on verse 12.

What Paul is saying therefore is that the way in which Scripture will become a blessing for ourselves and through us also for others, is to put it into practice.

In a thrilling conclusion to his book[398] Col. E. W. Starling emphasizes that for the sake of the welfare of ourselves and of our nation we must begin to take to heart that *Christianity is* not just a theory to be believed but *a living force*.

5, 6. May the God (who is the Source) of patient endurance and of encouragement grant y o u to live in harmony with one another, in accord with Christ Jesus, so that with one heart and mouth y o u may glorify the God and Father of our Lord Jesus Christ.

---

398. *Starling of the White House*, Chicago, p. 327.

In the present passage the two concepts "patient endurance" and "encouragement" are taken up again from verse 4. The apostle, addressing the membership of the Roman church and all others who then or later would be made acquainted with the contents of this epistle, utters the solemn prayer-wish that, through the practical and devotional use of the Scriptures, the addressed, being made the recipients of the aforementioned two precious blessings, may reach the goal of living in harmony with one another. Cf. 12:16.

He adds a phrase about which there has been much controversy, but which can probably best be rendered "in accord with Christ Jesus." Just what does he mean by this?

Some interpret the little phrase to mean "in accord with *the will* of Christ Jesus."[399] Others, "in accord with *the pattern example* of Christ Jesus."[400] If a choice as to be made between these two my preference would be for the latter, since the context twice refers to Christ as the believers' example (verses 3 and 7). However, is it not possible that "in accord with Christ Jesus"[401] is broad enough to comprise both ideas? Does it not mean, "in accord with that which Christ Jesus has revealed concerning himself both by precept and example"? To the present interpreter it would seem that Murray is correct when he states that what is after Christ's example must always accord with his will.[402]

Accordingly Paul is expressing the prayer-wish that true believers everywhere and of every variety, whether "strong" or "weak," may strive to reach the goal of living in harmony with one another and thus also with the example and will of Christ Jesus.

It is not necessary that Christians think exactly alike on every subject. But it is necessary that in the lives of all God's children the love of Christ Jesus be reflected and his will be done. Thus all will become truly united into one holy and powerful fellowship, one *body*. Cf. Eph. 4:1-6. Thus, and thus alone, the stated purpose will be realized, namely, that "with one heart and mouth (cf. Acts 1:14; 2:46) y o u may glorify the God and Father of our Lord Jesus Christ." On glorifying God see also Ps. 150; John 17:1; Rom. 11:36; I Cor. 10:31.

The expression "The God and Father of our Lord Jesus Christ" (cf. II Cor. 1:3; 11:31; Eph. 1:3; I Peter 1:3) should present no difficulty. The title "*God* of our Lord Jesus Christ" places the emphasis on Christ's *human* nature, and "*Father* of our Lord Jesus Christ" calls attention to the Son's *divine* nature, for not nativistic but trinitarian sonship is referred to here, a kind of sonship in which Christ, by whatever name he is called, is placed on a par with the

---

399. Cranfield, p. 737; Michaelis, Th.D.N.T., Vol. I, p. 669; Käsemann, p. 383.

400. Harrison, p. 152; Greijdanus, Vol. II, p. 621; Ridderbos, p. 322.

401. Original κατὰ Χριστὸν Ἰησοῦν.

402. Vol. II, p. 201.

Father and the Spirit. For more about this see pp. 253, 254 on 8:9-11; and p. 315 on 9:5. See also Matt. 27:46 (=Mark 15:34) and John 20:17.

If we should stop at this point, we still would not have done justice to the wonderful prayer-wish found in verses 5 and 6. To catch the true meaning of the passage it should be brought into relationship with the person of Paul, the apostle; that is, with his actual situation at the time he dictated this epistle.

As was shown earlier (pp. 14, 15), when Paul composed Romans he was working in Corinth. He was by no means living on Easy Street in that city; not now (Acts 20:3), nor earlier. For the earlier situation in Corinth see Acts 18:6, 12; cf. I Cor. 1:11 f.; 2:3; 3:1; 5:1 f.; 10:14; 11:20 f. Besides, even before composing Romans the apostle had experienced a series of afflictions (see pp. 11, 12) so sharp and bitter that we may well ask whether under comparable circumstances many a present-day pastor would not have sent in his letter of resignation.

Nevertheless, so firmly fixed is Paul's resolution to continue, come what may, that he even rejoices in the Lord, and here in Rom. 15:5, 6 speaks of God as the source of the believers' "patient endurance and encouragement." Moreover, when he thinks of the Savior his enthusiasm knows no bounds, so that his language builds up to the striking climax: "Christ" (15:3), "Christ Jesus" (verse 5), "our Lord Jesus Christ" (verse 6). What a marvelous Christian leader, this man Paul! Rather, what a marvelous God, this Source of patient endurance and of encouragement, this God and Father of our Lord Jesus Christ!

7. Accept one another, then, just as Christ accepted y o u, to the glory of God.

In connection with this passage the question has been asked, "Does 'to the glory of God' modify 'Christ accepted y o u,' or does it go with 'Accept one another'?" The right answer is probably, "In a sense it modifies both." What Paul is saying amounts to this, "Just as Christ accepted y o u in order that by means of that acceptance God might be glorified—for he certainly is glorified by the hearts and lives of the accepted ones—so, and with the same ultimate purpose in mind, y o u should accept one another."

The high ideal expressed in verses 5 and 6, namely, to live in harmony with one another and with heart and mouth to glorify God, here (in verse 7) becomes the basis for the exhortation that the addressed should accept one another. See what has been said with respect to this acceptance in connection with 14:1 (including footnote 372). However, here (15:7) the *reciprocal* character of this acceptance is stressed. Not only should the strong accept the weak (as in 14:1), but the weak must also welcome the strong.

Before leaving this passage it should be pointed out that between (a) Christ's deed of accepting sinners, transforming them into beloved sons and daughters, and (b) the believers' acceptance of one another there is an almost infinite qualitative difference. For Christ to be able to accept sinners meant nothing less than leaving the glories of heaven, entering into the miseries of earth, and undergoing a death so agonizing that words are lacking to describe it. For saved sinners to accept one another implies no such sacrifice. Hymn writers have given expression to the contrast between the divine sacrifice and human sacrifices; see especially Frances Havergal's "I Gave My Life for Thee" and Isaac Watts' "When I Survey the Wondrous Cross." And as for the ultimate purpose of all human activity that is acceptable to God see Fanny Crosby's "To God Be the Glory."

The duty of Jew and Gentile to live in harmony with each other to God's glory is re-emphasized in verses:

8, 9a. For I declare that Christ has become a servant of the circumcised for the sake of God's *truth*, to confirm the promises made to the fathers; but the Gentiles glorify God for the sake of (his) *mercy* . . .

Verses 8, 9a indicate that not only for the Jews (lit. "for the circumcision"; cf. 3:30; 4:12; Gal. 2:7-9; and see footnote 119 on p. 149) but also for the Gentiles Christ has become and continues to be a "servant." Cf. Isa. 42:1. It was to the Jews that, during his public ministry, Jesus turned his attention first of all (Matt. 10:5, 6; 15:24; John 1:11). To them he *ministered*; i.e., rendered humble, personal service (Matt. 20:28; Mark 10:45; Luke 22:27).

He did this in order *to confirm God's truth*, his reliability, his *faithfulness* to the covenant promise, the promise made to Abraham (Gen. 12:1-3; 15:1; 17:7; 18:19; 22:18), Isaac (Gen. 26:1 f.), Jacob (Gen. 28:13-15; 32:28; 46:2-4), and Israel as a people (Exod. 20:1; 24:8). Christ *confirmed* the promise by again and again causing it to be realized in hearts and lives. Note the plural, "promises," indicating *the various affirmations* of the one central promise.

However, not only Jews but also Gentiles were blessed by the work of Christ, for from the very start it was the divine intention to gather his elect also from the latter. See Rom. 4:9 f., pp. 149-152; and 9:23 f., pp. 330.

Therefore, though, strictly speaking, God originally established his covenant with Abraham, Isaac, Jacob, the people of Israel, all of them Jews, nevertheless his *mercy* extended also to the Gentiles; in fact, "to the ends of the earth" (Isa. 45:22; 52:10), to all its "families" (Gen. 12:3).

For the love of God is broader
Than the measure of man's mind;
And the heart of the Eternal
Is most wonderfully kind.
—from *There's a Wideness in God's Mercy* by F. W. Faber

So, in connection with the work of Christ for *Israel* it is especially God's *truth, his covenant faithfulness*, that stands out; and in connection with his work among *the Gentiles* it is predominantly his comprehensive, condescending *mercy* that shines forth.

It has been suggested that the reason Paul makes this distinction between Israel and the Gentiles is that he is still thinking about "the weak" versus "the strong," the former being mostly Jews, the latter mostly Gentiles. That suggestion may well be correct. But was there not, perhaps, a more basic reason for the distinction Paul draws? *To be sure, no one is saved except through God-imparted, personal faith in the Lord Jesus Christ!* (John 3:16; 14:6; Acts 4:12). But the *approach* to one group differs from that to the other. The distinction clearly spelled out here in Rom. 15:8, 9a must not be ignored.[403] Contrast Peter's *covenant-promise* appeal, as recorded in Acts 2:38, 39, with Paul's appeal to *the kindness or mercy of God* as described in Acts 14:17 and 17:24, 25. Both Peter and Paul were right in speaking as they did, but Peter was addressing a predominantly Jewish audience, while Paul, both at Lystra and in Athens, was speaking to Gentiles.

Before conversion has occurred the initial approach to Jews differs from that to Gentiles, though Acts 4:12 holds for both. But when Jews and Gentiles have become believers, they are *one* people, as Paul clearly teaches (Rom. 10:11, 12) symbolized by *one* olive tree (11:17 f.).

In view of Christ's mediatorial work, there is now *one* body of believers. The cementing of this unity (see verses 5-7) was one of the chief goals of this missionary to the Gentiles. See p. 23. Through the work of Paul and others God saw to it that also the Gentiles would be *glorifying* God, as 15:9b-12 is about to show.[404]

9b-12. as it is written:
"Therefore I will praise thee among the Gentiles,
and sing hymns to thy name."
And again, it says,
"Rejoice, y o u Gentiles, together with his people."
And again,
"Praise the Lord, all y o u Gentiles
let all the peoples praise him."
And again, Isaiah says,
"There will spring up the root of Jesse,
he who arises to rule over the Gentiles.
In him shall the Gentiles hope."[405]

---

403. For more on this see my little book *The Covenant of Grace*, especially pp. 9-11; 39-76.

404. It is probably best to regard both Χριστὸν . . . πατέρων and τὰ δὲ ἔθνη . . . θεόν as being directly dependent upon λέγω. So construed note contrasting parallels:

Jews	Gentiles
truth	mercy

405. *Details respecting the Greek text:*

Verse 9b

This is taken from what is Ps. 18:49 in our English Bible. In the Hebrew Bible it is found in Ps. 18:50; and in the LXX in Ps. 17:50. Paul's text here in Rom. 15:9b is in complete accord with the masoretic text. The LXX text adds the word κύριε (O Lord) after ἔθνεσιν (Gentiles, nations). See also II Sam. 22:50.

Verse 10

This is an exact quotation of the LXX version of (part of) Deut. 32:43.

Verse 11

This reflects what is Ps. 117:1 in our English Bible; LXX Ps. 116:1.

LXX (translated into English):	*Paul (word for word):*
Praise the Lord, all y o u Gentiles	Praise, all y o u Gentiles, the Lord
Praise him, all y o u peoples.	And let praise him, all the peoples.

Again, as so often, Paul appeals to Scripture for corroboration of what he has just now said (see verses 8, 9a). He quotes four very appropriate passages. The first and third are from the book of Psalms; the second is from the Law; the fourth, from the Prophets, so that the three main divisions of the Old Testament are all represented here. Note "as it is written"; also "And again *it* says," where "it" means Scripture.

The four quotations are not selected at random, but form a striking climax.[406]

In the first quotation (verse 9b; cf. Ps. 18:49) the Psalmist states that *he* will declare God's name among the Gentiles. In the second (verse 10; cf. part of Deut. 32:43) *the Gentiles are summoned to join* in praising God. In the third (verse 11; cf. Ps. 117:1) the Gentiles are called upon *independently* to praise God. And in the fourth (verse 12; cf. Isa. 11:10) the attention is fixed upon the (Shoot springing up from the) Root of Jesse, who will rule over the Gentiles, and in whom they will *hope.* He is the One apart from whom the promises made to the fathers (verse 8) would remain unfulfilled, and without whom the Gentiles (verse 9a) would never be able to glorify God.

With Paul "hope" is *justifiable expectation*. It is *the solid foundation for future bliss*. It is the mainspring of the believers' courage and stick-to-it-ive-ness. Not only for the writer of the letter to the Hebrews but certainly also for Paul Christian hope is "an anchor for the soul, firm and secure, and entering into the inner sanctuary . . . where Jesus is" (Heb. 6:19, 20). This very Jesus is the One apart from whom the promises made to the fathers (Rom. 15:8) would remain unfulfilled, and without whom the Christians from among the Gentiles (verse 9a) would never be able to glorify God.

It is not surprising, therefore, that *hope* is a subject on which Paul loves to dwell (Rom. 4:18; 5:2, 4, 5; 8:20, 24, 25; 12:12; 15:4; II Cor. 3:12; Gal. 5:5; Eph. 1:18; Col. 1:5, 23, 27, etc.). In fact, in the very next verse the apostle directs the attention of the hearers and readers once more to hope and to its Source.

13. May the God of hope fill y o u with all joy and peace, in the exercise of (y o u r) faith, so that by the power of the Holy Spirit y o u may overflow with hope.

Note the following:

a. Another earnest and impressive prayer-wish. Cf. verse 5.

b. "the God of hope."

This "hope" does not indicate a weak aspiration but a firmly rooted expectation. See Heb. 6:19, 20. The phrase "the God of hope" means: the God who is the Source of hope and imparts it to those who trust him.

A comparison of Paul's text with that of the LXX will show that he has made three minor changes: a transposition in the first line; and in the second the addition of "And" plus the substitution of the third for the second person.

Verse 12

For the quotation from Isa. 11:10 Paul follows the LXX text, but omits ἐν τῇ ἡμέρᾳ ἐκείνῃ (in that day).

406. So also Ridderbos, p. 326.

c. The object of this hope is God Triune as revealed in the Shoot springing up from the Root of Jesse; in other words, as disclosed in the Lord Jesus Christ. See also above, on verse 12.

d. "joy and peace." This is the "joy unspeakable and full of glory" (A.V. I Peter 1:8), and the "peace of God that surpasses all understanding" (Phil. 4:7). See pp. 169, 249.

Paul was well aware of the fact that *in the presence of such joy and peace no room would be left for quarrels between "the weak" and "the strong."*

e. "in the exercise of y o u r faith."

Faith is God's gift, indeed, but that does not cancel the fact that man must exercise it. See Luke 8:50; Phil. 2:12, 13; II Thess. 2:13.

f. Though it is man who must exercise faith, he cannot do so by his own power but "by the power of the Holy Spirit."

g. "y o u may *overflow* with hope."

In Paul's writings we find a constant emphasis on the *overflowing* or "super" character of redemption in Christ. See Rom. 5:20, p. 184; further also II Cor. 7:4; Phil. 4:7; I Thess. 3:10; II Thess. 1:3; I Tim. 1:14; etc. In our present passage note

"fill . . . all . . . overflow."

h. "with hope." See above, under b.

And will Christian hope "be emptied in delight"? Will it vanish at the moment when the soul enters heaven? The answer is found in I Cor. 13: "Now *abideth* faith, hope, and love, these *three* . . ."

What a marvelous prayer-wish!

Practical Lessons Derived from Romans 14:1—15:13

Verse 14:1

"Him who is weak in faith accept, but not with the idea of passing judgment on (his) opinions." Time flies. Elimination of quarrels about non-essentials would conserve time and energy for proclaiming the good news of salvation to a world lost in sin. Also, if you wish to cure a person of his error, first of all make him feel "accepted." If his error is not basic, he may see it and, with the help of God, correct it before you even mention it.

Verse 4

"Who are you that you dare pass judgment on someone else's servant?" See also Matt. 7:1. That brother on whom you pass judgment is *not your servant but God's.* Besides, it is God alone who knows all that needs to be known before a judgment can be pronounced. We have no right to try to play God!

Verse 15a

"For if your brother is seriously upset because of what you eat, you are no longer walking in love." Always bear in mind: One loving deed is more valuable than a hundred correct opinions.

Verse 15b

"Do not by your eating destroy your brother for whom Christ died." Remember: that brother whom you are offending is a very valuable person. He was bought with Christ's own blood! Be careful, therefore, how you treat him!

Verse 19

"Let us then pursue the things that lead to peace and to mutual edification." Before I make an attempt to argue with my brother about eating and drinking or any other matter of secondary religious significance, I should ask myself the following questions:

a. Am I sufficiently well-informed about this matter?

b. Will this debate be helpful to the brother? Will it really *edify* him?

Verse 21

"It is better not to eat meat or drink wine or to do anything else that will cause your brother to stumble." What you are doing or are about to do may be ever so *lawful*. The question, however, is, "Is it *helpful*?" See I Cor. 6:12; 10:23.

Verse 15:7

"Accept one another, then, just as Christ accepted y o u, to the glory of God."

A very appropriate text for a sermon . . . on any Sunday of the year, but perhaps especially at the beginning of a new year.

Theme: ACCEPT ONE ANOTHER

1. Universal Need
2. Generous Provision
3. Resulting Obligation
4. Ultimate Purpose

The first two points would be mainly introductory. See Rom. 3:10, 23 for point 1; and 3:24 for point 2. The main thrust of the sermon would center on point 3 (see Rom. 15:7a) and point 4 (see 15:7b).

Verse 13

"May the God of hope fill y o u with all joy and peace, in the exercise of (y o u r) faith, so that by the power of the Holy Spirit y o u may overflow with hope."

Even though, strictly speaking, this is not a prayer but a wish, this wish can easily be changed into a prayer, since it certainly implies the prayer, "O God of hope, fill us with all joy and peace . . . so that by the power of the Holy Spirit we may overflow with hope."

Note the following:

a. What kind of joy and peace? See I Peter 1:8 and Phil. 4:7. Why are these gifts very important? See 15:13d.

b. How are these blessings obtained? Answer: by exercising faith, which implies the work of the Holy Spirit in our hearts.

c. How generously are they supplied? Note: "fill," "all." In fact, God grants us even more than we ask. We ask for joy and peace. He grants us joy and peace *and hope*; in fact, a hope so abundant that it *overflows* the boundaries of our hearts and minds . . . and will never cease to do so. In this connection see my book *The Bible on the Life Hereafter*, pp. 70-74.

Summary of Chapter 14:1—15:13

This can be found on pp. 453, 454.

Outline (continued)

Practical Application

Conclusion

Closing Commendation and Explanation of Boldness in Writing
"I myself am convinced, my brothers, that y o u yourselves are rich in goodness . . . Nevertheless, I have written to y o u rather boldly . . . because of the commission God in his grace has granted me, to be a minister of Christ Jesus to the Gentiles"
15:14-16

Review of the Past
"From Jerusalem all the way around to Illyricum, I have fully proclaimed the gospel of Christ"
15:17-22

Plan for the Future
"Now . . . I am on my way to Jerusalem, in the service of the saints. . . . When I have completed this task . . . I will go to y o u on my way to Spain"
15:23-29

Prayer Request
"I exhort y o u, brothers, by our Lord Jesus Christ and by the love of the Spirit, to join me in my struggle by praying to God for me"
15:30-33

Commendation of Phoebe. Paul's Own Greetings and Those of All the Churches
"Greet Prisca and Aquila, my fellow-workers in Christ Jesus"
16:1-16

Final Warning
"I exhort y o u, brothers, to watch out for those who cause divisions"
16:17-20

Greetings of Friends
"Timothy, my fellow-worker, greets y o u"
16:21-23

Doxology
"Now to him who is able to establish y o u in accordance with my gospel and the proclamation of Jesus Christ . . . be glory forever through Jesus Christ! Amen."
16:25-27

CHAPTER 15:14—16:27

ROMANS

14 I myself am convinced, my brothers, that y o u yourselves are rich in goodness, amply filled with knowledge, and competent also to admonish one another. 15 Nevertheless, I have written to y o u rather boldly on some points, so as to remind y o u of them again. (I have done so) because of the commission God in his grace has granted me,[407] 16 to be a minister of Christ Jesus to the Gentiles, with the priestly duty of proclaiming the gospel of God, in order that the Gentiles might become an offering acceptable (to him), sanctified by the Holy Spirit.

Conclusion

Closing Commendation and Explanation of Boldness in Writing

"I myself am convinced, my brothers, that y o u yourselves are rich in goodness . . . Nevertheless, I have written to y o u rather boldly . . . because of the commission God in his grace has granted me, to be a minister of Christ Jesus to the Gentiles"
15:14-16

Approaching this part of Paul's Epistle to the Romans we should by all means avoid the mistake of thinking that what is found in 15:14—16:27 is *only* a conclusion, a kind of P.S., or Appendix, which, with very little loss, one could well afford to skip. On the contrary, neglecting or even underestimating the importance of 15:14—16:27 would amount to missing a very important part of the application of the doctrine of justification by faith.

We should bear in mind that the person who composed this letter had experienced, and was experiencing, the effects of this very basic doctrine in his own life. What kind of a person resulted? By means of the very spirit that is revealed in Rom. 1:1—15:13 Paul has already told us something about himself (see, for example, chapter 12), as he has done also in such individual passages as 1:8-16; 7:7-25; 8:38, 39; 9:1-4; 10:1; 11:1. Nevertheless, it must be admitted that by far the most of 1:1—15:13 is *doctrinal* in character. However beginning with 15:14 Paul becomes intensely *personal*. In a very natural—one might almost say unintentional—manner he shows us, by his own example, what kind of a person *he*, this justified-by-faith individual, has be-

407. Literally: because of the grace given me by God.

come. In reading even the opening verses of this Conclusion we are arrested by his *tact, modesty, prudence, humility, and concern for the feelings of others.*

Consequently here, indeed, is sermon material! Are not such qualities—in association, of course, with all-important trust in God—the very ones which should be in evidence in our lives? And if a minister should be afraid to dwell on these virtues, because he knows that in *his* own life these traits are not exactly outstanding, is not his very awareness of this fact all the more a reason why he should proclaim their necessity loudly and clearly. so that both his congregation and he himself may receive a transforming blessing?

As we read this Conclusion we are reminded of 1:5, 8-16. In the earlier verses Paul gave expression to his yearning to visit his friends in Rome. That thought returns here (15:23, 24, 32). In 1:5 he made mention of his "gift of apostleship." In 15:15 he again refers to this "commission which God in his grace has granted" him. Were we astounded by the depth of Paul's humility revealed in his earlier statement, "I am yearning to see y o u . . . in order that we may be mutually encouraged by each other's faith . . ." (1:11, 12)? We are no less astonished by his boundless generosity as he now writes, "I myself am convinced . . . that y o u yourselves are rich in goodness, amply supplied with knowledge, and competent also to admonish one another" (15:14).

But though what Paul writes in 15:14 f. is a somewhat amplified restatement of what he had written in the earlier part of his letter, there are also differences. In 1:13 he had merely stated that until now he had been prevented from visiting his Roman friends. Here, in 15:19-23, he gives at least a partial answer to the question what it was that had prevented him from coming. Moreover, in this later section he is far more explicit in revealing his traveling plans (15:23-29) than he had been earlier (1:8-15). Note also the prayer request now added (15:30 f.).

14. I myself am convinced, my brothers, that y o u yourselves are rich in goodness, amply filled with knowledge, and competent also to admonish one another.

Paul does not make use of flattery. He feels, however, that in view of the fact that he has pointed out certain weaknesses pertaining to groups and individuals within the church, he should now emphasize that these blemishes do not diminish his high regard for the church as a whole. He says, "I myself am convinced that y o u yourselves are *rich in goodness*"; that is, in kindliness, generosity of heart and action (cf. Gal. 5:22; Eph. 5:9; II Thess. 1:11). He adds, "filled with knowledge," practical discernment of every kind. He even credits them with being able independently—that is, without the help of Paul or anyone else—to caution one another against specific faults.

Today the word "counseling" is heard again and again. Ever so many books and articles have been written about it. Well, the apostle here reveals that also in this respect "there is nothing new under the sun." There was mutual counseling already in his day, and it was of a high character. By and large the members of the Roman church were "*competent* to admonish one another."

What makes Paul's remark even more heart-warming is the fact that in making it he addresses the members as being his "brothers." For this term of affection see on 1:13 (p. 52) and 7:1 (pp. 214, 215). Note strengthening modifier "my" ("my brothers") here (15:14), adding to the cordial nature of a passage which shows how filled to overflowing with love was this heart of Paul; better still, how rich were the fruits of the operation of the Holy Spirit in his life.

Paul continues: **15a. Nevertheless, I have written to y o u rather boldly on some points, so as to remind y o u of them again.**

The apostle had issued warning against such evils as antinomian tendencies (ch. 6), arrogance on the part of some (11:20, 21; 12:3), opposition to governmental authorities (13:2), the strong ridiculing the weak, and the weak condemning the strong (14:1 f.). Mercifully he adds, "so as to remind y o u," as if to say, "Of course, y o u knew all these things, and needed only a reminder."

What Paul is saying is not entirely the same as, but nevertheless reminds one of, lines in Pope's *Essay on Criticism*:

> Men must be taught as if you taught them not,
> And things unknown proposed as things forgot.

15b, 16. (I have done so) because of the commission God in his grace has granted me, to be a minister of Christ Jesus to the Gentiles, with the priestly duty of proclaiming the gospel of God, in order that the Gentiles might become an offering acceptable (to him), sanctified by the Holy Spirit.[408]

Note the following:

a. Paul has been outspoken not because he is unkind but because of his sense of duty as a minister of Christ Jesus to the Gentiles.

b. When the apostle says that he has written in this manner as "a minister of Christ Jesus to the Gentiles," does he not imply that most of the addressed were believers from the Gentiles?

c. ". . . with the priestly duty of proclaiming the gospel of God, in order that the Gentiles might become an offering . . ."

---

408. διὰ τὴν χάριν, because of the grace; that is, the *gift* imparted to me by God's grace. For more on χάρις see N.T.C. on Luke 2:40, p. 181.

With λειτουργός (here acc. s. -ν) cf. "liturgist." Others to whom the word "minister" is applied, either literally or by implication, are Zechariah (Luke 1:23), the "prophets and teachers" of Antioch (Acts 13:1, 2), holy angels (Heb. 1:7, 14), and even Jesus himself (Heb. 8:2, 6). In a somewhat broader sense the word is applied to those who contribute to the cause of Christian benevolence (II Cor. 9:12). For its use in connection with tax-collectors see on Rom. 13:6, pp. 436, 437.

ἱερουργοῦντα, acc. s. masc. pres. participle of ἱερουργέω, to perform priestly duty, offer as a priest; in the New Testament here only.

προσφορά (cf. Acts 21:26; 24:17; Eph. 5:2; Heb. 10:5, 8, 10, 14, 18). The noun is derived from προσφέρω, to bring to or forward.

Does Paul mean that by proclaiming the gospel to the Gentiles he himself, in such cases where the message was accepted by faith, has brought these Gentiles to God as a sacrifice? Or is he saying that the Gentiles offered themselves to God as a sacrifice?

The first interpretation would seem to be paralleled by a passage from Isa. 66:20, "And they will bring all y o u r brothers, from all the nations, to my holy mountain in Jerusalem, *as an offering to the Lord*." Since it has become evident again and again that Paul was thoroughly acquainted with the Old Testament—certainly also with the prophecies of Isaiah!—this may well be the correct interpretation.[409]

Of course, even then, Paul is not forgetting that these converted individuals would also offer themselves "as sacrifices, living, holy, and well-pleasing to God . . ." (Rom. 12:1).

d. Such sacrifices are "acceptable" (cf. I Peter 2:5) to God, being "sanctified by the Holy Spirit."

---

17. In Christ Jesus, then, I have the right to glory with respect to my work for God. 18 For I will not venture to speak of anything except that which Christ, in leading the Gentiles to God, has accomplished through me by what I have said and done. 19 (He accomplished it) by the power of signs and wonders (performed) through the power of the Spirit. So, from Jerusalem all the way around to Illyricum, I have fully proclaimed the gospel of Christ. 20 But it has always been my ambition to preach the gospel where Christ was not known, that I might not be building on someone else's foundation. 21 Rather, as it is written,

"Those who were not told about him will see,
and those who have not heard will understand."

22 That is why I have often been hindered from coming to y o u.

Review of the Past
"From Jerusalem all the way around to Illyricum, I have fully proclaimed the gospel of Christ"
15:17-22

17-19a. In Christ Jesus, then, I have the right to glory with respect to my work for God. For I will not venture to speak of anything except that which Christ, in leading the Gentiles to God, has accomplished through me by what I have said and done. (He accomplished it) by the power of signs and wonders (performed) through the power of the Spirit.[410]

Note the following:

a. The connection between this verse and the immediately preceding context is immediately clear. Paul has described himself as "a minister of Christ Jesus to the Gentiles." So he now continues, "In Christ Jesus, then, I have

---

409. The idea that people can be presented to the Lord as a spiritual sacrifice was not strange to the Jews. See, for example, also S.BK. I, p. 84; III, p. 153.

410. Variants, such as πνεύματος θεοῦ and πνεύματος ἁγίου are probably the result of scribal addition. There does not seem to be a good reason to reject the shorter text.

the right to glory," etc. Exultation is in order; that is, exultation "in Christ Jesus," not self-glorification.[411] Cf. I Cor. 1:29-31; II Cor. 10:17. Note Paul's humility. He does not say, "For I will not venture to speak of anything except that which I have accomplished through Christ," but "For I will not venture to speak of anything except that which *Christ . . . has accomplished through me* by what I have said and done."

b. "*Christ* . . . has accomplished . . . through the power of *the Spirit*." Equal honor and credit is ascribed to both. For more on this see p. 253.

c. "He [Christ] accomplished it by the power of signs and wonders."[412] Both "signs" and "wonders" are *miracles*, supernatural deeds. A miracle is called a "wonder" when the emphasis is on the effect it has upon the beholder, causing him to be filled with the sense of wonderment and awe. On the other hand, when the miracle points away from itself and *sign*ifies the qualities (power, wisdom, grace, etc.) of the One who performs it, it is called a "sign."[413]

d. By far the best commentary on this statement of Paul, in which he reviews his past labors for the Lord, is certainly the book of Acts. It is strange that even some of the finest books on Romans fail to refer to Acts in this connection. Nevertheless, without thoughtfully reading what Luke in that book tells us concerning the signs and wonders which accompanied Paul's labors we are in danger of missing the real meaning and importance of the apostle's statement.

These "signs and wonders" were great in number and enormous in effect. At this point the reader should turn to Acts and read the following sections: 13:6-12; 14:1-3; 14:8-10; 16:16-18; 16:25 f.; 19:11-16. As a result of these miracles ". . . when the proconsul saw what had happened he believed . . ." And as a result of the last ". . . the name of the Lord Jesus was magnified."

However, as Paul makes clear, many of the miracles that occurred during his lengthy pre-Romans ministry were the immediate results of *preaching* (note "by what I have *said* and done") applied to hearts and lives by the Holy Spirit. These successes were "gospel triumphs." Cf. II Cor. 2:14. In fact, in the book of Acts the emphasis is placed on these *spiritual* victories. See the following passages; Acts 13:42-44, 48, 49; 16:5, 14, 15, 32-34; 17:4, 11, 12; 18:4, 8, 27, 28. In spite of fierce opposition from the side of both Jews and pagans, even the enemies had to admit that Paul and his companions "were turning the world upside down" (Acts 17:6). The apostle's own inspired phraseology is much better: "Christ was leading the Gentiles to God."

---

411. The word καύχησις, glorying, boasting, reason for glorying, right to boast, pride (exact meaning here, as always, depending on the specific context), was used earlier in 3:27, and occurs also in I Cor. 15:31; frequently in II Corinthians, beginning with 1:12; and also in I Thess. 2:19 and in James 4:16. For the verb καυχάομαι and related forms see pp. 100-102, including footnotes 62-64.

412. Cf. II Cor. 12:12, "signs and wonders and mighty deeds."

413. In the original a *miracle* or *work of power* is a δύναμις a *wonder* is a τέρας, and a *sign* is a σημεῖον. For more information on this subject see R. C. Trench, *op. cit.*, par. xci.

19b-21. So, from Jerusalem all the way around to Illyricum, I have fully proclaimed the gospel of Christ. But it has always been my ambition to preach the gospel where Christ was not known, that I might not be building on someone else's foundation. Rather, as it is written,

"Those who were not told about him will see,
and those who have not heard will understand."

The expression "from Jerusalem all the way around to Illyricum" will have little meaning to the present-day reader unless he has a map or sketch of the indicated region in front of him. See it on p. 489. Note especially the line extending from Jerusalem in the southeast to Illyricum (Yugoslavia and Albania, p. 24) in the northwest. Although the book of Acts does not mention any missionary activity in Illyricum, Paul may have entered that territory, or may have reached its borders, on one of the occasions when he was in Macedonia; see especially Acts 20:2.

Why does Paul mention Jerusalem as the starting point for missionary activity? In view of the fact that all three great missionary journeys started out from Syrian Antioch (Acts 13:1-3; 15:40, 41; 18:22, 23), why does he not rather say, "from Antioch" instead of "from Jerusalem"? Was it because some of his early—though not the earliest—preaching had been done in *Jerusalem* (Acts 9:26-29)? Or because (after the first missionary journey) the leaders of the *Jerusalem* church had enthusiastically endorsed Paul and Barnabas as missionaries to work among the Gentiles (Gal. 2:9; cf. Acts 15:1-35)? Or, perhaps, because while praying in the *Jerusalem* temple the Lord had appeared to Paul and had told him, "Go, for I will send you far away to the Gentiles" (Acts 22:17-21)?

All of these facts are important, and one or more of them may have been part of the reason why Paul wrote as he did. Nevertheless, the main reason was probably the fact that not Syrian Antioch but Jerusalem was the southeastern limit of the region covered by the apostle on his journeys.

It will be recalled that the first journey covered a relatively small territory: Syrian Antioch to the island of Cyprus, to a group of Galatian towns;[414] and then, after virtually retracing his path through these towns, returning by sea to Syrian Antioch (Acts 13:1-14:26).

On the second journey Paul proceeded from Syrian Antioch via Galatia and Troas to Macedonia. Then turning toward the south and somewhere crossing the Jerusalem-Illyricum diagonal, he went to Athens and from there to Corinth. Later, by way of Ephesus and Caesarea he in all probability visited the church in Jerusalem,[415] and from there returned to Syrian Antioch. Thus on this trip he actually "went around" the diagonal (Acts 15:36—18:22).

The third journey outward bound somewhat resembled the second. This time, however, the apostle, again starting out from Syrian Antioch and revisiting the Galatian churches, entered Macedonia via *Ephesus, where he re-*

414. See N.T.C. on Galatians, pp. 4-14.

415. If, "the church" in Acts 18:22 means "the Jerusalem church," as is probable).

"From Jerusalem all the way around to Illyricum"
Rom. 15:19

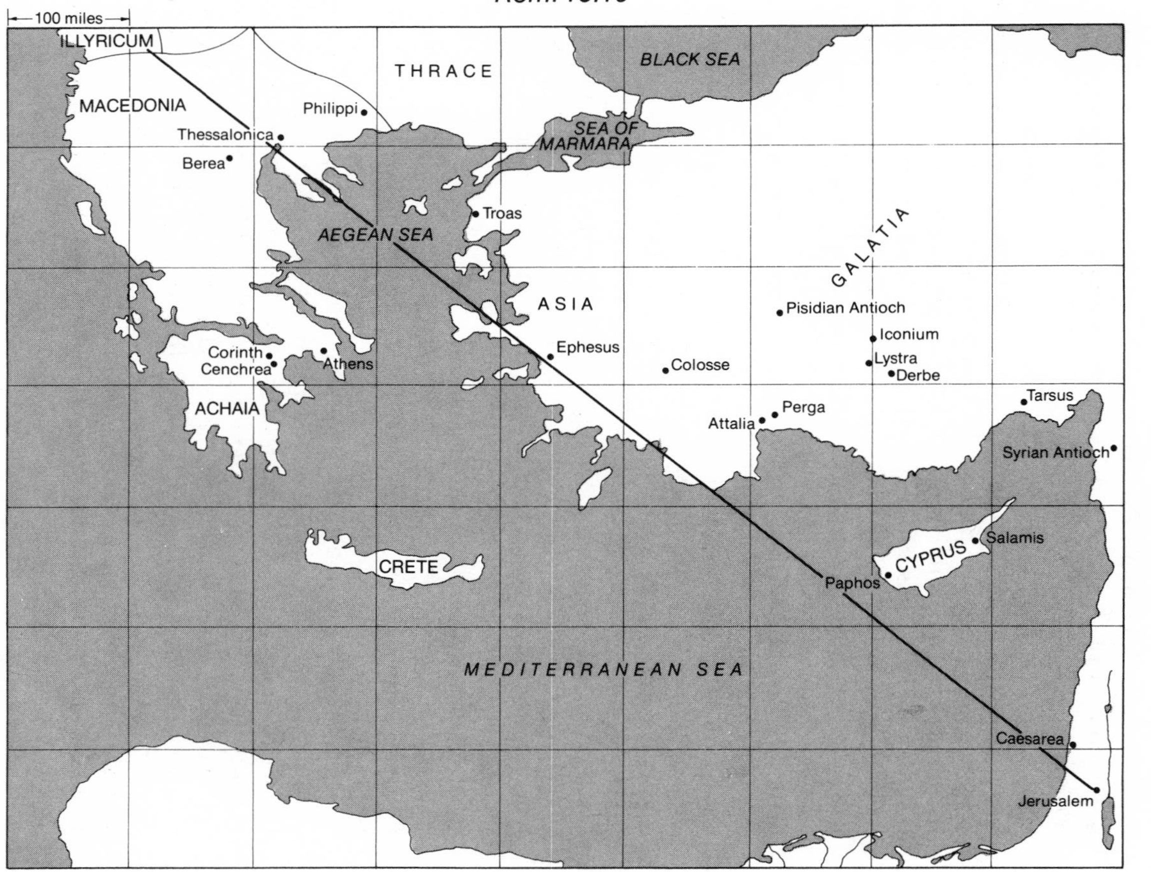

mained for a long time, instead of via Troas (as on the second trip). From Macedonia he proceeded to Corinth, where he is now, composing and dictating his epistle to the Romans (Acts 18:23—20:3a).

From this rapid review, accompanied by sketch, the expression "from Jerusalem to . . . Illyricum" is readily understood. In an age when travel was much slower than it is today, the area covered by Paul and his companions was certainly amazing in its extent.

Looking back, Paul is able to say, "I have fully proclaimed the gospel of Christ." This has been interpreted to mean, "In my gospel proclamation I have not omitted any important doctrine." In the present context that is, however, probably not the meaning, at least not the full meaning, the apostle is trying to convey. As will become clear in a moment, he is beginning to state the reason why he did not make an earlier visit to Rome. At least in part what he is saying amounts to this, "At an earlier time I would not have completed my gospel-blazing circuit. Now I have fulfilled or completed it." Verse 23 contains Paul's own explanation, "In these regions there is no longer any place for me to work."

Paul considered himself to be a trail-blazer for the gospel, a pioneer missionary, a founder of churches. He *planted*. Now let an "Apollos" come to *water* the seeds! See I Cor. 3:6. That this basic program did not in any way prevent the apostle from visiting an already flourishing congregation in order to enjoy and impart the blessings of Christian fellowship and even to preach a few sermons there, must be granted. But the apostle's main aim was to proclaim the good tidings to those who had not yet heard this uplifting message. His ambition was to establish new foundations (churches), not to build upon someone else's foundation.

He justifies this method of operation by very appropriately quoting Isa. 52:15, according to the LXX text, which in this case is a faithful rendering of the original Hebrew.

This portion of Scripture deserves a more detailed consideration than is generally given to it. It should be borne in mind that the fifty-second chapter of Isaiah immediately precedes Isaiah's most famous and familiar chapter, the fifty-third. The chapter division between 52 and 53 is not a happy one. Better would have been making the new chapter begin at 52:13. That new chapter (what is now 52:13-53:12) could then be given the title "From Suffering to Glory in the Life of the Coming Messiah." What are now the closing verses of chapter 52 contain a brief summary of this path from Humiliation to Exaltation, and what is now chapter 53 develops this theme in far greater detail.

There can be no question about the fact that, according to the New Testament, this prophecy refers directly to Jesus. See John 12:37; Acts 8:26-35; Rom. 10:16; I Peter 1:11; 2:24. In fact, Jesus himself so regarded it (Luke 22:37).

In describing Messiah's humiliation Isa. 52:14 predicts that "many will be appalled at him because of his disfigurement." Fulfilment: the physical abuse and mockery suffered by Jesus. But this humiliation gives way to exaltation: "He will be raised, lifted up, highly exalted." Think of Christ's resurrection, ascension, and coronation (taking his seat at the Father's right hand in heaven).

Isa. 52:15 shows that many nations will marvel because of his glory. Out of respect and reverence for him kings will keep silence before him. What follows is quoted by Paul here in Rom. 15, namely, "Those who were not told about him will see, and those who have not heard will understand."

That was the glorious prediction. Though many of his own people would reject the Messiah, Gentile kings and nations would listen to the wonderful tidings of salvation and would, by God's sovereign grace, hear and understand.

What Paul is saying, then, is that his prediction was being fulfilled in his own day; even more, that an important element was being realized in him as "the apostle to the Gentiles."

The question remains, "What was it that enabled Paul, writing from Corinth, after the completion of the first part of the third missionary journey—the part from Syrian Antioch, by way of Galatia, Ephesus, and Macedonia to Corinth—to believe and to state that he had now finished the great task of planting the gospel in the Jerusalem to Illyricum part of the Roman Empire? What was it that made it possible for him to say this *now* and not earlier; for example, after the completion of the second missionary journey? This belief and statement must have resulted from that which was accomplished on the third journey, during *the lengthy ministry at Ephesus.* It was from Ephesus that, by means of Paul *and his helpers*, one of them being Epaphras (Col. 1:7), the gospel had spread to the surrounding cities and towns; in all probability to Colosse and the other places located in the Lycus Valley, about 100 miles east of Ephesus (see the sketch), and to "the seven cities" mentioned in Rev. 1:11.

It would be difficult to exaggerate the results of the work of these church planters during this three-year period: "All the residents of [the province of] Asia heard the word of the Lord, both Jews and Greeks" (Acts 19:10. "In this way the word of the Lord spread widely and grew in power" (Acts 19:20). Not until this had been accomplished did Paul feel free to go to Rome. Or, in the words of Paul himself:

22. That is why I have often been hindered from coming to y o u.

---

23 But now that in these regions there is no longer any place for me to work, and since I have been longing for many years to see y o u, 24 (I plan to do so) when I go to Spain. I hope to see y o u in passing and to be helped forward by y o u after I have enjoyed y o u r company for a while. 25 Now, however, I am on my way to Jerusalem, in the service of the saints. 26 For Macedonia and Achaia have been pleased to make a contribution for the poor among the saints at Jerusalem. 27 They were pleased to do it and, indeed, they owe it to them; for if the Gentiles have come to share in the Jews' spiritual blessings, they owe it to the Jews to share with them their material blessings. 28 When I have completed this task, and have sealed this fruit to them, I will go to y o u on my way to Spain. 29 I know that when I come to y o u, I will come in the fulness of the blessing of Christ.

Plan for the Future
"Now . . . I am on my way to Jerusalem, in the service of the saints. . . .
When I have completed this task . . . I will go to y o u
on my way to Spain"
15:23-29

23, 24. But now that in these regions there is no longer any place for me to work, and since I have been longing for many years to see y o u, (I plan to do so) when I go to Spain. I hope to see y o u in passing and to be helped forward by y o u after I have enjoyed y o u r company for a while.

Note the following:

a. Paul mentions two reasons for his plan to visit the Roman church; the first relating to his task as a pioneer missionary; the second, to his love for the Roman Christians. The first: "there is no longer any place for me to work" (already explained); the second, "I have been longing for many years to see y o u." Cf. 1:10, 11.

b. the words "(I plan to do so) when[416] I go to Spain" show that visiting Rome's congregation is not the apostle's ultimate goal. That would be in harmony with his basic principle as expressed in verse 20. Nevertheless, visiting his Christian friends in Rome was certainly something to which he looked forward with eager anticipation.

c. Did Paul ever reach Spain? A definite answer cannot be given. We do, however, have the following early testimonies:

"Paul, having taught righteousness to the whole world, having gone to the limits of the West, and having given testimony before the rulers, thus was removed from the world and taken up into the Holy Place, having become the outstanding model of endurance" (Clement of Rome, I Corinthians V.vii). The expression "the limits of the West," most naturally refers to the western part of Europe; and in the present context, probably to Spain. This is especially true when, as in the present case, such a statement is made by someone who is writing from Rome.

"Luke relates them [these events] for the most excellent Theophilus because in his presence the individual events transpired, as he clearly declares by omitting the passion of Peter as well as the departure of Paul when the latter proceeded from the city (Rome) to Spain" (The Muratorian Fragment).

d. The words "I hope to see y o u in passing" should not be interpreted as if the apostle intends to rush through the city on his way to Spain. This expression simply reinforces the thought that Paul's ultimate destination is not Rome but Spain. That he intends to remain in Rome a while is clear from the very next line. Moreover, 1:11, 12, 15 show that the apostle looked

---

416. Greek ὡς ἄν = ὅταν followed by the pres. mid. subjunct. πορεύωμαι, "whensoever I go," indefinite; cf. "when I go to Rome, whenever that may be."

forward to enjoying sweet fellowship with the membership of the Roman church, and even to preaching the gospel in Rome.

e. "and to be helped forward by y o u." What does this imply? At this point some commentators restrict the meaning of the verbal form used by Paul[417] to *being commended to the grace of God* by the members of Rome's church (Acts 14:26; 15:40; implied in Acts 13:1-3). To be sure this is basic. Nevertheless, in accordance with the use of this verb elsewhere, some or all of the following items were probably also included: to be furnished with information, guides, provisions, money for the journey. The comprehensive meaning of the verb becomes clear when the following New Testament passages in which it occurs are read in light of their specific contexts: Acts 15:3; 20:38; I Cor. 16:6, 11; II Cor. 1:16; Titus 3:13; III John 6. See also Practical Lessons on Rom. 15:24, p. 524.

However, the addressees must not begin to think that Paul is about to make a straight course for Rome:

25-27. Now, however, I am on my way to Jerusalem, in the service of the saints. For Macedonia and Achaia have been pleased to make a contribution for the poor among the saints at Jerusalem. They were pleased to do it and, indeed, they owe it to them; for if the Gentiles have come to share in the Jews' spiritual blessings, they owe it to the Jews to share with them their material blessings.

Even though Paul regards preaching the gospel his main task (verses 16 and 20), he is deeply conscious of the fact that there is another very important obligation resting upon him, one that has to be discharged before he can wend his way to Rome, namely, that of helping to relieve the poverty of the Jerusalem saints. He knows that not only the soul but also the body must receive nourishment. The same Lord Jesus Christ who preached the Sermon on the Mount also fed the five thousand and the four thousand. The Savior's words recorded in Matt. 25:35, 36 are unforgettable.

Besides, the apostle remembered that some years earlier James, Peter, and John, leaders of the Jerusalem church, while extending to him the right hand of fellowship, in approval of his mission among the Gentiles, had added the words, "Only be sure to remember the poor," referring, of course, especially to the poor believers in Jerusalem.

This was also exactly in line with Paul's own thinking and planning (Gal. 2:10). He wanted to do it because he was a person with a loving heart, one who was eager to do something in return for the manner in which the Lord had blessed him. Besides, having himself been reduced to poverty again and again (II Cor. 11:27; Phil. 4:12), he was able to sympathize with those similarly afflicted. Last but not least, being a very practical person, he hoped that a gift coming from the Gentiles would contribute to the realization of his glorious purpose, namely, to break down once for all the terrible barrier

417. προπεμφθῆναι, aor. infin. pass. of προπέμπω, to send or help forward, to escort.

existing between Jew and Gentile, and to establish one holy universal church. Cf. Rom. 10:12; Eph. 2:14, 18; 4:4.

It deserves special attention that Paul tells the Romans that Macedonia and Achaia (see the sketch on p. 489)—meaning the Christians living in these provinces—*have been pleased* to make a *contribution*; that is, to give material expression to their participation in Christian *fellowship* with the believers in Jerusalem.[418] Though this was indeed a fact, it is worthy of note that Paul very generously omits to point out that he himself, by means of earnest and urgent exhortations (I Cor. 16:1-4; II Cor. 8 and 9), had contributed substantially to making it a fact.

The apostle points out, moreover, that the action of the Gentiles in relieving the need of Jerusalem's poor must not be viewed as cause for self-congratulation ("what good persons are we!") but rather as a moral obligation. The Gentiles have begun to share the Jews' spiritual blessings, those resulting from the acceptance of the gospel. Then should they not do their utmost to lighten the material burden under which their donors are groaning? In reality do not the spiritual blessings outweigh anything of a material nature that could be offered in return?

28, 29. When I have completed this task, and have sealed this fruit to them, I will go to y o u on my way to Spain. I know that when I come to y o u, I will come in the fulness of the blessing of Christ.[419]

The words, "When I have completed this task . . . I will go to y o u on my way to Spain" are clear. The explanation is found in verses 25, 26. See also Acts 24:17.

However, the expression "and have sealed this fruit to them" is among the most controversial in Romans. Rather than bother the reader with a description of all kinds of theories which I, along with many others, cannot accept, let me immediately present the view which strikes me as being the most reasonable.[420]

A church had been established in Jerusalem. By far the majority of its members were, of course, Christian *Jews*. They had accepted Jesus Christ as their Lord and Savior. For them it was difficult, however, fully to agree with the doctrine of "freedom in Christ." When they knew that Gentiles were no longer compelled to submit to circumcision or to avoid foods which in the law had been declared "unclean," some objected (Acts 15:1, 5). See what

418. It is interesting to observe that the word used in Gal. 2:9 to indicate *fellowship* is the same as that which here in Rom. 15:26 indicates a *contribution*. That Greek word—*koinonia*—has become so familiar in our circles that it is listed as an English word in Webster's Third International Dictionary.

419. εὐλογίας Χριστοῦ, supported by the leading MSS should be preferred to the expansion τοῦ εὐαγγελίου τοῦ Χριστοῦ, supported by later witnesses.

420. My view has much in common with that of the following authors:
S. Greijdanus, *op. cit.*, Vol. I, pp. 649, 650.
E. F. Harrison, *op. cit.*, pp. 158, 159.
H. Ridderbos, *op. cit.*, pp. 337, 338.
G. B. Wilson, *op. cit.*, pp. 239, 240.

has been said about this earlier, in connection with the subject of "the weak" and "the strong" (pp. 452-454). Besides, when these people noticed that the Gentile churches were rapidly increasing in membership, while they—their Jerusalem churches—were hard pressed to hold their own, they began to look askance at what was happening in the Gentile world.

There was really no excuse for their hesitancies, scruples, criticisms, and doubts. Had they only accepted *all* the teachings of Jesus, there would have been no problem. Had not Jesus pronounced a blessing upon the centurion, who did not belong to the people of the circumcision (Matt. 8:5-13)? And had not the Lord pronounced all foods "clean" (Mark 7:14-19)?

Now one of the reasons for organizing the drive for assistance to Jerusalem's poor saints had probably been to convince the Jerusalem Jews and others who agreed with them that they should accept Gentile Christians as equals. See Acts 10:1—11:18. When, therefore, the apostle now describes the contribution or collection as "fruit," he probably means that it must be regarded as a product of the Gentiles' genuine faith and of their sincere gratitude for the willingness of the Jewish believers to share with them their faith in Christ.

The gift from the Gentiles proved that the gospel was having a beneficial effect in their lives. It was the visible evidence of the operation of the Holy Spirit in the hearts and lives of the donors. And the handing over of this gift sealed or certified this gratifying fact to the Jewish recipients. Cf. Eph. 1:14, and see also N.T.C. on Philippians, pp. 61, 62, 208.

Do the words, "I know that when I come to y o u," etc. imply that Paul realized that the Romans might be somewhat disappointed about the news that he could not come to them directly but must first visit Jerusalem? However that may be, he now assures them that when he does come he will arrive "in the fulness of the blessing in Christ."

In view of 15:24 and also of 1:11, 12, 13b, 15, he must have had in mind such blessings as the joy of meeting and conversing with one another, his preaching in their midst, their listening to the apostle's report about divine blessings in other congregations, together planning the trip to Spain, etc.

When Paul was writing this, he had no way of knowing that his actual meeting with his friends in Rome would take place a few years later (see Acts 24:27; 28:11) than he had expected, and that he would be arriving as a prisoner. But even then a hearty welcome was in store for him (Acts 28:11-15), and he would receive much encouragement (Phil. 1:12-14), though some of the conditions in the Roman church would prove to be of a disappointing nature (Phil. 1:15a, 17).

---

30 I exhort y o u, brothers, by our Lord Jesus Christ and by the love of the Spirit, to join me in my struggle by praying to God for me, 31 that I may be rescued from the disobedient in Judea, and that my ministry to Jerusalem may be acceptable to the saints, 32 so that by God's will my coming to y o u may be a matter of joy, and that together with y o u I may be refreshed. 33 The God of peace be with y o u all. Amen.

Prayer Request
"I exhort y o u, brothers, by our Lord Jesus Christ and by the love of the Spirit, to join me in my struggle by praying to God for me"
15:30-33

What we have here is (a) an appeal, (b) a description of the character of the prayer requested by Paul, (c) an indication of its contents, and (d) of its purpose. All this is climaxed by (e) an appropriate and concluding prayer-wish.

A. *The Appeal*

30. I exhort y o u, brothers, by our Lord Jesus Christ and by the love of the Spirit . . .

The very wording indicates that Paul is deeply conscious of the need of the prayers of the church for him. Note the solemnity of the expression, "by our Lord Jesus Christ," referring to the Savior in all the fulness of his being and meaning for the church. Note especially "our," for he is both Paul's Lord and the Lord of the addressed.

Paul appeals to "our Lord Jesus Christ" because it was that same Lord who had sacrificed himself for Paul out of love for him (Gal. 2:20), and who had personally appointed him to be the apostle to the Gentiles (Acts 22:17-22).

He appeals also to "the love of the Spirit," probably indicating (though not all agree) that very love which the Spirit has poured out into the hearts of all those who belong to Christ (Rom. 5:5) and who therefore can be expected to pray for one another.

B. *Description of the Character of the Requested Prayer*

. . . to join me in my struggle by praying to God for me . . .

There is nothing superficial about genuine prayer. Isaiah describes it as a *taking hold* of God (64:7). For Jacob—that is, "Israel"—it was a *wrestling* with God (Gen. 32:24-30). And Paul here similarly calls it a *struggle*. Cf. Col. 2:1; 4:12. The apostle desires that the Roman believers join him in an intensely earnest and yearning petition.

C. *Its Contents*

The first requested petition is:

31a. that I may be rescued from the disobedient in Judea . . .

He refers here to the opposition he expects from the side of the unbelieving Jews in his own country. He calls them "disobedient" because of their refusal to subject themselves to the will of God as revealed in the gospel (Rom. 10:21; 11:30). That these Jews bitterly opposed Paul was made very clear when he was about to sail to Syria on his way to Jerusalem, and a plot by the Jews against his life was discovered. As a result traveling plans were changed, the apostle instead going to Jerusalem by way of Macedonia (Acts

20:3). Moreover, he had not forgotten that earlier too the Jews had made an attempt to murder him (Acts 9:29, 30). See also Acts 20:22, 23; 21:4, 10, 11, 27 f.

The second requested petition is:

31b. and that my ministry to Jerusalem may be acceptable to the saints.

Paul had worked long and hard for this "collection" or "contribution" from the Gentiles for the poor saints in Jerusalem. Nevertheless, he was afraid that those for whom it was intended might not even be willing to accept the gift. He knew but too well that, in spite of the decisions of the Jerusalem Council (Acts 15:19-29), opposition to himself and his gospel of freedom in Christ had never ceased. See Acts 15:1, 5; Gal. 3:1 f., 17; 5:1-4; 6:12. That explains his request for this earnest petition.

D. *Its Purpose*

32 . . . so that by God's will my coming to y o u may be a matter of joy, and that together with y o u I may be refreshed.

The prospect here visualized is very pleasing: the plots of the Jews are foiled, and the Jerusalem saints, emancipated from their prejudices, not only welcome Paul but are also delighted with the "benevolence" he brings. As a result Paul, filled with joy, heads for Rome, where he finds refreshment in the company of his dear friends!

But that is not entirely what happened. In some repects the very opposite occurred. We are reminded of the adage, "Man proposes; God disposes"; expressed just as succinctly in German: der Mensch denkt, Gott lenkt; cf. the Dutch: de mens wilkt, God beschikt.

What actually happened is recorded in Acts 21:17—28:16. What should be emphasized, however, is that Paul submits himself, with body and soul, for life, death, and eternity, to the wise and sovereign will of God. He writes "by God's will." In the present context God's decretive will is indicated. Result: even though events turned out in a manner Paul could not have anticipated, after he had been in Rome for a while he was able to write, "Now I want y o u to know, brothers, that the things that have happened to me in reality turned out to the advantage of the gospel . . ." (Phil. 1:12).

E. *The Prayer-Wish*

33. The God of peace be with y o u all. Amen.

Note the following:

a. Paul has been speaking about the Roman congregation, Jerusalem's Judaizers, the people of Macedonia and Achaia, his own traveling plans, etc. All of these are subject to change. Contingency is the universal rule. Stability is nowhere to be found. Nowhere? No, nowhere . . . except in God! That is why the present passage fits so neatly into this context; yes, *especially* here, where the apostle has just now revealed his uncertainty with reference to what might or might not happen to him in Jerusalem. Besides, in the immediately preceding line he has made mention of God's will. So also for this reason a reference here to "the God of peace" is very appropriate.

b. The expression, "the God of peace" must mean "the God who is the Author of peace," that is, who imparts peace. See II Thess. 3:16. Apart from close communion with him there is no peace.

c. The expression "the God of peace" is found also in Rom. 16:20; II Cor. 13:11; Phil. 4:9; I Thess. 5:23; and Heb. 13:20; the very closely related "Lord of peace" occurs in II Thess. 3:16.

d. The meaning of the word *peace* has been explained in connection with earlier passages (for example 1:7; 2:10; 5:1; 8:6; etc.). Basic to it is reconciliation with God through the death of his Son. As a result the person who has been thus reconciled has the inner assurance that past sins are forgiven, present events are being overruled for good, and in the future nothing will be able to separate him from the love of God in Christ. Consequently this person has received the richest blessing of all: salvation full and free, "prosperity," shālōm in its most comprehensive, religious sense, including serenity, the confidence: all is well.

e. When the apostle now expresses the prayer-wish that this God of peace be *with* those whom he addresses, he means that his inner desire—a desire to be realized in all who love the Lord—is that this God of peace may come so close to them that they may experience his peace in their lives, may meditate on it, possess it, rejoice in it. Compare the title *Emmanuel*, that is, "God *with* us," with the sick to heal them, with the hungry to feed them, and over-arching everything else, with the lost to seek and save them. See N.T.C. on Matthew, p. 141.

f. The apostle concludes this prayer-wish by adding the word of solemn affirmation and enthusiastic approval *Amen*. Cf. 1:25.

---

16 1 I commend to y o u our sister Phoebe, who is (also) a servant of the church at
Cenchrea, 2 I ask y o u to extend to her a welcome in the Lord that is worthy of
the saints, and to give her any help she may need from y o u, for she has been a
helper to many people and to me personally.
3 Greet Prisca and Aquila, my fellow-workers in Christ Jesus, 4 who risked their necks to
save my life, and to whom not only I but all the churches of the Gentiles are grateful. 5 (Greet)
also the church (that meets) at their house. Greet my beloved Epenetus, who is Asia's firstfruits
for Christ. 6 Greet Mary, who labored much for y o u. 7 Greet Andronicus and Junias, my
fellow-countrymen and (former) fellow-prisoners, who are outstanding among the apostles
and who were in Christ before I was. 8 Greet Ampliatus, my beloved in the Lord. 9 Greet
Urbanus, our fellow-worker in Christ, and (greet) my beloved Stachys. 10 Greet Apelles,
who is approved in Christ. Greet those who belong to the household of Aristobulus. 11 Greet
Herodion, my fellow-countryman. Greet those of the household of Narcissus who are in the
Lord. 12 Greet Tryphena and Tryphosa, who labor in the Lord. Greet Persis, the beloved,
who has labored much in the Lord. 13 Greet Rufus, the elect in the Lord, and his mother
and mine. 14 Greet Asyncritus, Phlegon, Hermes, Patrobas, Hermas, and the brothers (who
are) with them. 15 Greet Philologus and Julia, Nereus and his sister, and Olympas, and all
the saints (who are) with them. 16 Greet one another with a holy kiss.
All the churches of Christ extend greetings to y o u.

Conclusion

Commendation of Phoebe. Paul's Own Greetings and Those of All the Churches
"Greet Prisca and Aquila, my fellow-workers in Christ Jesus"
16:1-16

For the integrity of the text of Rom. 16:1-23 see Vol. I, pp. 26-28. On verse 24 see footnote 437, p. 513. As to the authenticity of 16:25-27 see Appendix, pp. 521-523.

A. *Commendation of Phoebe*

1, 2. I commend to y o u our sister Phoebe, who is (also) a servant of the church at Cenchrea. I ask y o u to extend to her a welcome in the Lord that is worthy of the saints, and to give her any help she may need from y o u, for she has been a helper to many people and to me personally.

The list of greetings is preceded by a note in which a certain lady named Phoebe is introduced and warmly commended to the church at Rome. It is reasonable to believe that it was Phoebe who, in departing for Rome, carried Paul's letter with her and delivered it to its destination. Some manuscripts even make mention of this in a subscript. We can easily understand that a note or letter of commendation, serving as a credential, was of great value both to the bearer and the addressed. Cf. II Cor. 3:1.

The lady's name *Phoebe* means *bright, radiant.* It is derived from pagan mythology, being another name for Artemis, the bright and radiant moon goddess, identified with the Roman goddess Diana. There are those who think that Phoebe must have been a Gentile Christian because—so they reason—Jews would certainly not give their children pagan names.

That reasoning may well be open to question, however, We should bear in mind that, as a result of Alexander the Great's conquest, with its accompanying spread of Hellenistic culture, names of Greek-pagan origin became popular all over the empire. Jews too soon adopted the habit of giving their children Greek names, just as even today Christian parents do not hesitate to name their children Dennis, Dion, Diana, Isadora, etc. And does anyone bother to change the pagan names of the days of the week?[421]

When Paul calls Phoebe "our sister," he means "our sister in the Lord." He continues, "who is (or "who is also")[422] a servant of the church at Cenchrea." Cenchrea was Corinth's seaport looking toward Asia. It was situated on the Saronic Gulf. See the sketch on p. 489. A few years earlier Paul had sailed from this port on his way from Corinth to Ephesus (Acts 18:18).

By calling Phoebe a *servant* of Cenchrea's church Paul probably means that she occupied a stable position, performed a definite and important function, in and for that church. She is accordingly called a *diakonos* of that

---

421. For more on this subject of pagan names see N.T.C. on Philippians, pp. 138, 139, footnote 116.

422. Whether καί is authentic is uncertain.

congregation. In Rom. 15:8 Christ was described as having become a *diakonos*, that is, a *servant*, of the circumcised. To them he *ministered*. However, the word *diakonos* can also be used in a more specialized or technical sense. In Phil. 1:1 and I Tim. 3:8 it refers, in the plural, to deacons.

If that technical sense pertains to the word as used here in Rom. 16:1, then Paul is calling Phoebe a *deaconess*. Now it must be granted that in a later century the ecclesiastical office of deaconess was not unknown.[423] The question, however, is "Does *the New Testament* either here (Rom. 16:1) or anywhere else, refer to such an ecclesiastical office, namely, that of deaconess?" On this subject there is a division of opinion. For details see footnote 424.

The absence of any mention of deaconesses in the rest of the New Testament is a fact. For I Tim. 3:11 see N.T.C. on Timothy, pp. 133, 134; and for Titus 2:3-5 see N.T.C. on Titus, pp. 364-366.

In order to discover what kind of specific function Paul has in mind when he calls Phoebe a *diakonos* of the church at Cenchrea, we should pay close attention to what he says; namely, "Extend to her a welcome in the Lord that is worthy of the saints," meaning, such a welcome as would be fitting for saints to give. He adds, "Give her any help she may need . . . for she has been a helper[425] to many people and to me personally."

This may well be the key to the solution of the problem we are discussing. In light of the facts reported in 16:1, 2, what kind of help would Phoebe need when she arrived in Rome, which was clearly not the place of her residence? Would it not be protection and especially hospitality? And what kind of help did those travelers need who were passing through, and stopping over at, the seaport Cenchrea, Phoebe's home-town, proceeding from west to east or from east to west? Is it not a fact that even today such very busy junctions make strangers feel somewhat uneasy? Was not what they needed a cordial word of greeting, good advice, protection against danger, and frequently even a friendly home in which to pass the night, or even the

---

423. See *Apostolic Constitutions* II 26, 57; III 7, 15. On this subject also consult S.H.E.R.K., Vol. I, p. 245.

424. Among those who favor the rendering *deaconess* here in Rom. 16:1 are the following: C. Hodge, p. 704; J. A. C. Van Leeuwen and Jacobs, p. 279; R. C. H. Lenski, pp. 898, 899; C. E. B. Cranfield, p. 781; A. Schlatter, p. 396; W. Sanday and A. C. Headlam, p. 417; O. Michel, p. 377; A. F. N. Lekkerkerker, Vol. II, p. 187; and, most recently, R. Y. K. Fung, "Charismatic versus Organized Ministry," *EQ*, 4 (1980), pp. 195-237.

On the other hand, B. H. Beyer, in his article on this word (Th.D.N.T., Vol. II, p. 93), states that it is an open question whether Paul is referring to a fixed office or simply to Phoebe's service on behalf of the community. J. Denny, p. 717, regards the rendering "deaconess" as being "too technical." S. Greijdanis (Vol. II, p. 657) also rejects "deaconess." H. Ridderbos points out that if Phoebe ministers to the saints, as is clear from verse 2, she would be a *servant* of the church. What Paul stresses is Phoebe's importance for the church. That the word *diakonos*, as here used, refers to an ecclesiastical office of deaconess cannot be proved. Ridderbos adds that nowhere else does the New Testament make mention of deaconesses (pp. 341, 342).

425. προστάτις, fem. of προστάτης, one who stands in front, protector, helper.

days and nights until the next ship would leave harbor on the way to their destination?

In a word it was *hospitality* that was needed at very busy Cenchrea. And it was *hospitality* Phoebe knew how to offer. Is it not probable that, like Lydia (Acts 16:11-15, 40), Phoebe was a well-to-do Christian lady, blessed with an alert mind and with a heart overflowing with the spirit of kindness and helpfulness? Perhaps, also like Lydia, Phoebe was a businesswoman.

We can well understand that Paul must have referred many a "case" to Phoebe. For that reason, and probably also for other reasons, Paul is able to say, "For she has been a great help to many people and to me personally."

For a list of worthy women, including Phoebe, mentioned in Scripture, see N.T.C. on I Timothy, pp. 133, 134. The lesson is clear. Two extremes should be avoided: (a) that of ordaining women to an ecclesiastical office when there is no warrant for doing so in Scripture; and (b) that of ignoring the very important and valuable services devout and alert women are able to render to the church of our Lord and Savior Jesus Christ.

B. *Paul's Own Greetings*

In connection with the greetings (16:3-16a), the question, "How could Paul have known so many persons in Rome, since he himself had never been there?" has been answered. See p. 27 (under *3a*) and p. 28 (under *As to 3a*). The following facts should also be taken into consideration:

1. Several of these very names occur on inscriptions found in or near Rome (on tombstones, etc.). This does not necessarily mean that the same name refers to the same person. It does indicate that we can no longer be surprised about the occurrence of the name in Paul's epistle to the *Romans*.
2. Some of the names are definitely Latin: Junias, Ampliatus, Urbanus.
3. Mark, writing to the *Romans*, mentions "Simon, the father of Alexander and Rufus," as if to say, "people with whom y o u, in Rome, are well acquainted." Cf. Rom. 16:13, "Greet Rufus."
4. All the codices contain this list of names as part of Paul's epistle to the *Romans*.

Anent the reason for the inclusion of all these greetings, as was indicated previously (p. 28), the very fact that Paul had not been in Rome himself made it advisable warmly to greet those members of the congregation with whom he was acquainted, in order thus to gain an entrance into the hearts of the entire Roman church.

3-5a. Greet Prisca and Aquila, my fellow-workers in Christ Jesus, who risked their necks to save my life, and to whom not only I but all the churches of the Gentiles are grateful. (Greet) also the church (that meets) at their house.

Aquila was a Jew, a native of Pontus. We may assume that his wife, Prisca (in Acts called Priscilla), was also Jewish.[426] These two are always mentioned

426. Meaning of names: Aquila=eagle; Prisca=old woman; Priscilla =little old woman.

together. Their names are mentioned three times by Paul (Rom. 16:3; I Cor. 16:19; II Tim. 4:19), and also three times by Luke (Acts 18:2; 18:18; 18:26).

They were great travelers, moving often from one place to another, as has been indicated (pp. 16, 17). When Paul first met them they had recently come from Rome, having been expelled from that city by the decree of emperor Claudius, who had ordered all the Jews to leave Rome (Acts 18:2).

The two were tentmakers, as was Paul. Better still, they were Christians. Was it Paul who had been instrumental in bringing about their faith in the Lord Jesus Christ? Here in Rom. 16:3 Paul calls them "my fellow-workers in Christ Jesus." So all three—Paul, Prisca, Aquila—were partners both in daily vocation and in gospel proclamation. It is not surprising that in Corinth Paul had made his home with them (Acts 18:3).

When Paul, during his second missionary journey, homeward bound, departed from Corinth in order to make a quick stop at Ephesus, with a promise to return there later, Prisca and Aquila went with him. But when Paul departed from Ephesus and sailed to Caesarea, Prisca and Aquila remained at Ephesus (Acts 18:18-21). In that city there was work for them. It may be described as laying the foundation for the apostle's subsequent lengthy ministry in that city, described in Acts 19.

One day a famous and fervent preacher, an Alexandrian Jew, named Apollos, arrived in Ephesus. When Prisca and Aquila noticed that in spite of his eloquence and great learning there was something lacking in his knowledge of "the way of God," they invited him to their home and gave him further instruction (Acts 18:24-26).

It was toward the close of Paul's lengthy ministry at Ephesus that he wrote I Corinthians. Now he was with Prisca and Aquila again, as is clear from the fact that in his greetings he includes this item, "Aquila and Prisca greet y o u warmly in the Lord, and so does the church that meets at their house" (I Cor. 16:19).

Here in Rom. 16:3-5a Paul causes the salutation to Prisca and Aquila to be the first of a lengthy list. Not only is it the first, it is also the fullest and the longest of the greetings. It now appears that the couple had "risked their necks" for Paul; that is, had hazarded their lives for his sake. Did this happen during the riot at Ephesus described in Acts 19:23-41? Cf. I Cor. 16:9, 19; II Cor. 1:8-10. We cannot be certain about this. What is clear, however, is that the devout couple was and remained loyal to Paul to the nth degree.

Paul, in turn, was not slow in letting everybody know what Prisca and Aquila had done for him. Our passage shows that from all over, wherever Gentile churches had been established, messages of praise and gratitude poured in for this self-sacrificing loyalty of Prisca and Aquila. Note also that now the couple is back in Rome again, to which the apostle is addressing this letter. Once more, as in Ephesus, the home of Prisca and Aquila is a meeting-place for the congregation. On the subject of house-churches see pp. 22, 23. So Paul adds, "(Greet) also the church (that meets) at their house."

It appears from II Tim. 4:19 that at a later time the two left Rome once more and returned to Ephesus. The reason for this return may have been the Neronian persecution. It was from his prison in Rome that Paul, shortly before his death, sent one last greeting to these two loyal partners.

It is worthy of note that in two of the three instances in which Paul mentions this couple the name of Prisca occurs before that of Aquila. Similarly, in two of the three passages in Acts Priscilla is mentioned first. We wonder why this is so. Could the reason be that in this case the wife ranked even higher than the husband in her labors for Christ? However that may be, from the list of honorable women mentioned in Scripture Prisca (=Priscilla) must not be omitted. She deserves to be mentioned in one breath with Lydia, Phoebe, and all the others. And her husband too was fully committed to the cause of Christ.

It must have been with special emphasis—his heart probably throbbing a bit faster, his eyes brimming with tears of love and gratitude—that Paul wrote, "Greet Prisca and Aquila."

During his missionary career Paul had colleagues and fellow-workers. But he deemed it necessary to oppose Peter to his face (Gal. 2:11 f.). With Barnabas he had such a sharp disagreement that the two parted company (Acts 15:39). There was a time when Paul refused to allow Mark to remain one of his companions (Acts 15:38). He was going to reprimand Euodia and Syntyche (Phil. 4:2). And Demas was going to desert him (II Tim. 4:10). But even though Prisca and Aquila in a sense stood closer to him than any others—for they were his companions both in trade and in faith—as far as the record shows, between Paul, on the one hand, and Prisca and Aquila, on the other, there was always perfect harmony!

5b. (Greet) my beloved Epenetus, who is Asia's firstfruits for Christ.

Epenetus means praiseworthy.[427] It is fitting that Epenetus (or Epaenetus), who is Asia's[428] "firstfruits" or "first convert for Christ," is mentioned right after the greeting addressed to Prisca and Aquila, who were deeply involved in missionary activity carried on in that general region, the western part of Asia Minor, with its leading city Ephesus.

The very expression "firstfruits" implies that many others were to follow, which was actually what happened (Acts 19:10, 20). For the word "firstfruits" see also on 8:23 (p. 270) and on 11:16 (p. 369). Note "for Christ" because believers belong to him, since he has bought them with his precious blood (I Cor. 6:20; 7:23; II Peter 2:1), in order that they might glorify God.

It is easy to imagine that whenever Paul or any of his fellow-workers, such as Prisca and Aquila, looked back upon the tremendous expansion of Christianity in and around the Roman province of Asia, they must have said, "And it all began with Epenetus; he was *the firstfruits*." That may well have been

427. Cf. ἔπαινος, praise, Rom. 2:29.

428. not "Achaia's" (cf. A.V. "of Achaia"), for which there is no solid textual justification, and which probably arose because of confusion with I Cor. 16:15.

one reason why the apostle, his heart overflowing with profound emotion, writes, "(Greet) *my beloved* Epenetus." Of course, there may also have been other reasons why Paul makes use of the modifier "beloved" here and in connection with Ampliatus (verse 8), Stachys (verse 9), and Persis (verse 12), reasons which we cannot now discern.

6. Greet Mary, who labored much for y o u.

"Mary" (or Miriam) is a Semitic name borne also by several other women mentioned in the New Testament: the mother of Jesus (Matt. 1:16), the mother of John Mark (Acts 12:12), Mary of Bethany (Luke 10:42; John 11:1), the mother of James and Joses (Matt. 27:61; cf. John 19:25), and Mary Magdalene (Luke 8:2). How did Paul know that this particular Mary (Rom. 16:6) had labored much for the Roman church? The answer is found in Acts 18:1, 2, "After this, Paul departed from Athens and went to Corinth. There he met a Jew named Aquila, a native of Pontus, *who had recently come from Italy with his wife Priscill* because Claudius had ordered all the Jews to leave *Rome*." Paul did not remain uninformed about what was happening in the various churches. See also verse 19 and cf. 1:8.

7. Greet Andronicus and Junias, my fellow-countrymen and (former) fellow-prisoners, who are outstanding among the apostles and who were in Christ before I was.

An attempt should be made to answer the following questions with respect to which opinions vary:

a. Should we read Junias (masc.) or Junia (fem.)?[429] In the latter case Andronicus and Junia could be husband and wife.

b. Did Paul say, "my fellow-countrymen" or "my relatives"?

c. Does "who are outstanding among the apostles" mean "outstanding in the estimation of The Twelve" or does it mean, "who, as apostles, are outstanding"?

I suggest the following answers:

As to a. The continuation which can be rendered "men of note among the apostles" (R.S.V.) favors the conclusion that both were men.[430]

As to b. When for the first time in Romans the apostle uses the word in question,[431] namely, in 9:3, it must mean fellow-countrymen; that is, fellow-Jews. No good reason has been shown for adopting a different meaning for this word as used here in 16:7. It is hard to believe that Paul had three "relatives" (verses 7 and 11) in Rome, and three other "relatives" (verse 21) around him in Corinth. When Paul became a Christian, by far the most of his "relatives" must have given up on him. Cf. Phil. 3:7.

As to c. The Twelve are not in the picture here. Besides, in the New Testament the word *apostle* is used in a looser and in a stricter sense. According to the broader application of the term, such men as Barnabas, Epa-

---

429. That is, should we adopt the accentuation 'Ιουνιᾶν or 'Ιουνίαν?

430. The original reads ἐπίσιμοι ἐν τοῖς ἀποστόλοι.

431. the pl. of συγγενής.

phroditus, Apollos, Silvanus, and Timothy are all called "apostles." They all evangelize. They can be described as missionaries or itinerant Christian evangelists. What Paul is saying, then, is this:

Extend greetings to Andronicus and Junias, fellow-countrymen of mine; that is, fellow-Jews, former fellow-prisoners (cf. II Cor. 6:5; 11:23), men who are apostles, and as such, of note, and who were Christians even before I was."

The possibility must be allowed that what Paul meant was that the very fact that these men had embraced Christ even before he did made them outstanding among apostles.

8. Greet Ampliatus, my beloved in the Lord.

Ampliatus is a Latin name meaning *amplified*, enlarged. The name was common among slaves. Between Paul and fellow-Jews there was a strong attachment (9:1-4a), but between the apostle and fellow-believers the bond was far stronger. Ampliatus is Paul's "beloved *in the Lord*." Thus, in a sense, the attachment of the one to the other is similar to that between David and Jonathan (I Sam. 20:41, 42). In this connection see on verse 5b above, and by all means read II Cor. 6:14-18.

9. Greet Urbanus, our fellow-worker in Christ, and (greet) my beloved Stachys.

Urbanus, again a Latin name, means *urbane*, elegant, polite. Men of every social class bore that name. The fact that Urbanus is called "our" fellow-worker, in distinction from Prisca and Aquila who are called "my" fellow-workers (verse 3), may indicate that the relation between Urbanus and Paul was not as close as that between Prisca-Aquila and Paul. It should be recalled that the apostle had made his home with the two, but not, as far as is known, with Urbanus. Thus "our" may indicate that at one time this brother in Christ had been one of Paul's personal fellow-workers but was now a Christian worker in Rome; or it may simply indicate that since Urbanus is engaged in evangelistic work in Rome, a work which, wherever it was performed, was close to Paul's heart, he for that reason says, "*our* fellow-worker," a fellow-worker engaged in a cause that is *dear to all of us*.

"And . . . my beloved Stachys." Note again, as in verses 5, 8, and 12, that precious modifier, "beloved"; here, as in verses 5 and 8, even "*my* beloved." Stachys, meaning *ear of grain*, is a Greek name, but not very common.

10a. Greet Apelles, who is approved in Christ.

Apelles is a Greek name, borne also by Jews. Paul adds, "who is approved in Christ," meaning that amid difficult circumstances Apelles had remained true to the faith, dependable. It may be recalled that Paul was going to tell Timothy, "Do your utmost to present yourself to God *approved*" (II Tim. 2:15). See also I Cor. 11:19; II Cor. 10:18. An approved person is someone who, after thorough examination by the Supreme Judge, has the satisfaction of knowing that God is pleased with him and commends him. For the opposite of "approved"—therefore "unapproved, disqualified, rejected"—see I Cor. 9:27.

This is all we know about Apelles, but the manner in which Paul causes him to be greeted is certainly very encouraging.

10b. Greet those who belong to the household of Aristobulus.

Was this Aristobulus a grandson of Herod the Great? The expression "*the household* of Aristobulus" probably refers to the slaves of the person Paul has in mind. If the conjecture mentioned above should be correct, then it would seem that Aristobulus himself was not a Christian or that he had already died when Paul composed Romans. At their master's death these slaves were kept together and became the property of the emperor. This theory, in turn, might indicate that when Paul continues (in verse 11) by saying, "Greet Herodion," he is referring to a freed slave of Aristobulus or otherwise to someone whose name implies "associated with" or "having admiration for" the family of Herod. But this entire reconstruction[432] is full of hypotheses.

11a. Greet Herodion, my fellow-countryman.

Like Andronicus and Junias, Herodion was Paul's fellow-countryman, accordingly a Jew.

11b. Greet those of the household of Narcissus who are in the Lord.

The name Narcissus may remind us of (a) a bulb plant with smooth leaves and with clusters of orange, white, and yellow; or of (b) a beautiful (mythological) youth who pined away for love of his own reflection in a spring; and so also of (c) any person characterized by excessive self-love. But Paul's passage may especially remind us of (d) a freedman who, during the period when Claudius was emperor, became very rich and powerful. However, whether even this Narcissus was the man whom Paul had in mind cannot be established. All we can say is that the name sounds very natural in a letter directed to the church in *Rome*. Not all those who belonged to the household of Narcissus were believers, as is clear from the fact that Paul sends his greetings to those of this household who were "in the Lord."

12a. Greet Tryphena and Tryphosa, who labor in the Lord.

Tryphena (=delicate) and Tryphosa (=dainty, or perhaps luxurious), were they sisters? They may well have been; see, for example, also Mary and Martha (John 11:1); and today: Hilda and Mathilda, Ruth and Rachel, Joan and Jean. Parents often give their daughters like-sounding names.

But though Tryphena and Tryphosa may well have belonged to a family living on Easy Street, they themselves did not live a life of ease. Whenever Paul thinks of them his soul is filled with admiration. Therefore he makes sure that this high regard he has for them will be reflected in the greeting they receive; hence, "Greet Tryphena and Tryphosa, *who labor in the Lord*." They were workers for the Lord to whom they had surrendered their lives.

12b. Greet Persis, the beloved, who has labored much in the Lord.

Persis=Persian lady. Like Ephenetus (verse 5), Ampliatus (verse 8), and Stachys (verse 9), this sister in the Lord is described as being "beloved." In

---

432. See also J. B. Lightfoot, *St. Paul's Epistle to the Philippians*, reprint Grand Rapids, 1953, pp. 172-175.

fact, in the present case, "*the* (not just *my*) beloved," perhaps stressing the fact that she is the object of God's love and of the love of the entire church.

Like Mary (verse 6) she is described as one who "labored much." Does the distinction in tense:

Tryphena and Tryphosa *labor* (verse 12a)
cf.
Persis *has labored* (verse 12b)

indicate that the frailties connected with old age have caught up with Persis, so that no longer is she able to labor as diligently as was once the case? If so, Paul takes care that her past labors are not forgotten. A lesson for us all to remember!

13. Greet Rufus, the elect in the Lord, and his mother and mine.

This passage immediately reminds us of Mark 15:21, according to which the legionnaries, exercising their right of requisitioning, forced a Cyrenian, Simon, the father of Alexander and *Rufus*, to carry Christ's cross. Since Mark in all probability wrote his Gospel in Rome for the Romans, and since here, in Paul's letter to the Romans, a man by the name of *Rufus* is mentioned by name, the popular opinion, dating back to the early centuries, that the two sources refer to the same individual, *may* well be correct. We cannot be sure, however.

The interpretation of the phrase "the elect in the Lord" varies all the way from Cranfield's view that it does indeed mean "chosen by God, elect," to Lenski's that it has nothing to do with election unto eternal life but simply indicates that Paul regarded Rufus as being a choice Christian.[433]

It cannot escape notice that of Simon's two sons (Alexander and Rufus) only Rufus (=red) is mentioned by Paul. The reason for this *may* have been that, when the apostle composed Romans, Alexander had already died, or that this son of Simon was not living in Rome. Simon is also left unmentioned. Had he died?

There are, of course, also other possibilities. One of them is that while Alexander was not a Christian, Rufus was, and this not because of any innate goodness on his part but because he was "the elect in the Lord."

Also we should not forget that *whether Rom. 16:13 and Mark 15:21 refer to the same family is not at all certain.* Whatever be the truth in this matter, there would seem to be no good reason for interpreting the expression "the elect" in any sense other than it has elsewhere in Paul's writings (Rom. 8:33; Col. 3:12; II Tim. 2:10; Titus 1:1; and for the cognate verb see I Cor. 1:27, 28; Eph. 1:4). So the meaning "chosen by God, elect" must stand.

---

433. See Cranfield, p. 794; Lenski, p. 911. Murray (p. 231) also flatly states that "chosen in the Lord" does not refer to election in Christ, giving as a reason for his opinion that this would apply to all saints mentioned in this chapter. This argument is not very convincing, for one might also say that "beloved" would apply to all believers; yet the word is used only in connection with Epenetus, Ampliatus, Stachys, and Persis.

Note also "and his mother and mine," probably meaning, "and his mother (hence the wife or widow of Simon of Cyrene, *if* Mark 15:21 applies here), who has been a mother to me also." Exactly where and when it was that the mother of Rufus had mothered Paul we do not know. Fact is that here, as often, the apostle again proves that he appreciates what the female members have done and are doing for himself and for the church, to the glory of God.

14. Greet Asyncritus, Phlegon, Hermes, Patrobas, Hermas, and the brothers (who are) with them.

About these five men—were they slaves or freedmen?—we have no further information. The expression "and the brothers (who are) with them" probably refers to the other members of the same house-church.

15. Greet Philologus and Julia, Nereus and his sister, and Olympas, and all the saints (who are) with them.

Among slaves of the imperial household there were many named Philologus and Julia. These two may have been husband and wife, and the next two their children. "Olympas, and all the saints (who are) with them" may perhaps be considered to have been the other members of a house-church.

16a. Greet one another with a holy kiss.

There are three sets of passages in which the New Testament refers to the kiss or/and kissing.

The first is found in Luke 7:36-50, where Jesus tells his host, Simon the Pharisee, "A kiss you did not give me, but she (the penitent woman), from the moment I came in, has not stopped kissing my feet." The lesson is: not only should there be affection but it should be *expressed*. There should be a token of affection; for example, a kiss.

The second is described in Luke 22:47, 48 (cf. Matt. 26:47-49; Mark 14:44,45). Jesus says to Judas, "Is it with a kiss that you are betraying the Son of man?" Not only should love be expressed but this love should be *real*; the kiss should be *sincere*.

The third concerns the kiss interchanged between the members of the Christian community, the church. It is this kiss to which there is a reference here in Rom. 16:16 (=I Cor. 16:20) and also, with transposition of two words, in II Cor. 13:12. Not only should there be a kiss and not only should it be a symbol of genuine affection but it should also be *holy*. In other words, it should never imply less than three parties: God and the two who kiss each other. The holy kiss symbolizes Christ's love mutually shared.[434] It is indeed as indicated in I Peter 5:14, "a kiss of *love*," hence also a kiss of *harmony, peace*. If this is rightly understood believers will not deliberately omit kissing those whom they do not happen to like. They will *love* even those whom they do not *like*. The holy kiss is for *all* the members (I Thess. 5:26).

---

434. So also E. F. Harrison, *op. cit.*, p. 165.

Among the Fathers of the church it is Justin Martyr who first mentions this kiss. He indicates the very moment in the liturgy when this kiss was given, persons of the same sex kissing each other. He writes, "At the conclusion of the prayers we greet one another with a kiss."[435]

C. *Greetings of All the Churches*

16b. All the churches of Christ extend greetings to y o u.

On his travels from place to place Paul came into contact with ever so many churches. From them he would gather information to be passed along to others. It is reasonable to suppose that the churches visited by the apostle would ask him to transmit their greetings to the brothers and sisters in Christ he would meet elsewhere.

Paul was eager to comply with this request, for he himself, at every opportunity, was stressing the unity of all believers in Christ. See what has been said about this in connection with Rom. 9:24, pp. 330, 331.

Moreover, as an apostle of Jesus Christ he had been clothed with authority to promote this unity. "The entire Church of God on earth *one* body, with many members," was a theme on which he loved to dwell. The idea of keeping the various local congregations informed about each other, to encourage them to help each other in their respective needs, both physical and spiritual, and therefore also to forward the salutations of one congregation to as many of the others as possible, was in line with all this.

One day Rome was going to become the world's mightiest fortress of Christianity. For the purpose of welding together the various parts of that gradually arising empire, greetings, that is, tokens of loving concern reaching out from one division of that vast area to another, were effective tiebeams.

---

17 I exhort y o u, brothers, to watch out for those who cause divisions and put obstacles in y o u r way that are contrary to the teaching y o u have learned. Avoid them. 18 For such people are not serving our Lord Jesus Christ but their own bellies; and by smooth talk and flattery they deceive the hearts of the simple. 19 For the report of y o u r obedience has reached everyone, so that I rejoice over y o u; but I want y o u to be wise about what is good, and innocent about what is evil. 20 The God of peace will crush Satan under y o u r feet soon! The grace of our Lord Jesus (be) with y o u.

Final Warning

"I exhort y o u, brothers, to watch out for those who cause divisions"

16:17-20

17. I exhort y o u, brothers, to watch out for those who cause divisions and put obstacles in y o u r way that are contrary to the teaching y o u have learned. Avoid them.

---

435. *The First Apology*, Chapter 65, quoted from *The Fathers Of The Church* (tr. by T. B. Falls), New York, 1948, p. 105; also footnote 1 on that page. In the quotation of this sentence (concerning the holy kiss) as it appears in *The Ante-Nicene Fathers* (edited by A. Roberts and J. Donaldson), Vol. I, p. 185, Grand Rapids, 1950, there is a footnote informing the reader that the holy kiss passed into common Christian usage, was continued in the Western Church until the thirteenth century, and is still continued in the Coptic Church.

There are those who maintain that the passage, verses 17-20, cannot have been a part of Paul's epistle to the Romans because its tone is different from that found in the rest of this letter. They maintain that it is "out of context." (Something has been said about this on pp. 27, 28.) They ask:

"Since the apostle has been lavishing effusive praise upon the membership of the Roman church (1:8; 15:14), how could he then now, all of a sudden, be scolding them?"

Those who so reason should look again. On closer examination they will discover that what Paul says here in 16:17-20 is definitely "in context." In the preceding verse he has instructed the addressed to greet one another "with a holy kiss." This kiss was clearly a token of love, unity, harmony. So now in verse 17 he warns the congregation to watch out for people whose purpose it is to disturb this harmony and to create divisions. The connection is close.

Again Paul has just now referred to "all the churches of Christ." Is it even possible that, while reflecting on the conditions in these several churches, he could have dismissed from his mind the fact that some of them were being, or had recently been, disturbed by false teachers who followed him at his heels and did their utmost to overthrow the doctrine of salvation by grace alone? They were constantly causing divisions and putting *obstacles* (see on 14:13, p. 461, footnote 384) in the way, with the purpose of obstructing the true teaching the Romans had learned.

Nowhere does the apostle say or imply that these troublemakers were members of the Roman church. They were probably outsiders, traveling propagandists of error.

It is not necessary to believe that they were all of one kind. Some may have been legalists (Judaizers), others antinomians or perhaps ascetics, or advocates of a combination of two or more disruptive isms.

Paul does not say, "*Oppose* them"; for, though some of those whom he addresses might have been able to do this successfully, others could easily have been led astray if they had entered into a debate. Therefore Paul urges the *brothers* (on which see 1:13, p. 52; 7:1, pp. 214, 215) to *avoid* these dissenters altogether. He knew that the possibility that some of the members might otherwise have lost their bearings was real, especially in view of the clever methods employed by the propagandizers, as indicated in verse

18. For such people are not serving our Lord Jesus Christ but their own bellies; and by smooth talk and flattery they deceive the hearts of the simple.

The expression used in the original for "such people" in this case contains a touch of contempt. It could perhaps be rendered, "folks of this ilk," or "this sort of individuals." Paul clearly considers them to be imposters, quacks.

By stating, "For such people are not serving our Lord Jesus Christ but their own bellies," the apostle is, as it were, saying, "We either serve our Lord Jesus Christ"—note fulness of this glorious title—"or we serve ourselves. To do both at the same time is impossible. We pledge our allegiance to one or to the other." Cf. Matt. 6:24.

Thus within the compass of just a few words Paul exposes the basic error of the gang against which he is issuing a warning. Since in the case of these false teachers the first alternative, namely, serving our Lord Jesus Christ, is out, it must be that they are serving their own bellies. Cf. Phil. 3:19. Does "their own bellies" necessarily mean that these disturbers are all libertines, sensualists? Probably not, for in that case the warning would be directed against only one kind of troublemakers. The real meaning is therefore probably, "self-servers of any description, people who are slaves of their own ego." Whether they be Judaizers, antinomians, ascetics, or what not, how they love to hear themselves talk! They are filled with an exalted opinion of themselves (cf. Col. 2:18, 23). They are living "according to the flesh," allowing their lives to be determined by the cravings of their sinful human nature (cf. Rom. 8:4, 5).

That this is true follows also from the methods they employ to capture their audiences. They make use of smooth talk and flattery. Cf. Jude 16. They are what some would consider "eloquent orators," though in reality "slick shufflers." They are not really helping anybody, though they pretend to do so. They are deceivers, for they lead people away from the fulness of salvation in Jesus Christ. It is the hearts of the simple, unsuspecting, naive, gullible, that are led astray by these charlatans.

The question may be asked, "Is the warning of verses 17, 18 all that is needed in order to cause those addressed to continue to live lives to the glory of God the Father and the Lord Jesus Christ (15:6), lives rich in goodness (15:14), and in accordance with the teaching they have learned (16:17)?" Probably not. So Paul adds,

19a. For the report of y o u r obedience has reached everyone, so that I rejoice over y o u . . .

It is clear that the apostle is mentioning another incentive to Christian conduct: departure from the path of faith and obedience would be a deep disappointment, and this not only to Paul himself but to believers everywhere. The faith of the Romans was being talked about throughout the entire world, so that the apostle is constantly thanking God for them and rejoicing over them (1:8). They certainly would not wish to stop this thanksgiving and rejoicing, and to spoil the reputation they now enjoy.

Note the words, "the report of y o u r obedience." *Obedience* is a term of which Paul is fond (1:5; 6:16; 15:18; 16:26).

In order to make it easier for the hearers-readers to continue in the right path, the apostle lays down a simple yet comprehensive rule, namely,

19b. but I want y o u to be wise about what is good, and innocent about what is evil.

This passage immediately calls to mind several other Pauline texts; such as, I Cor. 14:20; Phil. 2:15; and I Thess. 5:21, 22; as well as the familiar saying of Jesus, "Therefore be keen as the serpents, guileless as the doves"

(Matt. 10:16), which, however, does not mean that Paul was necessarily quoting Jesus.

The wisdom Paul here advocates is more than knowledgeability. It is a spiritual as well as a mental quality. Cf. 11:33. It results from sanctified experience. Paul wants the Romans to live in such a manner that they will be equal to the task of choosing what is good in the eyes of God, and that they will be innocent or guileless[436] about what is evil. They should be wise for the purpose of doing and promoting what is right, and should not get "mixed up" with anything that, in God's sight, is wrong.

In verses 17-19 Paul has been telling the Romans how they should conduct their lives. That is very important. In ever so many passages Scripture stresses *human responsibility*. But *divine sovereignty* must not be ignored. In fact, man can do nothing apart from the strength imparted to him by God.

An instructive example of giving due recognition to both of these truths is found in the life of the youth David:

"David said to the Philistine, 'You come against me with sword and spear and javelin, but I come against you in the name of the Lord Almighty, the God of the armies of Israel, whom you have defied. This day the Lord will deliver you into my hands . . . that all the earth may know that there is a God in Israel.' . . . Reaching into his bag and taking a stone, he slung it and struck the Philistine on the forehead. The stone sank into his forehead, and he [Goliath] fell facedown on the ground" (I Sam. 17:45-49, quoted in part).

David did not forget to ascribe all the glory to God . . . but neither did he forget to sling the stone! Conversely, here, in Rom. 16:17-20 Paul exhorts *those whom he addresses* to do the following: watch out . . . avoid . . . obey . . . be wise . . . and be innocent. In other words, *Shoulder y o u r responsibility*! But he follows this up immediately by emphasizing that if there is going to be a victory—and yes, there will be one—it is *God*, he alone, who will achieve it:

20a. The God of peace will crush Satan under y o u r feet soon!

God will exercise his sovereign will in the interest of his people! For the term "God of peace" see on 15:33, p. 498. The apostle has been speaking about those who cause divisions, disharmony, strife. Over against them stands the Almighty, who is "the God of peace." In connection with that which this God of peace will do three items are mentioned:

a. He will *crush* Satan. In other words, he will fulfil the promise of Gen. 3:15. Not Satan but God is Victor.

b. He will crush him *under y o u r feet*. Those who are co-heirs (8:17) are also co-conquerors. The saints will participate in God's victory over Satan. See Rev. 19:13, 14.

c. He will do so *soon*. In a sense it is true that God is crushing Satan right along. A most decisive victory was won on Calvary. There can be no doubt about it, though, that the present passage has reference to the final, escha-

---

436. ἀκεραίους, ἀ-priv. plus κεράννυμι, to mix; hence, unmixed, unadulterated.

tological victory of God over Satan, a victory that will take place in connection with Christ's glorious return (II Thess. 2:8). That this great blessing for the elect will indeed be imparted to them *soon* no longer creates any real problem. See above, on 13:11, pp. 444-447.

d. God's triumph over Satan proves that for his people he is "the God of peace," that is, of complete salvation.

20b. The grace of our Lord Jesus (be) with y o u.

Note the following:

a. *Grace* is God's unmerited favor. For a word-study of this concept see N.T.C. on Luke, pp. 181, 182.

b. Here "our," not just "the" as in I Cor. 16:23. "Our" is here the word of trustful self-appropriation.

c. "Lord Jesus." Jesus means Savior, but in order to be our Savior he must be acknowledged as our Lord, the One who, having purchased us with his blood, owns us, and whose sovereignty over us we acknowledge with joy.

d. the word "be"—in "(be) with y o u"—is not in the text but is understood. The benediction is not a mere wish. It is a promise which becomes a reality in the lives of those who have embraced "our Lord Jesus" with a living faith. Cf. the Aaronitic benediction, to which is added, "So shall they put my name upon the children of Israel, *and I will bless them*." For more on this see N.T.C. on I Thess. 1:1, pp. 42-45. Other Pauline benedictions can be found in I Cor. 16:23 (already mentioned); II Cor. 13:14; Gal. 6:18; Eph. 6:23, 24; Phil. 4:23; I Thess. 5:28; II Thess. 3:18; I Tim. 6:21; II Tim. 4:22; Titus 3:15; and Philem. 25.

e. It is surely remarkable that in God's providence Paul's epistle to the Romans has come down to us in such a manner that while in 15:33 we have a prayer-wish, and here in 16:20 a closing benediction, the glorious doxology, certainly very appropriate for such a basic and marvelous epistle, is saved for the very last few verses (25-27). For more on the genuine character and placement of these verses see Appendix, pp. 521-523.

---

21 Timothy, my fellow-worker, greets y o u; (so do) Lucius and Jason and Sosipater, my fellow-countrymen. 22 I, Tertius, who wrote down this letter, greet y o u in the Lord. 23 Gaius, who is host to me and to the entire church, greets y o u. Erastus, the city treasurer, and our brother Quartus, greet y o u.[437]

Greetings of Friends
"Timothy, my fellow-worker, greets y o u"
16:21-23

The sending of personal greetings is resumed at this point; with this difference, that the previous greetings were Paul's own (verses 1-16a) and those

---

437. Verse 24 "The grace of our Lord Jesus Christ be with y o u all. Amen." is not adequately supported by textual evidence.

of "all the churches of Christ" (verse 16b) while, by contrast, the present greetings (verses 21-23) are those from individuals who, in one way or another, were associated with the apostle.

There certainly is not any good reason to find fault with this arrangement. In fact, one might even argue that grouping together all the greetings, so that what is now found in verses 21-23 would have followed immediately upon verses 1-16, with the painful warning of verses 17-20 introducing the doxology of verses 25-27, would not have been any improvement. The arrangement as we now have it is surely the best.

21. Timothy, my fellow-worker, greets y o u; (so do) Lucius and Jason and Sosipater, my fellow-countrymen.

Among those who are sending greetings Paul mentions Timothy first of all. A most remarkable person was Timothy or Timotheus. His character was a blend of amiability and faithfulness, in spite of natural timidity. It was concerning him that, a few years later, Paul was going to write, "I have no one likeminded . . . As a child (serves) with (his) father, so he served with me in the gospel" (Phil. 2:19-22). The apostle was going to call Timothy "my beloved child" (II Tim. 1:2). That Paul, writing from Corinth, would make mention of Timothy as one who was in his company, is not surprising. From the book of Acts we learn that on the second missionary journey, outward bound, Paul and Silas, having arrived at Lystra, took Timothy with them. On that same journey Timothy, having been separated from Paul for a little while, joins him again at Corinth, the very city from which the apostle, on his third journey, is now composing Romans. It is not strange, therefore, that also at this time Timothy was with Paul and sending greetings. For more on Timothy see N.T.C. on I Timothy, pp. 33-36. By calling Timothy "my fellow-worker" Paul was making a true statement. It was, however, an understatement. Timothy was indeed a fellow-worker, but to Paul he meant far more than that.

Another person who sends greetings is Lucius. There is no valid reason to identify this person either with the Lucius mentioned in connection with the church of Syrian Antioch (Acts 13:1) or with Luke, though Luke seems, indeed, to have been with the apostle at this time. See Acts 20:5 f. But nowhere does Paul call him "Lucius." See Col. 4:14; II Tim. 4:11; Philem. 24.

The Jason mentioned here could be the one to whom reference is made in Acts 17:5-9, and the Sosipater may be the Sopater of Acts 20:4. The apostle calls Lucius, Jason, and Sosipater "my fellow-countrymen." In other words he describes them as being Jews (one more reason for not identifying the Lucius of this passage with "the beloved physician"). For justification of the rendering "fellow-countrymen" instead of "relatives" see on verse 7, p. 504.

22. I, Tertius, who wrote down this letter, greet y o u in the Lord.

For an author of a letter to have a secretary was not at all unusual. That Paul also had one and would at the very close affix his own signature, at times even adding a few words, is clear from Gal. 6:11; II Thess. 3:17. See also I Cor. 16:21; Col. 4:18.[438]

In the present case the secretary, Tertius, being himself a Christian—Paul certainly would not entrust this kind of task to an unbeliever!—feels the need of adding his own personal greeting, a greeting definitely, like all the others, "in the Lord," that is, expressed as one who is included in that mystic and marvelous fellowship which unites all believers with Christ.

It is the Lord alone who knows how greatly indebted are writers of letters *and/or of books* to their faithful and competent Christian secretaries!

23. Gaius, who is host to me and to the entire church, greets y o u. Erastus, the city treasurer, and our brother Quartus, greet y o u.

This Gaius may well be the same person as the one mentioned in I Cor. 1:14. He should not be identified with the "Gaius from Derbe" of Acts 20:4. When Paul calls Gaius his *host*, he probably means that, since Prisca and Aquila were no longer in Corinth, it was this very man, Gaius, with whom the apostle was making his home. The added expression, "who is host . . . to the entire church" probably does not mean that from every section of Corinth believers crowded into the home of Gaius to attend the worship services. It may simply mean that Gaius was always standing ready to offer hospitality to any believer in need of it. We are thinking especially of travelers. This does not exclude the possibility that the home of Gaius may also have served as a house-church for *part* of the congregation.

"Erastus, the city treasurer." Much has been written about him. Some authors, and even translators, identify him with the man of the same name who on a Corinthian inscription is called *aedile*; that is, commissioner of public works. Such an officer was in charge of buildings, roads, public games, etc. But an *aedile* is not the same as an *oikonomos*, which is the term used here in Rom. 16:23. Cf. the English word *economist*, which causes one to think rather about a *treasurer*. Those who cling to the translation "commissioner of public works" will sometimes answer that Erastus could have performed both functions, that of commissioner of public works and that of city treasurer. But even if this be granted, does it justify any rendering other than "city treasurer" here in Rom. 16:23?

To identify the present Erastus with the one mentioned in Acts 19:22, connected with Ephesus, is also difficult. Or, perhaps, with the Erastus mentioned in II Tim. 4:20? On this see N.T.C. on II Timothy, p. 331, footnote 184.

About Quartus we know nothing beyond what is found here. He is called "our brother," which is certainly a term of endearment, in the present context meaning "our fellow-Christian." Probably Quartus had acquaintances in Rome, and accordingly sends Christian greetings.

---

438. Also A. Deissmann, *op. cit.*, pp. 171, 172.

25 Now to him who is able to establish y o u in accordance with my gospel and the proclamation of Jesus Christ, in conformity with the revelation of the mystery hidden for long ages past 26 but now manifested, and in accordance with the command of the eternal God clarified through the prophetic Scriptures in order to bring about obedience of faith among all the nations, 27 to the only wise God, through Jesus Christ, (be) glory forever! Amen.

Doxology

"Now to him who is able to establish y o u in accordance with my gospel and the proclamation of Jesus Christ . . . be glory forever through Jesus Christ! Amen."

16:25-27

This is a lengthy doxology. Nevertheless, the New Testament contains other doxologies equal in length (Rom. 11:33-36; Heb. 13:20, 21). Even those of Eph. 3:20, 21 and Jude 24, 25 are not exactly short.

For exegetical purposes the paragraph may be divided into two parts: verses 25, 26; verse 27.

25, 26. Now to him who is able to establish y o u . . . in order to bring about obedience of faith among all the nations . . .

Various concepts introduced in the opening of Romans (see 1:1-11; especially 1:1-5) return here in 16:25, 26; such as:

a. establish or strengthen (16:25), cf. 1:11;

b. my gospel (16:25), cf. the gospel of God (1:1);

c. the mystery hidden for long ages past (16:25, 26), cf. the gospel which he promised beforehand (1:1, 2);

d. through the prophetic Scriptures (16:26); cf. through his prophets in (the) sacred Scriptures (1:2);

e. to bring about obedience of faith among all the nations or Gentiles (16:26 and 1:5).

But even though the connection between the present passage (16:25-27) and the beginning of the epistle is close, that between the present passage and verses 17-20 is also close. Note especially, in verse 19, the expression "the report of y o u r obedience" and here in 16:26 "In order to bring about obedience of faith."

In connection with verses 25, 26 note the following:

a. "Now to him who is able to establish y o u"

As in 1:11 so also here Paul is referring to spiritual strengthening, not to the impartation of any specific charismatic gift, such as speaking in tongues.

b. "in accordance with my gospel"

As in 2:16 and II Tim. 2:8, so also here, Paul has a right to describe the good news as being "my gospel," for it had been revealed to him by the Lord; and he, Paul, loved it (cf. I Cor. 9:16), proclaimed it, and was trying, by God's grace, to show its effect in his own life. See also I Cor. 15:1; Gal. 1:11; 2:2, 7; Eph. 3:6, 7. For "our gospel" see II Cor. 4:3; I Thess. 1:5; II Thess. 2:14.

c. "and the proclamation of Jesus Christ"

What Paul meant was "my gospel, that is, the proclamation of Jesus Christ."[439] It was by means of the good news, as loved and proclaimed by Paul, that God was able to confirm the addressed.

d. "the *proclamation*"

True preaching is the earnest and enthusiastic outcry of *the herald* as he announces the coming and arrival of the King, and as he urges the people to welcome him with joy and to be in subjection to him. See what has been said on this subject in connection with 10:14, 15, p. 350. As the apostle sees it, it is in connection with, and by means of, such a gospel proclamation that God is able to establish those who are here being addressed. It is that kind of *good news* to which Paul gave the name *my gospel*.

e. "in conformity with the revelation of the mystery hidden for long ages past but now manifested"

A mystery, as the apostle uses the term, *is something that*—in some cases even someone who—*would have remained unknown if God had not revealed it*; or, if the mystery is a person, if God had not revealed *him*.

The apostle is going to say three things about this mystery: first, that it was hidden for long ages past (verse 25b); secondly, that it has now been made manifest (verse 26a); and thirdly, that, in accordance with the command of the eternal God, it was being clarified through the prophetic Scriptures, in order to bring about obedience of faith among all the nations or Gentiles (verse 26b).

f. The essence of the mystery was this, that one day the Gentiles would not only be entering God's kingdom in large numbers but would be fellow-sharers, participants on equal terms, with the elect from among the Jews. "Christ in y o u, the hope of glory" (Col. 1:27) would be the solid basis for present salvation and future eschatological glory for *everyone*, regardless of race, who would, by God's sovereign grace, place his trust in the Savior. On this see also Eph. 2:11-22.

It was this mystery that had been hidden for long ages past, for though the decision had been made in God's eternal plan and though even during the old dispensation there had been foreshadowings of the realization of God's promise of salvation for both Gentile and Jew, the period of fulfilment on any large scale had not been reached until now. But *now*, the new dispensation having arrived, and the gospel being proclaimed far and wide, this mystery was being made manifest, was becoming abundantly clear. It was being manifested in *the fulfillment* of prophecy. Think of Gen. 12:3; 22:18. For more on this see N.T.C. on Eph. 3:5, 6, pp. 154, 155.

Was not this very epistle being addressed to a church consisting of both Jews and Gentiles, *unitedly* serving God? Think of Pentecost and its significance (Acts 1:4-8; ch. 2).

---

439. "of Jesus Christ" = "concerning Jesus Christ" (objective gen.).

But not only did the facts of salvation shed light upon ancient prophecies; in turn, these prophecies were now clarifying salvation truths and salvation events. A believer who would now turn to Isa. 53 and read about Messiah's substitutionary sacrifice and its meaning for his (the believer's) life would certainly exclaim, "Now, in light of Isa. 53, I see far more clearly than ever before what Messiah's death means for me!" See also Eph. 1:9-14; 3:1-13.

g. "to bring about obedience of faith among all the nations (or Gentiles)"

That was the purpose or goal of the indicated clarification. God delights to see in any person the kind of obedience that is based on childlike trust in him. For the concept "obedience of faith" see p. 45 (on 1:5). Note also "among *all* the nations," understandable in light of 10:12 and of Matt. 28:19; John 3:16; Acts 2:21.

Paul concludes this paragraph, this chapter, and in fact, the entire epistle, with the words of verse

27. to the only wise God, through Jesus Christ, (be) glory forever! Amen.[440] Here the thought of verse 25 is resumed; hence, "Now to him who is able . . . to the only wise God," etc.

When Paul reflects on what, by inspiration, he has composed, he is filled with amazement. So he must needs add this concluding line to his doxology.

He has been speaking about a love of the Holy One for those who in and by themselves are completely unworthy; a love of the Self-sufficient One reaching out toward those who are thoroughly unable to give anything in return that would enrich the Giver; a love of One who did not wait to extend help until those desperately in need of this love would be favorably disposed to him but who anticipated their love; a love altogether sovereign, unique: "But God demonstrated *his own love* for us in this, that while we were still sinners Christ died for us" (Rom. 5:8). Cf. II Cor. 5:19-21; I John 4:10.

What fills the apostle's soul with astonishment, as he concludes his epistle, is the fact that God was able to rescue *such* sinners; in fact, not only to *rescue*

---

440. Literally what Paul writes is, "to the only wise God, through Jesus Christ, to whom (be) glory forever." That is what he writes *if* ᾧ is authentic. So interpreted, the glory would seem to be ascribed not to God but to Christ, and the first part of the sentence, referring to God, would be "hanging in the air." Now it is true that Paul at times starts a sentence without immediately completing it; e.g. in Rom. 5:12 and in Eph. 2:1. But in such instances he takes up the thought again a little later, so that it is not left incomplete. In the case of Rom. 5:12 he does this in verse 18 of that chapter; and for Eph. 2:1 see 2:5. In the present case, however, he would have completely forgotten the thought with which he began. That can hardly be true. It is therefore far more reasonable to believe that the relative pronoun, if authentic, refers to God. Nevertheless, because of the position of the pronoun in the sentence, where it immediately follows the designation "Jesus Christ," a translation into English that retains the word-order of the original would cause the apostle to ascribe the glory not to God but to Jesus Christ, and would leave the sentence unfinished.

Therefore the translator might just as well omit the relative pronoun entirely, as happens in several published translations.

The 26th edition of Nestle-Aland *Novum Testamentus Graece*, Stuttgart, 1979, places brackets around all of verses 25-27, with explanation of these signs on p. 44* of the Introduction. For the reason to believe that it was Paul himself who was responsible for the closing doxology see the Appendix of the book you are reading, pp. 521-523.

them but to open for them the gateway to everlasting glory and to bring them inside . . . and at such a cost (Rom. 8:32)!

It is with all this in mind that Paul concludes his strikingly beautiful and impressive epistle by exclaiming, "To the only wise God, through Jesus Christ, (be) glory forever!" The fact that God was able and willing to rescue such sinners fixes Paul's attention on the divine *wisdom*; that is, on God's ability to employ the best means for the attainment of the highest goal, namely, the glory of God being ascribed to him by the hearts, lives, and lips of the redeemed. For more on this concept of *wisdom* see on 11:33, p. 386. See also I Cor. 2:6-13.

Note the exact wording: "To the only wise God, through Jesus Christ, (be) glory forever!" It was indeed through Jesus Christ (his departure from the realm of everlasting delight and honor, his self-sacrifice even unto death, death on a cross, victory over death and hell, etc.) that sinners were, are, and are going to be saved. And it is also "through Jesus Christ" that the redeemed ascribe never-ending praise to their Benefactor, God Triune. To him, therefore, be the glory forever. For other ascriptions of glory to God see 11:33-36; Gal. 1:4, 5; Eph. 3:20, 21; Phil. 4:20; I Tim. 1:17; I Peter 5:11; and Jude 24, 25.

As he had done before, namely, at the conclusion of Part I of this letter (11:36), so also now, at the close of the entire letter, Paul adds the word of solemn and enthusiastic affirmation and approval, AMEN.

APPENDIX

in connection with 16:25-27

Did Paul write 16:25-27? That he did not is the view of many New Testament scholars. That he did is vigorously defended by others.

Because of their anti-Rome and anti-Old Testament bias Marcion and his followers were not favorably impressed with references to Rome in 1:7, 15, and to the Old Testament in 15:4, 8, 9 f. Some believe that it was Marcion himself who mutilated the text of Romans. It was Origen who stated, "Marcion, by whom the evangelical and apostolic writings were falsified, removed this section [16:25-27] completely from the epistle, and not only so, but deleted everything from that place where it is written, 'whatsoever is not of faith is sin,' [14:23] right to the end."[441]

But whether the removal of the final two chapters of Romans was done by the heretic himself, as Origen believed, or by others, makes little difference.

As a result, in part, of manipulation some manuscripts bear witness to the existence, at one time or another, of a Romans in 16 chapters, some to a 15-chapter epistle, and some to one containing only 14 chapters.

A suitable *conclusion* was considered necessary for most of the editions. As many see it, such an ending was composed by an editor or by an editorial committee. It was then attached to several editions. However, there still remain some rather early witnesses which attest to the complete omission of the doxology (our 16:25-27); also some in which this passage occurs twice; that is, first after 14:23, then after 16:23 (24).

The result was the coming into existence, at one time or another, of the following five groups of textual witnesses:

a. doxology after 16:23 (24): ℵ B C D E 81 436 630 1739 1962 2127 syr^{p} cop vg, etc.

b. doxology after 14:23: L Ψ 181 326 330 451 460 614 1241 1877 1881 1984 1985 2492 2495 *et plur.*^{40} syr^{h} goth^{41}, etc.

c. doxology after both 16:23 (24) and 14:23: A P 5 17 33 104 109.

d. doxology after 15:33: p^{46}.[442]

e. no doxology: G F 629 g E 26 Marcion, etc.

---

441. *Commentaria in epistolam ad Romanos* (re Rom. 16:25-27), in Migne, *Patrologia Graeca* XIV, 1290 AB.

442. This is the famous Chester Beatty Papyrus dating from around the beginning of the third century.

There have been scholars who, while crediting Paul with the composition of all 16 chapters, defended the thesis that it was he himself who was responsible for the appearance of this epistle in a longer and in a shorter form. According to this view the apostle realized that by far the most of what he had written in this letter—that is, everything with the exception of chapters 15 and 16—was of importance to every church and could therefore serve as a kind of circular letter. So he himself made his Romans available in two editions, one containing 14, the other 16 chapters.

The insuperable objection is, of course, that by so doing the apostle would have sliced in half the argument of 14:1-15:13 (concerning the strong and the weak). That theory must therefore be rejected.

There have been many other theories, equally objectionable, for which consult the older commentaries.

All of these studies have, however, become somewhat outdated by the appearance of a doctoral dissertation (revised) by Harry Gamble, Jr., namely, *The Textual History of The Letter to The Romans*, Grand Rapids, 1977. We shall now direct our attention to that work.

The dissertation is written in excellent style. The author, though handling a difficult subject, has thoroughly mastered the art of capturing and holding the attention of the reader from the very beginning to the end of his book. Moreover, the arrangement of the material is logical. Gamble presents a good deal of valuable information; for example, with respect to the Hellenistic letter-writing pattern and its influence upon the authors (including Paul) of the New Testament books.

On p. 92 and elsewhere he shows that only if what we now recognize as The Epistle to the Romans was actually addressed to the Romans—not, for example, to the Ephesians—does the peculiar character of the greetings of Rom. 16 make any sense. In fact, as the reader can see for himself by making a comparison, some of Gamble's arguments in favor of a Roman (not Ephesian) address for the letter are substantially the same as those found on pp. 27, 28 of the commentary he (the reader) is now studying.

On pp. 15-55 Gamble examines the textual evidence for the three major forms in which Romans has appeared: the 14-chapter, 15-chapter, and 16-chapter form. He concludes that the 16-chapter form is authentic.

Another excellent feature of the dissertation is that it defends the position according to which Romans is not a general letter, that is, one which could just as well have been addressed to any other church, but that its author reveals specific knowledge about the situation *in Rome*, p. 136.

And on p. 53 he presents a very fair appraisal of the Chester Beatty Papyrus, and maintains that it cannot be regarded as proving that the 15-chapter book of Romans was the original text.

With respect to one important point Gamble's dissertation has failed to convince me. Let the reader by all means check on this item for himself. Let him not just depend on my criticism.

It is Gamble's position that the passage, Rom. 16:25-27, is unauthentic. The reasons he gives are as follows:

a. The testimony of the manuscripts favors the placement of the doxology after chapter 14, not after chapter 16. The conclusion of a letter with a *doxology* stands in clear contrast with Paul's habit of concluding with a *grace benediction* (pp. 67, 123).

b. In agreement with Harnack, Gamble believes that the doxology is constructed with a certain *awkwardness* and pleonastic style (p. 108).

The answer to this might be as follows:

How do we know that the original did not contain the doxology at the end of the letter? At any rate the Alexandrian witnesses staunchly favor this position. And as to Paul's habit of concluding an epistle with a grace benediction, in I Cor. 16:23 the grace benediction does not occupy the final position, as Gamble himself admits. Also some of the other New Testament books do not end with a benediction. II Peter closes with a doxology; so does Jude.

It is very clear that Paul's epistle to the Romans is divided into two large sections: chapters 1 through 11, *doctrinal*; chapters 12 through 16, *practical.* The first large section definitely ends with a doxology (11:33-36), one of (about) 52 words. Then why should not the second large section similarly end with a doxology (16:25-27), of about the same number of words? Must we really take for granted that Paul would close his epistle—in which he sets forth the unmerited grace of Christ in such marvelous terms—with "Erastus, the city treasurer, and our brother Quartus, greet y o u"? Would not that be *awkward*?

For the rest, barring a few passages in which Gamble casts doubt on the authenticity of Colossians and II Thessalonians, without furnishing proof for the legitimacy of this doubt (p. 80), I recommend the reading of this very informative and interesting dissertation.

Practical Lessons Derived from Romans 15:14—16:27

CHAPTER 15

Verse 14

"I myself am convinced, my brothers, that y o u yourselves are rich in goodness, amply filled with knowledge, and competent also to admonish one another." The apostle has pointed out certain weaknesses characterizing the members of the Roman church. Therefore all the more he is quick to mention also their virtues. If that method would be adopted in every church today, would it not result in blessings for many and better relations all around?

Verse 15

"Nevertheless, I have written to y o u rather boldly on some points, so as to remind y o u of them again. (I have done so) because of the commission God in his grace has granted me . . ." In our democratic society we are apt to look down on ideas such as "office," "authority," etc. Such an attitude is clearly in conflict with Scripture. The person who has been invested with an office should faithfully discharge the duties pertaining to it and should, by God's grace, adorn that office with a godly life. And, on the other hand, church members benefited by the institution of this office should honor the office-bearer, remember him in their prayers, and wherever possible co-operate with him.

Verse 24

"I hope . . . to be helped forward by y o u . . ." Paul had the right idea, namely, to get the membership of the Roman church to become involved in the glorious work of Christian missionary endeavor. People will become enthusiastic about a cause to which they themselves have contributed.

Verse 27

". . . if the Gentiles have come to share in the Jews' spiritual blessings, they owe it to the Jews to share with them their material blessings." In order to receive a blessing one should strive to be a blessing!

Verse 31 (and 16:19)

"(Pray to God for me) that I may be rescued from the *disobedient* in Judea . . . For the report of y o u r *obedience* has reached everyone . . ."

In a day in which so much emphasis is placed on *freedom* of thought, speech, and action, it should not be forgotten that God requires *obedience* to his commands. It is our *duty* to love and worship God. To be sure, it is our privilege to do this, but it is also our obligation. We sometimes hear, "We do not try to influence our children with respect to their religion. We leave that entirely to them." Is that course really the right one? The Word of God teaches differently. See Gen. 18:19; Deut. 6:4-9; Eph. 6:1-4. Such *obedience* should spring from love and gratitude.

Verse 30

"the love of the Spirit . . ."

For that *Holy* Spirit to dwell in our sinful hearts he must be loving indeed! Note also:

a. The Father loves us (I John 3:1)

b. The Son loves us (Rom. 8:35)

c. The Holy Spirit loves us (Rom. 15:30)

And these three are ONE. What a blessing! And what an inducement in return to love The Triune God!

CHAPTER 16
Verse 12

"Greet Tryphena and Tryphosa, who labor in the Lord." With respect to them note the following:

a. They are women, perhaps sisters. They may even have been twins. Kingdom work needs women as well as men.

b. These women not merely worked, they labored, worked hard, toiled.

c. Similarity in name is interesting. Similarity in religious ardor and devotion is best of all.

Verses 19b, 20a

". . . I want y o u to be wise about what is good, and innocent about what is evil. The God of peace will crush Satan under y o u r feet soon!"

The Practical Lesson: give both human responsibility and divine sovereignty their due; see the illustration, found on p. 512.

Summary of Chapter 15:14—16:27

In close connection with the immediately preceding prayer-wish Paul assures the Romans that he recognizes their excellent spiritual qualities. Nevertheless, he has at times felt it necessary to express himself rather boldly for their own benefit, exercising his duty as a minister of Christ Jesus to the Gentiles, his aim being to bring the Gentiles to God (15:14-16).

In pleasing humility, ascribing all the glory to God alone, the apostle describes *not* what *he* has done but what *Christ* has accomplished through him in leading many Gentiles to God. He had been privileged to proclaim the gospel of Christ all the way from Jerusalem round about to Illyricum (Yugoslavia-Albania). By means of signs and wonders, performed through the power of the Holy Spirit, that work had been signally blessed. Paul had been a trail-blazer for the gospel. From the very beginning his purpose had been to proclaim the gospel in places and regions where Christ was not known (cf. Isa. 52:15). That explains why he had not been able to make an earlier visit to Rome (verses 17-22).

Paul informs the Romans that since his work of establishing churches in the eastern part of the Roman Empire is finished and since for many years he had been yearning to visit his fellow-believers in Rome, he plans to do so on his way to Spain. However, he cannot come immediately, for he must first of all supervise the handing over of a generous bounty which the Gentile believers of Macedonia and Achaia had been collecting for the needy saints in Jerusalem. He adds, "They were pleased to do it and, indeed, they owe it to them; for if the Gentiles have come to share in the Jews' spiritual blessings, they owe it to the Jews to share with them their material blessings. When I have completed this task . . . I will go to y o u on my way to Spain. I know that when I come to y o u, I will come in the fulness of the blessing of Christ" (verses 23-29).

In need of the intercession of the church, Paul asks the Romans to remember him in prayer:

a. that he might be rescued from the plots of the unbelieving Jews;

b. that his ministry to Jerusalem—a ministry of benevolence—might be acceptable to the Jews, so that

c. his coming to the Romans might be a matter of joy, and, together with them, he might be refreshed.

This prayer was certainly answered, though not, in every respect, in a manner Paul had been able to foresee.

As to a, there was indeed a plot against his life by the Jews, but it was discovered in time, so that traveling plans were changed (Acts 20:3);

As to b, Acts 21:17 reports that the brothers in Jerusalem did indeed extend a hearty welcome to Paul and his companions, and glorified God when they heard Paul's report about the results of mission work among the Gentiles. Whether the Jerusalem saints also received the generous collection with grateful enthusiasm is not reported.

As to c, that petition too was granted, though not at the time and in the manner Paul had envisioned. But see Acts 28:11-15; Phil. 1:12.

The little paragraph ends with the prayer-wish of verse 33 (verses 30-33).

The apostle warmly commends to the church Phoebe, a servant of the church at Cenchrea, a seaport of Corinth. In all probability she was the lady who delivered the letter to the Roman Church.

Next, he extends his own greetings to many persons—men and women, Gentile and Jewish believers—members of the Roman Church and known to Paul. The list of individuals to whom greetings are sent begins with Prisca and Aquila with whom Paul had made his home when this couple was still living in Corinth. They were tent-makers as was Paul. But of even greater importance was the fact that they were "fellow-workers in Christ Jesus." So very loyal had they been to Paul that once they had even hazarded their lives for his sake. That may have happened during the riot of Ephesus described in Acts 19:23-41. But we cannot be certain about this.

Paul adds, "(Greet) also the church (that meets) at their house." It seems that wherever Prisca and Aquila were living—whether in Corinth, Ephesus, or Rome—they were always inviting their fellow-believers to meet with them for the worship service.

Next, Paul sends greetings to Epenetus, "Asia's firstfruits for Christ." Among several others to whom greetings are extended is also Rufus. Paul adds, "and his mother and mine," indicating that the mother of Rufus had been a mother to the apostle also; that is, had rendered motherly service to him. This Rufus reminds us of the Rufus mentioned in Mark 15:21, but whether the same person is indicated in both places is uncertain. At the conclusion of the list Paul writes, "All the churches of Christ extend greetings to y o u" (16:1-16).

Paul now tells the Roman church to watch out for false teachers. Let the members be on their guard, and this especially for two reasons: (a) by means of smooth talk and flattery these troublemakers try to deceive the hearts of the unsuspecting; and (b) the Roman believers should not spoil the good reputation (for obedience to the truth) they have gained everywhere. Using an expression that reminds us of a saying of Jesus (Matt. 10:16), the apostle adds, "I want y o u to be wise about what is good, and innocent about what is evil." In addition to placing emphasis on the *responsibility* the Romans should shoulder, he comforts them by reminding them that God, in the exercise of his *sovereignty*, will crush Satan under their feet soon. He adds, "The grace of our Lord Jesus (be) with y o u" (verses 17-20).

The greetings which friends are sending to the Roman church follow. The greeters include Timothy, a very dear friend and fellow-worker of Paul; Tertius, the apostle's secretary, to whom the apostle had dictated the letter; and Gaius, at whose home Paul was staying and who was ever ready to reveal his hospitality in the interest of the entire church (verses 21-23).

By means of a very impressive doxology, one which in many ways reflects the opening verses of the epistle, Paul brings his marvelous epistle to an appropriate close (verses 25-27).

BIBLIOGRAPHIES

Select Bibliography on Romans 9—16

A. *On Romans 9*

Bavinck, H., *The Doctrine of God* (translation of *Gereformeerde Dogmatiek* Vol. II, pp. 1-425), Grand Rapids, 1955; Edinburgh, 1979; see especially pp. 337-407.

Berkhof, L., *Systematic Theology*, Grand Rapids, 1949, pp. 100-125.

Calvin, J., *Commentaries on the Epistle of Paul the Apostle, to The Romans*, translated and ed. by J. Owen, Grand Rapids, 1947, pp. 332-380.

———. *Institutes of the Christian Religion*, translated by John Allen, Philadelphia, 1928, Vol. II, pp. 140-149.

Klooster, F. H., *Predestination: A Calvinistic Note* (Perspectives on Evangelical Theology), Grand Rapids, 1979, pp. 81-94.

Murray, J., *The Epistle to the Romans* (The New International Commentary on the New Testament), Grand Rapids, 1959; Vol. II, pp. 1-45.

B. *On Romans 11*

Lenski, R. C. H., *The Interpretation of St. Paul's Epistle to the Romans*, Columbus, 1945, pp. 678-743.

Robertson, O. P., *Is There a Distinctive Future for Ethnic Israel in Romans 11?* (Perspectives on Evangelical Theology), Grand Rapids, 1979, pp. 209-227.

C. *On Romans 10, 12-16*

Calvin, J., *Romans* (for full title see under A.), pp. 381-407; 449-556.

Cranfield, C. E. B., *A Critical and Exegetical Commentary on the Epistle to the Romans* (The International Critical Commentary), Vol. II, Edinburgh, 1979, pp. 512-542; 592-814.

Murray, J., title as under A.; Vol. II, pp. 46-64; 109-268.

General Bibliography

Aalders, G. Ch., *Het Boek Genesis* (Korte Verklaring), 2 vols., Kampen, 1949.

Abelard, P., *Commentarii super S. Pauli epistolam ad Romanos* (Minge, Patrologia Latina), Paris, 1844-64.

Althaus, P., Der Brief an die Römer, Göttingen, 1949.

Ambrosiaster, *Commentaria in XIII spistolas beati Pauli* (Minge, Patrologia Latina), Paris, 1844-64.

Ante-Nicene Fathers, ten vols., Grand Rapids, 1950, for references to Irenaeus, Origen, Tertullian, etc.

Asmussen, H., *Der Römerbrief*, Stuttgart, 1952.

Augustine, *Epistolae ad Romanos* (Minge, Patrologia Latina), Paris, 1844-64.

Barclay, W. *The Letter to the Romans* (Daily Study Bible), Edinburgh, 1957.

Barret, C. K., *A Commentary on the Epistle to the Romans* (Black's New Testament Commentaries), London, 1957.

Barth, K., *Der Römerbrief*, Zürich, 1954.

_________. *A Shorter Commentary on Romans* (tr. of *Kurze Erklärung des Römerbriefes*, 1956), London, 1959.

Batey, R. A., *The Letter of Paul to the Romans*, Austin, 1969.

Bavinck, H., *Gereformeerde Dogmatiek*, 4 vols., Kampen, 1918.

Beck, J. T., *Erklärung des Briefes an die Römer*, 2 vols., Güterslo, 1884.

Beet, J. A., *A Commentary on St. Paul's Epistle to the Romans*, London, 1902.

Berkhof, L., *Systematic Theology*, Grand Rapids, 1949.

Berkhouwer, G. C., *Dogmatische Studiën* (the series), Kampen, 1949, etc.

Best, E., *The Letter of Paul to the Romans* (Cambridge Bible Commentary), Cambridge, 1967.

Black, M., *Romans* (New Century Bible), London, 1973.

Boylan, P., *St. Paul's Epistle to the Romans*, Dublin, 1934.

Brakel, W. a, *Redelijke Godsdienst*, 2 vols., Leiden, 1893.

Bruce, F. F., *The Epistle of Paul to the Romans* (Tyndale Bible Commentaries), Grand Rapids, 1963.

Brunner, E., *The Letter to the Romans* (English tr. of *Der Römerbrief*, 1956), London, 1959.

Burton, E. D., *Syntax of Moods and Tenses in New Testament Greek*, Chicago, 1923.

Buttz, A., *Epistle to the Romans in Greek*, New York and Cincinnati, 1876.

Calvin, J., *Commentaries on the Epistle of Paul the Apostle, to the Romans* (tr. and ed. by J. Owen, Grand Rapids, 1947.

_________. *Institutes of the Christian Religion* (tr. by John Allen), Philadelphia, 1928.

Chamberlain, W. D., *The Meaning of Repentance*, Philadelphia, 1943.

Cranfield, C. E. B., *A Critical and Exegetical Commentary on the Epistle to the Romans* (The International Critical Commentary), 2 vols., Edinburgh, 1975, 1979.

Denney, J., *St. Paul's Epistle to the Romans* (The Expositor's Greek Testament), Vol. II, Grand Rapids, n.d.

Dibelius, M., *Die Geisterwelt im Glauben des Paulus*, Göttingen, 1909.

Dodd, C. H., *The Epistle of Paul to the Romans* (Fontana Books), London, 1959.

Doekes, G., *De Beteekenis van Israëls Val*, Nijverdal, 1915.

Donfried, K. P., (ed. & contributor), *The Romans Debate*, Minneapolis, 1977.

Erdman, C. R., *Epistle of Paul to the Romans*, Philadelphia, 1925.

Flynn, L. B., *Did I Say That?*, Nashville, 1959.

Foakes Jackson, F. J., and Lake, K., *The Beginnings of Christianity*, Vols. IV and V, Grand Rapids, 1965, 1966.

Fraser, J., *A Treatise on Sanctification*, London, 1898.

Fuchs, E., *Die Freiheit des Glaubens: Römer 5-8 ausgelegt*, Munich, 1949.

Gamble, H., Jr., *The Textual History of the Letter to the Romans*, Grand Rapids, 1977.

Gifford, E. H., *The Epistle of St. Paul to the Romans*, London, 1886.

Gispen, W. H., *Exodus* (Korte Verklaring), Kampen, 1932.

________. *De Spreuken van Salamo* (Korte Verklaring), Kampen, 1954.
Godet, F. *Commentary on St. Paul's Epistle to the Romans* (tr. from the French), 2 vols., Edinburgh, 1880, 1881.
Gore, C. *The Epistle to the Romans*, London, 1907.
Greijdanus, S. *De Brief van den Apostel Paulus aan de Gemeente te Rome* (Kommentaar op het Nieuwe Testament), 2 vols., Amsterdam, 1933.
Haldane, R., *The Epistle to the Romans*, London, 1966.
Hamilton, F. E., *The Epistle to the Romans*, Grand Rapids, 1958.
Harder, R. C., a chapter in *De Heilige Geest*, ed. by J. H. Bavinck, P. Prins, and G. Brillenburg, Wurth, Kampen, 1949.
Harrison, E. F., *Romans* (The Expositor's Bible Commentary), Grand Rapids, 1976.
Hendriksen, W., *Beginner's Book of Doctrine*
________. *Israel in Prophecy*
________. *More Than Conquerors* (on the book of Revelation)
________. *New Testament Commentary*: a volume on each of the four Gospels, and volumes on all of Paul's Epistles (except I and II Corinthians)
________. *Survey of the Bible*
________. *The Bible on the Life Hereafter*
________. *The Covenant of Grace*
________. *The Doctrine of God* (my translation of H. Bavinck's *Gereformeerde Dogmatiek*, Vol. II, pp. 1-425)
Place of publication of all the above: Grand Rapids
________. The Meaning of the Preposition ἀντί in the New Testament (unpublished dissertation, Princeton Seminary, 1948).
Hodge, C., *A Commentary on the Epistle to the Romans*, Grand Rapids, 1886 (reprinted 1950).
Hoeksema, H., *God's Eternal Good Pleasure*, Grand Rapids, 1950.
Huby, J., *Saint Paul: Épître aux Romains*, Paris, 1957.
Hunter, A. M., *The Epistle to the Romans* (Torch Bible Commentaries), London, 1954.
Jowett, B., *The Epistles of St. Paul to the Thessalonians, Galatians, and Romans*, London, 1855.
Käsemann, E., *An die Römer* (Hand buch zum N.T.), Tübingen, 1973; English translation, *Commentary on Romans*, Grand Rapids, 1980.
Kelly, W. *Notes on the Epistle to the Romans*, London, 1873.
Kirk, K. E., *The Epistle to the Romans* (Clarendon Bible), Oxford-1937.
Klooster, F. H., *Predestination: A Calvinistic Note* (Perspectives on Evangelical Theology), Grand Rapids, 1979.
Knox, J., *The Epistle to the Romans* (The Interpreter's Bible), New York, 1954.
Kühl, E., *Der Brief des Paulus an die Römer*, Leipzig, 1913.
Kümmel, W. G., *Römer 7 und die Bekehrung des Paulus*, Leipzig, 1929.
Kuyper, A., *Het Werk van den Heiligen Geest*, Kampen, 1927.
Lagrange, M. J., *Saint Paul: Épître aux Romains* (Etudes Bibliques), Paris, 1950. This book contains a long list of commentaries of the Greek and Latin church-fathers.
Lange, J. P., *The Epistle of Paul to the Romans*, tr. from the German (Lange's Commentary on the Holy Scriptures), Grand Rapids, 1869.
Leenhardt, F. J., *The Epistle to the Romans*, tr. from French, London, 1961.
Lekkerkerker, A. F. N., *De Brief van Paulus aan de Romeinen*, 2 vols., Nijkerk, 1971.
Lenski, R. C. H., *The Interpretation of the Acts of the Apostles*, Columbus, 1944.
________. *The Interpretation of St. Paul's Epistle to the Romans*, Columbus, 1945.
Liddon, H. P., *Explanatory Analysis of St. Paul's Epistle to the Romans*, London, 1893.
Lietzmann, H., *An die Römer* (Handbuch zum N.T.), Tübingen, 1933.
Lightfoot, J. B., *Notes on the Epistles of St. Paul: The Epistle to the Romans*, chapters 1-7, London, 1895.
________. *St. Paul's Epistle to the Philippians*, Grand Rapids, 1953.
Lloyd-Jones, D. M., *Romans* (Exposition on Romans 3:20-8:39), 6 vols., Grand Rapids, 1971-1976.
Loane, M. L., *The Hope of Glory (an Exposition of Romans 8)*, London, 1968.

ROMANS

Luther, M., *Lectures on Romans*, tr. by W. G. Tillmanns and A. O. Preus (from German, Weimar edition of Luther's works, Vol. 56), Volume 25 of *Luther's Works*, ed. by H. C. Oswald, St. Louis, 1972.

Manson, T. W. *Romans* (Peake's Commentary on the Bible), London, 1962.

Meyer, H. A. W., *The Epistle to the Romans*, tr. from German, Edinburgh, 1884.

Michel, O., *Der Brief an die Römer* (Kritisch-exegetischer Kommentar über das N.T.), Göttingen, 1966.

Moule, H. C. G., *The Epistle of Paul to the Romans* (The Expositor's Bible, Vol. 5), Grand Rapids, 1943.

Murray, J., *The Epistle to the Romans* (The New International Commentary on the New Testament), 2 vols. Grand Rapids, 1959.

Nygren, A., *Commentary on Romans*, London, 1952.

Parry, R. St. J., *The Epistle of Paul the Apostle to the Romans* (Cambridge Greek Testament), Cambridge, 1912.

Ridderbos, H., *Aan de Romeinen* (Commentaar Op Het Nieuwe Testament), Kampen, 1959.

Robertson, A. T., *The Epistle to the Romans* (Word Pictures in the New Testament, Vol. IV, pp. 320-430), New York and London, 1931.

Robertson, O. P., *Is There a Distinctive Future for Ethnic Israel in Romans 11?* (Perspectives on Evangelical Theology), Grand Rapids, 1979.

Robinson, J. A. T., *Wrestling with Romans*, Philadelphia, 1979.

Sanday, W. and Headlam, A. C., *A Critical and Exegetical Commentary on the Epistle to the Romans* (International Critical Commentary), Edinburgh, 1911.

Schlatter, A., *Gottes Gerechtigheit: ein Kommentar zum Römerbrief*, Stuttgart, 1952.

Schmidt, H. W., *Der Brief des Paulus an die Römer* (Theologischer Handkommentar zum N.T.), Berlin, 1962.

Steele, D. N. and Thomas, C. C., *Romans, an Interpretive Outline*, Philadelphia, 1963.

Taylor, V., *The Epistle to the Romans* (Epworth Preacher's Commentaries), London, 1956.

Thomas, W. H.G., *St. Paul's Epistle to the Romans*, Grand Rapids, 1956.

Trench, R. C., *Synonyms of the New Testament*, Grand Rapids, 1948.

Van Andel, J., *Paulus' Brief aan de Romeinen*, Kampen, 1904.

Van Leeuwen, J. A. C., and Jacobs, D., *De Brief aan de Romeinen*, Kampen, 1932.

Vaughan, C. J., *St. Paul's Epistle to the Romans*, London, 1880.

Vine, W. E., *The Epistle to the Romans*, London, 1957.

Volbeda, S., *De Intuitieve Philosophie van James McCosh*, Grand Rapids, n.d.

Von Hagen, W. V., *The Roads that Led to Rome*, Cleveland and New York, 1967.

Vos, G., *The Pauline Eschatology*, Princeton, 1930.

Warfield, B. B., *Biblical and Theological Studies*, Philadelphia, 1954.

Wilson, G. B., *Romans, A Digest of Reformed Comment*, Edinburgh, 1977.

Wood, L. J., *The Prophets of Israel*, Grand Rapids, 1979.

Zahn, T., *Der Brief des Paulus an die Römer* (Kommentar zum Neuen Testament), Leipzig, 1910.